COMING OUT
CONSERVATIVE

COMING OUT CONSERVATIVE

CONSERVATIVE

An Autobiography

BY

MARVIN LIEBMAN

CHRONICLE BOOKS
SAN FRANCISCO

1992

The publisher gratefully acknowledges Penguin USA for
permission to reprint excerpts from the story
"Hands" by Sherwood Anderson.

Printed in the United States of America.

Library of Congress Cataloging in Publication Data

Liebman, Marvin.
    Coming out conservative : a founder of the modern conservative
movement speaks out on personal freedom, homophobia, and hate
politics / Marvin Liebman.
        p.   cm.
    Includes index.
    ISBN 0-8118-0073-3
    1. Liebman, Marvin.   2. Politicians—United States—Biography.
3. Gay politicians—United States—Biography.   4. Conservatism—
United States—History—20th century.   5. Homosexuality—United
States.   I. Title.
E840.8.L47A3   1992
324'.08'664—dc20   92-3036
                                                              CIP

Book design: Engdahl Typography
Composition: Mackenzie-Harris Corporation
Jacket design: Kathy Warinner
Back jacket photograph: Doug Hinckle

Distributed in Canada by Raincoast Books,
112 East Third Avenue, Vancouver, B.C. V5T 1C8

10 9 8 7 6 5 4 3 2 1

Chronicle Books
275 Fifth Street
San Francisco, CA 94103

For

Wing Biddlebaum

Acknowledgments

I needed a lot of help to begin and finally complete this book, and I take this opportunity to express my deep appreciation to some of my friends who generously gave of their time to make it all happen: Allan Berube; Betty Berzon; Robb Bettiker; Carol Buckley; John Buckley; Priscilla Buckley; William F. Buckley, Jr.; Jane Dystel; Judy Feiffer; Jeffrey Hart; Paul Hasse; Geoffrey Hoefer; Peter Ivancie; Dorothy Kemper; Gregory King; Alberta Lebihan; Brenda Mack; Ed Marston; Shepard Rifkin; William A. Rusher; Jay Schaefer; Norman Sherman; and Karen Silver.

Thanks also to the Historical Research Foundation, Fund For American Studies, Young America's Foundation, the Archives at Indiana University and Purdue University in Indianapolis, and the Hoover Institution Archives at Stanford University.

And, finally, to all those who were inadvertently left out of the above. Thank you, all.

Table of Contents

Prologue

FOR ALMOST four decades, I was one of the leading anticommunist and conservative activists in the United States. During most of those years, I worked in close coordination with my friend William F. Buckley, Jr., whom I consider to be the founder of modern American conservatism and the prime articulator of its philosophy.

A little more than a month before my sixty-seventh birthday—on June 7, 1990—I wrote to him, and asked that he publish a letter in his magazine, *National Review*. The letter announced that I was gay.

After asking me if I had fully considered the personal ramifications of such a disclosure, Bill agreed to run my letter. He said that he felt he must also publish his reply.

We'd known each other for almost thirty-five years. I assumed he knew that I was gay, but I never brought up the subject. And it never seemed to matter so long as the word was never spoken—certainly not to Bill or his wife, Pat, or to my other straight friends. Just don't talk about it, for heaven's sake.

In the spring of 1990, however, it did matter very much to the American Right, an amalgamation of several constituencies: dedicated anticommunist groups; the "religious Right," always seeking more money-raising ideas; the tively new "traditional American family values" organizations; and the politicians whose jobs and appeal depend on their ability to promote fear and bigotry and then convince their constituencies that they are the only ones who can hold the fort against whatever enemy they have created.

These far-right groups have little in common with the conservative philosophy that is primarily based on the sanctity and power of the individual over the state. It is this conservative philosophy, espoused by Bill Buckley and his brilliant colleagues who founded *National Review*, for which I worked and in which I believe.

When communism began its demise with the fall of the Berlin Wall, a frenzied search began within the American Right for something to replace anticommunism as the central issue that held the "conservative movement" together for more than thirty years. The standard old bogeymen—Jews, Catholics, blacks, foreigners—were still around. But they were well organized and far more difficult to use as scapegoats.

But there was one group that could be used as a target: homosexuals. The spreading AIDS epidemic and the growing activism of the gay and lesbian community provided the hate-mongers with the perfect victims at a perfect time.

The campaign began, using the very same rhetoric that had worked so well at stirring up public passions in the past against communists, leftists, Catholics, and Jews. *They* have infiltrated every segment of American society; they are taking over the American schoolroom so as to poison the minds of our children against "traditional American family values"; they wield too great an influence on the mass media and are changing the traditional culture of America; and they are the cause of every other conceivable social ill.

On June 6, 1990, a research fellow at the "conservative" Free Congress Foundation told the *Washington Times* that the spread of AIDS in large cities "could be the greatest impetus for euthanasia we've ever seen." The rhetoric of bigotry was building.

My letter to Buckley said:

Anti-Semitism is something that, happily for the history of the last three decades, *National Review* helped to banish at least from the public behavior of conservatives. *National Review* lifted conservatism to a more enlightened plane, away from a tendency to engage in the manipulation of base motives, prejudices, and desires; activity in my view which tended to be a major base of conservatism's natural constituency back then. Political gay bashing, racism, and anti-Semitism . . . are waiting to be let out once again. I worry that the right wing . . . will return to the fever swamps.

I saw the bigots hovering in the distance, waiting to take over a rudderless conservative movement that had lost its focus.

At that particular time, in the spring of 1990 when bigotry publicly came out of its closet again, I felt like a Jew in Germany in 1934 who had chosen to remain silent, hoping to be able to stay invisible as he watched the beginning of the Holocaust. In my letter I said how I regretted all those years of compliant silence. I continue to regret them, but they are over and unsalvageable. I will never be silent again.

It was in the closing months of the 1980s that the forces of the new bigotry were mobilized to concentrate on a single incident: the showing of some photographs by Robert Mapplethorpe in the Corcoran Gallery of Art in Washington, D.C., that was part funded by a small grant from the National Endowment for the Arts. This provided the New Bigots with the opportunity they were looking for. They were able to promote fear and hatred of gay and lesbian Americans and, at the same time, provide themselves with a *raison d'être* for their money-raising, beating the drums for "traditional American (white Christian) family values" under attack by the vanguard of the homosexual menace.

Their effort to impose a New Morality had begun. I feared that there would be no stop to the bigotry and hatred that would sweep America. This was my political motive in writing my letter to Buckley and coming out so publicly.

Bill Buckley took on a personally difficult task when he committed himself to reply publicly to my coming out letter. I'm certain I caused him great pain. He is a devout and doctrinaire Roman Catholic bound by the theological strictures with which he grew up and to which he still holds fast. Eleven years before, he had been my sponsor when I entered the Catholic church.

In his reply he said,

I honor your decision to raise publicly the points you raise . . . but you too must realize what are the implications of what you ask. Namely, that the Judaeo-Christian tradition, which is aligned with, no less, one way of life, become indifferent to another way of life. . . .

National Review will not be scarred by thoughtless gay bashing, let alone be animated by such practices . . . You are absolutely correct in saying that gays should be welcome as partners in efforts to mint sound public policies; not correct, in my judgment, in concluding that such a partnership presupposes the repeal of convictions that are more, much more, than mere accretions of bigotry. You remain, always, my dear friend, and my brother in combat.

Betty Berzon, psychologist, and author of *Permanent Partners* and other books, and my friend of forty years, urged me to supplement my letter with a statement to the gay community through the *Advocate*, the gay and lesbian national magazine. She became my mentor in this new phase of my life and encouraged me to explain publicly my personal as well as political reasons for coming out. I agreed with her. I wanted to make my coming out, my work, and my life as meaningful as I possibly could.

For over half my life, I have been a professional activist in the anticommunist/conservative movement in America. I organized activities that gave the movement focus, credibility, and viability. In the 1950s and 1960s I developed the fund-raising techniques that fueled the campaigns and committees—including Young Americans for Freedom and the American Conservative Union—that fostered the strong, consistent, anticommunist core of the American Right.

My sense of political theater and my ability to dramatize issues provided some of what was needed to translate the right wing in America from a fringe element into a historic force. I was a conservative insider who knew what it was like to come in from the cold. In my youth, I had been a member of the American Communist party; of numerous left-wing front groups; of the Israeli underground organization, the Irgun Zvai Leumi; and of many more conventional liberal groups in the United States.

I have moved from place to place, from idea to idea, from person to person, from left to right, from Jew to Catholic, from middle class to bohemian and back again, and from youth to age, looking for a family, a place, a home where I could be me. I have achieved "security" in these later years, and something that my father always dreamed of for me, a government job.

The temptation was great to leave well enough alone and live out whatever years I have left in anticipation of respectful obituaries. Why now? These were the thoughts that kept crowding in.

Then I realized what all the searching, all the changing, was about. I was looking for *me*, trying to find out just who *I* was, unable to fit the separate parts of my life together. For all those years, I was hiding from the world and from myself. And that's the reason I moved about so much physically and intellectually.

As I thought about the new me, I recalled stories, anecdotes, good times and bad. They were divided among three lives. There was my professional life of causes, organizations, movements, and politics that spilled over into social activities—particularly with Bill and Pat Buckley and their friends. Until I moved to Washington, and even for the first few years there, I had spent almost every weekend of the past thirty years with them—almost a lifetime!

Then, there was my private gay life, from my bohemian friends in the 1940s in Greenwich Village to the close gay men friends in my later years, with none of whom I had sex.

Finally, there was my secret promiscuous sexual life. It started out when I was a desperately lonely, frightened boy, knowing he was "different" but not knowing why or how. And then walking the countless streets of countless cities into the early hours of the morning, searching, seeking.

I wanted to bring these parts of myself together, and I had to do it publicly.

My first television appearance after my coming out was on a San Francisco TV talk show, *People Are Talking,* with the Rev. Lou Sheldon, founder and head of the Traditional Values Coalition in California. Reverend Sheldon believes that homosexuality is some kind of a disease, that it is learned, that it can be cured, that homosexual "preference" is just that.

As he spoke, I began to realize in an entirely new, more visceral way, that it was not "them" he was speaking of, but "us," "we," *me*. Sitting there under the hot studio lights in front of the TV cameras, I felt for the first time that I was part of a family at last. I had finally come home.

This moment was in sharp contrast to another, during the Thanksgiving weekend of 1976. Ronald and Nancy Reagan were the Buckleys' guests at their house in Stamford, Connecticut, along with their young son Ron Reagan, then a student at Yale, Christopher Buckley, and myself. The weekend was fine, except that I sensed tension between young Ron and his parents.

After dinner on Saturday night, Reagan, Buckley, and I were standing around in the kitchen having a nightcap, joking and telling stories. Reagan suddenly turned uncharacteristically serious. He looked away and then back to us and said, "I haven't told Nancy yet, but young Ron has told me he's going to quit Yale and become a . . . ballet dancer. Now, I don't care what the kid does so long as it's legal and makes him happy, but . . ."

He turned directly to me and said, "But, aren't dancers . . . aren't dancers sort of . . . funny?" He meant homosexual, of course, but couldn't say it. What do you tell a troubled father when he fears his son is gay and can't ask, can't even bring himself to say the word, when you yourself are in the closet?

I told him that some dancers were "funny," of course, but that many were not. I told him then that some male ballet dancers were notorious womanizers—both graceful and lustful and their lust directed toward women. I mentioned that Baryshnikov was one of the sex idols of our time, immensely attractive to women, and Reagan seemed relieved. I mentioned dancers he knew—Gene Kelly and Fred Astaire.

That reassured him. He smiled again, said he was ready to break the news now to "Mommy," and he moved quickly toward their bedroom. I did not bother to tell him that many of his wife's best friends and his own good friends were also "funny." He must certainly have known that, I thought, but denial can be a peaceful form of retreat.

Bill and I put our glasses in the dishwasher without further discussion of dancers, and I headed off to my room. I didn't feel as jolly as before. Once again, for the thousandth time, I had stood quietly and achingly a gay man in the closet, competent to deal with Ronald Reagan's fears about his son, unable to deal openly with the facts of my own life. I had failed to tell him that many of us were "funny" and that there would be nothing degrading about it if "unfunny" people, like him, did not make it so.

Now I see that incident as bringing many themes of my life together—politics, important people, dear friends, fathers and sons, family and home. But, because of my fears, I was still an outsider. To be myself and truly belong, I would have to tell my secret, violate the code of never discussing one's "plumbing" in public. It took me almost four-teen more years to break the silence and begin integrating the different parts of my life.

Chapter 1

Beginnings

*I*N LATE 1990, I went to the Old Mount Carmel Cemetery in Queens to see the family. I hadn't been there for nearly twenty-three years, since we buried my mother.

So many graves and tombstones. Some room left yet in the Liebman plot. My father was buried in 1955. My mother, lying next to him, buried in 1968. Uncle Harry, Uncle Izzy, Uncle Sammy and their wives, Fanny, Mary, and Bernice. My paternal grandfather, Moses, and all the others, *tantes*, *fetahs*, cousins.

We never really knew my father's age; he was probably sixty-eight or sixty-nine when he died, about my age now. He came to the United States as a small child around 1889. His mother had inconveniently died and left her husband with four very young sons: Max, Sam, Izzy, and Benjamin, my father. Like other immigrants, my grandfather was helped by relatives living in America. They emigrated from Hadonkovitz, a village in Galecia, and landed in New York's Lower East Side ghetto on Rivington Street. My grandfather opened a stable and married his second wife, Rachel, who took over as mother to his four sons and produced a daughter, Mary, and two more sons, Harry and Sammy.

My father, Benjamin, aka Benny, was the rebel of the family. He never went to school and ran away from home, fleeing the mean streets of New York's ghetto when he was only twelve. He went out West and ended up living in San Francisco. He never talked much about his travels or the past at all.

He returned to New York just before the First War. Somehow, he and all his brothers avoided military service in World War I. They worked in their father's stable, which they eventually turned into a garage. My father opened his own garage in Brooklyn, where he met my mother.

My mother, Rose Schorr, was also born in Galecia, in a small *shtetl* in 1893 near the village where my father was born. It seems that all Jews from that part of the world are related, and the Liebmans and the Schorrs were no exception. My mother had three brothers—Sam, Henzel, and Saul. She spent her first nineteen years in the village, except for a short time at a Jewish girls' seminary in the city of Lemburg. Her parents obviously thought enough of her intellect to send her to a private school they could barely afford.

In 1913, my grandfather's brother, David, safely ensconced in New York City, sent money for the two oldest children to come to America. My nineteen-year-old mother, Rose, and her sixteen-year-old brother Sam arrived at Ellis Island and within a day they went to work in their Uncle David's hat factory. His wife, Tante Rivka, didn't like "greenhorns" so my mother went to live with Tante Fanny in Brooklyn and Uncle Sam went to live with Tante Paulie in Newark—both Liebman-Schorrs by birth and marriage.

It was their families rather than love that paired my mother and father in marriage. My mother was twenty-eight; my father was in his early thirties. When a woman and man of their ages were unmarried, ways had to be found to avoid the shame of having an old maid and, God forbid, a bachelor in the family. The problem was solved among relatives, and that's how in 1921 my mother and father became husband and wife.

My father became business partners with my mother's brother, and within the year they opened the Sunshine Garage in the Bay Ridge section of Brooklyn. The full-service garage was open twenty-four hours a day. My father's work uniform was always an Army wool khaki shirt and trousers, a fedora, a suede jacket, and a cigar that he always chewed rather than smoked. Throughout his life, he worked hard and put in longer hours than necessary, perhaps to stay away from my mother's constant nagging. I was born in 1923, and we lived in an apartment house adjoining the garage. My father was proud to have a son, and renamed the garage the Marvin Garage. The next year we moved to a two-family house on Eighty-seventh Street, between Third Avenue and Ridge Boulevard, a block lined with other two-family houses. When I was three, and already wearing glasses, my father renamed the garage Sunshine.

Bay Ridge was a polyglot community of middle-class families—mostly Scandinavian, with a few Irish, Italian, German, and Greek —holding on to whatever they could during those terrible depression years. The small number of Jews all gathered at the Bay Ridge Jewish Center, the synagogue where I was bar mitzvahed. My grammar school, PS 185, was on the corner. I lived in this neighborhood until I was drafted in World War II.

On hot evenings people would sit on their stoops chatting with each other. The Borden's milkman came by in his horse and wagon, as did the iceman Tony—they were always called Tony. Girls skipped rope and played "potsie" (hopscotch) on the sidewalk—sometimes they'd let me play, too. The boys played stickball or "ring-a-levio" in the street or in the schoolyard. But not me. I watched them behind too-large glasses from the window, a picture book on my lap.

On a typical Sunday, as I remember it, we would go to one of the aunts' or they would come to our house. There would be Aunt Goldie, Little Aunt Mary, Big Aunt Mary, Aunt Fannie, and Aunt Bernice. The uncles—Uncle Izzy, Uncle Sam, Uncle Sammy, Uncle Ben, and Uncle Harry. The women would busy themselves in the kitchen. The food was usually Brooklyn-Jewish "chow mein," boiled vegetables, chicken or beef, soy sauce, and my favorite—dried noodles—which they bought at the local Chinese restaurant. The men would play pinochle in one room. The women would gossip, and all the cousins would be together. Within the larger family I was less an outsider—in fact, I was admired and loved by my aunts and uncles. I could draw, I could write stories, and I thought, as did my mother, that I was the smartest.

At home we would eat in the kitchen, my sister in the high chair, me, my father, my mother, and—in spite of hard times—a live-in maid. I remember Helen Walker from Scotland, Nora Quinlan from Ireland, and the assorted other immigrants and young black women whose names I don't even remember. They ate at the table with us, black and white.

That kitchen was a battleground. I remember, as a three- or four-year-old boy, the screaming, the angry shouts that were almost blows. "You dirty son of a bitch, bastard!" (in English) and "May God break your legs and your arms so that you are in eternal pain!" (in Yiddish) and Polish curses I couldn't understand. Always about money, money, money. One time my father actually ripped up dollar bills and threw them at my mother. She did most of the shouting, all-powerful fury aimed at him, making him seem smaller forever in my eyes. I would hide wherever I could, in a closet, under a bed, my small hands over my ears, desperately frightened. I don't remember crying; I was too scared.

The most terrible fight of all was in June of 1927. I was not yet four years old, and mother was in her sixth month of pregnancy with my sister, Eleanor. My mother wanted to visit her family in Poland, whom she hadn't seen in fourteen years. She told happy stories of her days in Europe, when she was a girl: the gypsies who came through town each year, the geese she tended. And she told one that frightened me: about a pogrom in which Polish peasants beat their neighbor, my grandfather, with a chain for no reason other than that he was a Jew. My mother, her brothers, and my grandmother all watched, terrified, unable to do anything to help him. He was crippled.

As important as this trip back home was to my mother, my father refused to give her the money (the garage business was not flourishing), and they had a great row. So she pawned her engagement ring to get money for the trip. We sailed on the *Leviathan*, one of the great transatlantic liners of the time. My mother later told me that I disappeared from our third-class cabin the second day out. She was frantic, and the entire ship was alerted. They finally discovered me in the first-class billiards room, the darling of all the gentlemen: a skinny kid holding a bottle and nipple, wearing oversized horn-rimmed glasses and the ubiquitous tweed cap. How could they resist me?

We landed in Cherbourg and took a train to Paris, then to the little village of Kapitchinicz. My grandmother, grandfather, and my mother's brothers and their families were all waiting to welcome us at the railroad station. My mother leaped off the train to embrace those dear people she had feared she would never see again. Amid the tears, kisses, and hugs, they forgot all about me. When the train started up, they saw that I was still on it, and Uncle Saul came to my rescue.

I stayed in that small *shtetel* for the whole summer. I felt wanted and at home in the undemanding love of my grandmother and grandfather. I vaguely remember my grandfather, with his long beard, cutting black bread for me as I sat on his lap. My tiny grandmother, with her wig (*sheitl*) covering her hair, protected me no matter how bad I was or how annoyed my mother got at my antics. I learned little-boy Yiddish then, and a few words of Polish, so I could talk to them.

In late August my father came over to make amends to my mother and to take us back to the United States. He arrived unexpectedly, driving a rented open touring car, wearing a straw hat, and smoking a big cigar clenched in his teeth. Everyone greeted him as if he were a film star. My mother bid her family a tearful farewell and returned just in time to give birth to my sister. Except for her brother Henzel and his family, who emigrated to Chile, my mother never saw any of her family again.

When the Nazis invaded, my mother's parents and her brothers hid out in a cave with the other Jews of the village for several months. After the war, a survivor from their village came to see my Uncle Sam and my mother in Brooklyn to tell them what happened to the village. When their money and possessions ran out, they left their cave and were captured and taken to the village square. The men were forced to dig a trench outside the square. Then all the Jews were lined up—men, women, children—stripped naked in the freezing winter, and shot—not by the Nazis but by the Poles who had crippled my grandfather some thirty years before.

We arrived back in Brooklyn barely a month before my sister Eleanor was born in September. It was in these early years that I first began to feel different.

I was always attracted to boys, but most of the time they frightened me. They thought I was a sissy, and I guess I was. Except for those who were mean to me, I loved the other boys but wasn't sure what I wanted from them. When I played at all, it was with the girls my age. I hated my name Marvin, which sounded like a sissy name. Fortunately, my parents and everyone else called me "Sonny" until I was a grown man.

There was an empty lot on the corner where some of the kids built a shanty of tar paper and old boards as the headquarters for their "gang." I was terrified of them, but I was also envious. One day, four members of the "gang" asked whether I would like to be a member.

Suspiciously, I asked, "What do I have to do?"

"Nothing," they said. "Just an initiation."

"What kind of initiation?" I asked.

"We're playing 'house on fire.' All you have to do is make believe you're on fire."

That didn't sound too difficult. They took me to the lot and blind-folded me. I fluttered my hands and squeaked, "Help, Help, I'm on fire, I'm on fire."

The minute they heard that, about seven of them put me out by peeing on me. I was too stunned to be angry—I just felt rejected and ashamed.

When I was about seven, my mother took me to see Eva La Gallienne and Josephine Hutchinson in *Peter Pan* at La Gallienne's Civic Repertory Theater on Fourteenth Street. I will never forget when Peter Pan flew from the balcony across the audience onto the stage, over my head—really flew. It was then I decided that somehow I would be a part of this thing that made real people fly: the theater.

A few years later, my father insisted that I join the Boy Scout troop at the Bay Ridge Jewish Center. I was outfitted in everything a Boy Scout would ever need. I loathed those terrible meetings; I felt I was surround-ed by enemies. A favorite game of the troop was called "horsey." One boy would get on the shoulders of another boy, and they would rush at each other trying to knock the top boys off. I would see to it that I was knocked off in seconds so I wouldn't have to keep playing. I was clumsy at making knots and barely got even one merit badge. But I became good friends with Melvin, who was my own age, and we'd spend half the time comparing each other's things and seeing how big they would grow and what other tricks they could do.

I had my first orgasm—self-inflicted—just before I was bar mitz-vahed, probably when I was twelve or so. I thought I was the only one in the whole world who did it—and I loved it. The boys at Hebrew school would buy little comic books printed in Cuba that had the sexual escapades of our favorite comic book characters, Popeye and Olive Oyl, Maggie and Jiggs, Dick Tracy and Tess Trueheart. These were tremendously erotic to me and to the other boys, and they served the same purpose that *Playboy* does today. There was much measuring and testing and giggling with the boys from the Bay Ridge Jewish Center. This was the only time that I could ever really participate in any activities with them.

Some days I would skip school and use my milk money for a subway ride to Times Square. There I was, a child of eleven, wearing his knickers and cap, wandering around Times Square, peering out of thick glasses. In those days, it wasn't the sleazy area it has become; but it was a crowded, bustling place, full of bright lights and wonderful sights for me to see.

When my mother found out I was playing hooky, she beat me. She was always ready with her hand or a wooden spoon—her favorite weapon. I avoided any confrontation with her and hated her for what she did to my father and what she might do to me. She loved me, but I was frightened of her temper, which kept me from getting close to her—except in her last years.

I knew that my mother loved me deeply, better than anyone. But she could never understand or accept me. She knew I was "different." It was a secret that we might have shared if, growing up, I could have figured out what the secret was. At times, she loved me for being different. At other times, she must have hated me because I wasn't like the other boys, the sons of her friends. She couldn't brag about me.

Toward the end of my mother's life, I was able to do things for her, to give her something to brag about. I bought her a mink coat and jewelry and went with her once (paying for the trip) to see her brother Henzel in Chile. I was so overcome at the sadness of their leave-taking that I bought two more tickets to enable Henzel and his wife to visit their brother and sister in America some months later. My mother enjoyed me in her later years, and I enjoyed her. I was planning a big celebration for her seventy-fifth birthday in 1968. Just the day before, she had a heart attack and died.

I never knew what dreams my father had for me or, indeed, what dreams my father had for himself. I always knew that I was a disappointment to him, that I couldn't be what he wanted me to be, that he really didn't know what he wanted me to be. At first, it was, "Why can't you be like the other boys? Why don't you have friends? Why don't you play ball?" And then, later, it was, "Get a job. Get a government job where you will be secure; make a life, be like everyone else." In the end, I finally achieved his dream of the government job for me, but I could never live up to his expectations which remained undefined. Whenever I was with my father, I felt a terrible loneliness, a devastating aloneness, the total inability to communicate.

He did try to break through a few times. Once, he took me to the Loew's Alpine—just the two of us—to see my first "talkie." It was *The Unholy Three*, starring Lon Chaney, a particular favorite of his. I remember Daddy buying me ice cream afterward and walking home with me hand in hand—he with his fedora and cigar and suede jacket, me with enormous glasses on a little face, a cap, knickers, and the hated long brown stockings fastened to my underwear to keep them up. That night, I felt loved by him.

The most memorable time I had with my father was when I was seven or eight. I had the whooping cough, and my father took me to a farm in the Catskills that took in boarders. I recall winter and my father and me walking up a snowy hill. He was chewing on a cigar and wearing his suede jacket and fedora, with a muffler under the hat tied at his throat. I was bundled up with a wool cap and earflaps that tied under my chin and pushed my glasses down my nose. He built a fire and roasted potatoes, and we ate the wonderful charred hot potatoes outside in the cold. I never felt closer to my father. He, probably, never felt as close to his son.

I wanted my father to love me. But he always seemed shy around me, as if he were afraid to touch me. He never hugged me. Not so with my sister, with whom he was affectionate. I couldn't respect him because he wasn't really a father figure—he was a person who was yelled at by my mother. He was an immigrant Jew who wanted his son to be Jack Armstrong, All-American Boy. What he got was me—an underweight, scrawny bookworm. He never had the son he wanted. I never had the father I wanted. I spent the rest of my life looking for fathers—as well as for a family where I would be accepted for who I was.

The men who worked at my father's garage gave me some of the affection that I didn't get from him. I liked to visit them when my father wasn't there. His partner, Uncle Sam, liked me and always had Lucky Strike cigarettes that I could steal. Both black and white mechanics kidded around with me—John, the Marxist neighbor across the street, who had spent four years in the USSR with his family; the eccentric Kalody, a carpenter and handyman and a communist, and his friend Polo. They all loved to talk politics, and I loved to listen, not always understanding what they were saying. The *Daily Worker*, the newspaper of the U.S. Communist party, was always in the garage office, and I sometimes took a look at it.

I was bar mitzvahed in September 1936 and graduated from PS 185 on June 24, 1937. I started New Utrecht High School in Brooklyn in September of 1937. I had just turned 14, and my life began to change immediately. In grammar school I had been a solitary outsider. But in high school, I was a star almost from the beginning.

My first-year civics class was taught by a leftist, probably a member of the Communist party. Our first assignment was to discuss and act out the trial of Tom Mooney, a radical labor leader who was arrested for allegedly planting a bomb at a Preparedness Day parade in San Francisco in 1916. A number of people were killed. His trial became a cause célèbre in the 1920s. He was sentenced to life imprisonment. Mooney became an instant hero of mine, a man working for the working man against the rich and powerful establishment.

The classroom was set up as a courtroom, and I was assigned to be Mooney's defense attorney. That classroom became my first stage; that role, my first performance. It let me be someone I could be proud of. I loved the show, the drama, the performance, and I wanted my own life to have that kind of magic, even if I had to make it up.

My classroom performance was a hit with my student audience and my "director," Mrs. E. Although I did do some research, I made up a lot to make it look good, and I succeeded in winning Mooney's acquittal! I had a victory all my own.

My performance and conviction caught my teacher's attention. I was thrilled when she invited me, along with some of the other kids involved in the trial, to her apartment, which faced Prospect Park. She flattered us all by talking to us as if we were adults. She told us we should get involved in the American Student Union (ASU). She introduced me to a boy named Stanley, a leader of that group, on whom I immediately developed a major crush.

At my first meeting, I was welcomed enthusiastically by the other kids. I had found a new family and a cause. The ASU was the noncommunist front for the Young Communist League. It was also an affiliate of the American Youth Congress, which had a number of other communist youth fronts involved along with religious and other groups that ignored the obvious communist control. I went to all the meetings. I was accepted. I composed leaflets and talked about the working class, the dust bowl farmers, the Negroes, dialectical materialism, the Spanish civil war. We listened to and sang along with Keynote records of the Red Army Chorus, the Lincoln Brigade, Woody Guthrie, Beatrice Kay, and Earl Robinson.

Soon afterward I was invited to join the Young Communist League. This was probably one of the great moments of my young life. To me, it was like an honorary secret society limited to the very best, to the people I admired the most. I became a full-fledged member of the YCL. I attended classes on Marxism and dialectical materialism in Communist party headquarters, over the Worker's Bookshop on Thirteenth Street. I paid scant attention to regular schoolwork. The Worker's Bookshop and the Cameo Theater on Eighth Avenue (which showed Soviet films) became my hangouts.

Politics wasn't the only reason I went to the movies. I made many brief forays to Times Square, and this time I knew what I wanted. I found it in the seedy movie houses on Forty-second Street: amorous encounters with other boys and men in the pitch black theaters. It didn't make any difference who because it was too dark to see anything anyway. A tentative hand on the thigh of whomever you sat next to—and then it was show time. This was something that I could never mention to anyone—certainly not my parents, and especially not the young comrades, who were as puritanical as they could be, scorning such bourgeois excesses as sex, and especially homosexuality. Here I was, deflowering the working masses, one by one. I never quite understood my comrades' puritanism, but I kept my mouth shut.

Bernard Malamud, who was to become one of the great American writers, was my first English teacher. He was teaching his first high school class. I became his protégé. He encouraged me to write. He introduced me to his literary heroes Matthew Arnold and Sherwood Anderson, and to Anderson's story "Hands" from *Winesburg, Ohio*, about Wing Biddlebaum, who was driven out of town for being too affectionate with boys, for being "different." Although Malamud never said anything, I'm sure he gave me the story because he knew I was homosexual and he thought it might help me.

I soon became an active member of the Young Communist League and was assigned to various citywide projects. Stanley, who recruited me, became my immediate and unrequited love object. They were a wonderful group of young people, especially Beatrice, a rather plain English girl I was sure was a lesbian. She was my special pal and "bohemian," which brought us closer to each other. If she hadn't been so homely then, she too might have been a love object. Even though our hormones were running riot, you avoided sexual contact with any of your friends. It wasn't the workers' way.

Happily, our group was transferred almost intact from New Utrecht to become the first class (sophomore) at Lafayette High School. Mr. Grady, our assistant principal, hated the young leftists and made our lives difficult. Every few months, my mother had to go to school to plead with him to keep me in. We were all under constant threat of suspension. Mr. Grady, a devout Catholic, detested Jews and communism, in that order.

I became a student volunteer at *New Masses* magazine, selling the magazine outside Macy's on Thirty-fourth Street. Another kid, a little older, was selling *Social Justice*, the magazine of Father Coughlin's *Christian Front*. I would shout, "Get the *New Masses!* Get the worker's magazine!" and he would shout "Stop the Antichrist!" and we would scream at each other. Although I hated his politics, I thought he was cute-looking in his corduroy knickers; I liked his freckles and his very Christian upturned nose. After our fifth screaming encounter, we finally spoke. "You want to take a break?" I asked. "Sure," he said, "if you want to." We walked up to the men's room at Macy's, went into one of the stalls, put our propaganda on the floor, shut our eyes, and began to fool around. The Christian anti-Semitic and Jew-communist movements merged for a brief moment—if only in secret, in this most unlikely of closets.

I became a sort of mascot at *New Masses*. I met all my heroes: Ruth McKenney, who wrote *My Sister Eileen;* Bruce Bliven, her husband and editor of the magazine; Paul Robeson, the great singer and actor; "Mother" Ella Reeves Bloor, whose sons were killed in a union massacre, a plump white-haired old woman who was brought out at all the rallies; Elizabeth Gurley Flynn and William Z. Foster, leaders of the Communist party; the cartoonist Sam Gropper; and the writer Mike Gold. I even shook hands with Earl Browder, the head of the Communist party. I was beside myself with joy. I was in the forefront of the movement to help all the outcasts of the world. The future was mine! I belonged!

Happy day, the May Day parade of 1939. I was one with thousands of other marchers singing union songs, our placards, banners, and flags waving; bands were playing "The International"; and my heroes on the platform were waiting for us to arrive. I was marching in the right cause, warmly embraced by my new family: comrades against the world.

In 1939, I attended the American Youth Conference in Washington, D.C., my first trip to the capital. I had to fight for money and permission to go. My father didn't like my new communist activism; he thought it would hurt my future. When he refused to give me the money I needed, I began to weep. It was almost the last time I was able to cry—the next was in a mental ward in Egypt some five years later. My mother finally gave me twenty-five dollars, a lot of money in those days.

Although I could have paid for a hotel room, I slept in a phone booth in the Labor Department building so as not to appear too bourgeois. President Roosevelt addressed us on the White House lawn. He said that our claim that Finland had invaded the Soviet Union (which we firmly believed) was "twaddle." Our entire group, several hundred, booed him. It made headlines.

Mrs. Roosevelt spoke to us the next day, and she just about apologized for her husband. She was followed by John L. Lewis, head of the United Mine Workers. It was a triumphant meeting and a great time for me.

I read a lot. I thought Richard Wright's *Native Son* was the best thing ever written. *The Grapes of Wrath*, *Johnny Got His Gun*, Romain Rolland, Céline, all the Russian writers—I read everything I could get my hands on, not only the Marxist literature from the Worker's Bookshop (which bored me), but any novel, including Fannie Hurst and Edna Ferber. I read *The Well of Loneliness*, Radcliffe Hall's novel about lesbians, but that didn't make much of an impression then.

I started writing short stories and fancied myself a writer. I would be the leading proletarian writer, following in the footsteps of Theodore Dreiser, Jack London, and Mike Gold. Mike was a columnist for the *Daily Worker* and wrote one of my favorite books at that time, *Jews Without Money*.

I read everything and did everything—except schoolwork. I flunked economics and math and had to take the courses over again in summer school to get my diploma, which I got in September 1941, three months late.

My father paid my way to New York University at the Washington Square campus. There I got my first taste of the Village and hung around, searching unsuccessfully for bohemia. I was once again without a family. As the war heated up, the YCL and the Communist party went underground. I attended few classes and received incompletes in just about every course I took.

The break in my unhappiness came when I met Paul Friedman at the NYU student union and quickly became "best friends." He lived in the Williamsburg section of Brooklyn, where his father and mother ran a small grocery store. I adored Paul. We spent hours together, reading poetry to each other and listening to records. His favorite was Sibelius's *The Swan of Tuonela*. My favorite was *The Student Prince*, because he was *my* student prince. I played that over and over again, and our theme song became "Overhead the Moon Is Beaming."

We did everything that lovers did but sleep together. I never had the courage to tell him I was gay. Paul, of course, was straight, or he thought he was. We held hands and massaged each other—after all, we were poets and friends. We went out on double dates together. I'd drop off my date; he'd go in with his girl to her apartment, and I would wait outside. I imagined him doing with the girl what I wanted him to do with me. When he came outside, we walked to the subway hand in hand. Those moments of closeness made up for all the waiting.

In February 1942, two months after Pearl Harbor, I went with Paul and some of our friends to enlist. We had visions of fighting together like the comrades in *Beau Geste*. They were all accepted—I wasn't, because of my eyes. I was devastated. Once again I was losing a family, and, worst of all, my beloved Paul.

Chapter 2

Going to War

IT WAS DECEMBER 1942 when the draft notice arrived. I was elated; now I could be one of the boys. But, because of my eyesight, the Army Air Corps wanted me for "limited service" only. I had to sign a disclaimer relieving the United States government of any responsibility if I was sent overseas and killed. That made me feel like half a man, half a soldier.

On the morning in January that I left home, I could see the icy trees and sidewalks from my bedroom window when I woke up, I shivered a bit at what the day would bring. I could smell lox and onions frying and eggs cooking. I had to face my parents and younger sister, waiting for me in the kitchen.

I tried to eat something to cheer them up. We all nervously avoided each other's eyes. My parents could be proud of me; their son was going to war. Now they could be like the Vavoulis family downstairs and the Jacomochis next door. The tasseled square of cloth with a blue star already hung in a window of our Brooklyn apartment as a symbol of my parents' pride in my service and their patriotism.

My mother and sister cried, and my father, who worked at being manly, gave me mini-lectures about the Army, of which he knew nothing. My mother kept disappearing into another room to cry, returning with redder eyes each time.

Finally, I shook hands with my dad and kissed the slippery cheeks of the women, refusing my father's offer of a lift to the draft board office,

terrified of being humiliated by public good-byes. I left with an overnight bag containing a few clothes and personal belongings and a honey
cake my mother had baked for me, wrapped in waxed paper.

From the draft board office, an Army bus took about forty of us to
Grand Central Station. Most of us were leaving home for the first time.
By the time we were lined up by the sergeant in the station concourse,
others looked as I did—pale, scared, insecure. I could only think over
and over again, What am I getting into? It's going to be the Boy Scouts all
over again, only worse.

My discomfort grew when I spotted my father looking around for me,
standing in his work clothes, khaki shirt and pants, the old suede jacket
and hat. At least he didn't dress up, I thought. He was such a lonely
sight, wanting to see me off yet clearly not wanting to embarrass me or
himself. I went to him as soon as I could. For the first and last time in my
life, I embraced him and kissed him on the cheek. He was still standing
alone, staring after me, as we departed.

We arrived at the induction center at Camp Upton on Long Island late
that night and marched off through a torrential rain to check in. We once
again called out the details that identified but did not really describe us:
name; birth date; religion. When asked my religion, I said, "Jewish,"
and the clerk marked *H* on my form. I was amused at the idea that there
are no Jews in the service, only Hebrews.

It was the only funny moment of the day. We were issued our dog tags
and, of course, uniforms that didn't fit. I was a caricature of a soldier. My
helmet was too big and kept sliding down my face over my glasses. My
gas mask fell into the mud, and by the time I crawled into my bunk, I was
exhausted by the emotion, travel, and chaos of my day. I had already
forgotten the dos and don'ts that began the day and knew only that I was
in the wrong place.

My first morning in camp began not with a bugle call but with a tough
sergeant bellowing the standard greeting as though he had made it up
himself: "OK, men, drop your cocks, pick up your socks, get out of your
fart sacks, you poor, sad motherfuckers!" It was all too crude. A simple
"Wake up, lads" would have done.

The crudeness of army life was confirmed when I went to the latrine:
twenty toilets on each side of a long room, knees practically touching the

man across from you, no partitions, no doors, no privacy. A sign on the wall announced, "Long Crap Help Jap," and I stared at it to focus my gaze. To help the war effort and avoid the scene, I practically stopped using the latrine (I only used it when I thought no one would be there—like 3:00 A.M.).

Shots and a medical examination followed, part of the abuse. The "three-day generals," recruits who had already undergone all the indignities and were waiting to go to basic training, warned us about the first shot, which they called "the hook."

"What's that?" we asked, terrified.

"That's to test you for clap. They stick a long needle up your prick, and then, when it's up there as far as it will go, it opens up like an umbrella and they yank it out." The toughest of us turned white, and several men literally passed out in the mud. Of course, it wasn't true, but few of us knew enough to question the possibility.

From there, we were taken to see *Mickey Mouse*, a film about venereal diseases and how to use a disinfecting brown soap to avoid them. "Stay away from whores" was the message. The hidden message was, if you ever had to have it, take the matter in your own hands, so to speak. I had no difficulty in doing what they asked.

I left Camp Upton three days later. I had survived the inoculations. My career in the United States Army Air Corps had begun.

I was sent to Atlantic City, New Jersey, where the Air Corps had taken over all the major hotels and turned them into dormitories, four soldiers in each room. Basic training made me long to be back in the Boy Scouts, where you were only pushed and kicked and thrown around once a week. Here we were marched—a mile at first, twenty-five miles by the end—along the beach and out of the city, freezing cold and wet in the winter days. Then it was target practice, gas mask drills, and more of the endless marching. "Hut, two, three, four" filled the air in a mindless repetition.

My helmet never did fit. It kept knocking my glasses off, so that I had to search blindly for them in the mud or snow. I was so inept that the men in my small group began to look after me. They taught me to become a goldbrick: how to fake a fever by keeping brown soap under my armpits, and how to miss KP duty by cutting a finger. Instead of getting angry, when I successfully avoided any onerous duty I seemed to feel a sense of victory.

Once, on a five-mile march, exhausted by the weights I carried, I collapsed by the side of the road after the second mile, and sat gloomily watching the other soldiers march past.

"What are you doing?" snarled the sergeant.

"I sprained my ankle," I said. I was soon picked up by an ambulance, along with some other goldbricks along the road, and driven back to my hotel in style. I avoided long marches by putting my glasses on the floor and ramming a broom handle into one of the lenses. When it was time to line up for the march, I would plaintively explain, "My glasses broke." I spent far more time on sick call getting new glasses than I did on the road.

Toward the end of January, my group was drilling just below the boardwalk next to our hotel. I could never do the "left flank" or the "right flank" properly and would invariably move in the wrong direction. Toward dusk a light snow fell, and I was cold and wet and miserable, laden down with a heavy outer coat, a gas mask, a pack on my back, a rifle, and that damn helmet.

When my incompetence was too much for him to handle, the drill sergeant gave me two sticks, one red, one blue. "The red is left, and the blue is right, you fucking idiot," he snarled, and put me in front of the others to drill. I did a left flank and faced the boardwalk as I turned. I couldn't believe my eyes. I saw my mother, weeping, of course, and Mrs. Flannigan, whose son was also in my unit. She was beaming at the spit and polish of her child. They were leaning over the boardwalk railing, their faces red with the cold. Then, my mother waved to me. Waved!

The drill sergeant continued to shout orders, and to his amazement, and mine, I now did everything perfectly. In another ten minutes or so, we marched back into the hotel. "Sonny, Sonny," my mother said, as she plucked at my sleeve in the lobby. I pretended not to know her until my fellow soldiers moved on.

"Sonny, it's me," she said.

"What are you doing here?" I hissed.

"I was so proud of you, Sonny, leading all those soldiers," she said, beaming. We talked for a short while. She soon left with Mrs. Flannigan. I was relieved to see her go and be left alone again. In February, on another cold and miserable day, my father and sister also came to see me. Somehow that visit went easier, though I was glad when they left.

When I finished basic training, I went to cooking school in Fresno, California, a town known to GIs as the "asshole of the Republic." From Atlantic City to Fresno was an uncomfortable four- or five-day train ride, and then Fresno lived up to its billing. It was hot beyond description. The fields where we drilled were covered with wood chips, and they seemed to smoke in the heat of the day, a little bit of dusty hell under our feet.

My finest hour in Fresno came on the firing range, where I won a "Sharpshooter" medal. After we fired at our targets, we were sent to bring them back to the sergeant in charge for evaluation. None of my shots had hit any part of the target. I was so humiliated that I poked some holes in the bull's-eyes with a pencil. The sergeant either didn't notice or didn't care, and I got my very first and last medal defending my country and democracy.

Because I looked vaguely intellectual and said I was a writer, I was assigned to draft a manual on how to run a field kitchen. The manual never was completed—it barely got started. This was not my idea of creative writing.

It all seemed absolutely hopeless. One night I decided to commit suicide. I swallowed fifty or so aspirin, a whole bottle, and lay down on my bunk to die. For the next two hours I was desperately sick—cold sweat and uncontrollable shaking. I panicked and ran to the infirmary, where I was diagnosed as having the flu and given two aspirin.

I spent a lot of time in town, as often as I could get away from the base. I liked Fresno because it was the birthplace of William Saroyan, a writer I admired, and I wandered about pretending to be part of that Saroyan world. I spent most of my time in the bar at the Omar Khayyam Hotel, where I earned a reputation as a great beer drinker.

It was at that bar that I met Bob, a GI from Chicago. If I ever knew his last name, I have long since forgotten it. I doubt he knew mine. He picked me up at the bar and led me out into the night. His arm steadied me as we walked to a nearby park. He knew where we were going; I did not. Hidden from public sight, I had "grown-up" sex with a man for the first time, someone I barely knew, emotionally safe in the anonymity of the occasion, in the darkness of an open space. It was brief, more elaborate than the movie theaters, and nerve-racking because I was sure we would be seen.

I made several trips to Los Angeles from Fresno ostensibly to visit my father's brother, Uncle Sam, and his wife, Aunt Goldie. I did visit them once, but I spent much more time walking up and down Hollywood Boulevard, watching men cruising for men during the late night hours, literally hundreds of soldiers and sailors waiting for a pickup in doorways and on street corners. I would look, but I didn't dare do anything. I walked endless miles during those long nights—my own private "long marches"—titillated by desire and so many opportunities, overwhelmed by fear.

Cooking school came to an end, and, as low as Army standards for cooks were, I didn't pass the test. I was transferred to Buckley Field in Denver where I was assigned as a writer on the *Buckley Armorer,* the base newspaper. Then I was transferred to clerk-typist school at Fort Logan, also in Denver. I kept up my long marches there. I would go into town and walk for hours, torn between my desire and my fears, afraid that the minute I did "it" I would forever become one of "them." I wasn't sure if I was ready for that, though shortly afterward I stole an angelic-looking young blond boy from a fat old sergeant about to pick him up. I took him to my cheap hotel room, and we slept in the same double bed, but I didn't touch him. I felt sorry for him because he was so young.

At Fort Logan I was promoted to private first class, my highest rank, and took my picture in one of those little booths that dispensed four frames for a quarter. I put my arm across my chest and under my chin so my stripe showed and sent a picture home. I'm sure my mother cried and my father smiled when they got it. It was lucky I got the picture when I did because I was busted soon after for drinking beer in the PX when I should have been in class.

To punish me more, my commanding officer assigned me to an all-Negro squadron. "Negroes" (the term blacks was not used in those days) were about as low on the Army's scale as anyone could be. They hated me at first because I was white, but as a communist, I felt it was my duty to show them culture and life. Liberals and communists were the most patronizing to Negroes, sometimes even more so than white Southerners who were open in their bigotry.

My Negro friends began to accept me as an eccentric white person who cared about them and their lives. But the limits of our relationship became painfully clear when I took some of them to Boulder to visit my United Mine Workers friends, who were putting on a social event to indoctrinate/recruit Negro soldiers. Boulder was a university town but, like America generally, was still "Jim Crow." A woman union organizer I knew arranged with a local hotel for the black soldiers to stay there.

I ended up in a room with a Negro soldier my age from New Orleans. There was only one bed. Both of us focused on it when we opened the door. I was horrified. He took a shower and got under the sheets. I smoked countless cigarettes and finally took my own shower. I had to get in the bed sooner or later. My fears were not sexual, but racial. I was a communist who knew all men were equal, yet I was nervous about being so close to a Negro. I had never touched a black man, and I slept fitfully at my edge of the bed.

In the morning, I felt I had to tell him of my concern. "You know, I really felt strange sleeping with a Negro, and I'm really ashamed of that feeling." He said, "How did you think I felt. It was the first time I ever slept next to a white boy." It hadn't occurred to me to wonder about his feelings.

Denver was not a bad interlude in my Army career, but I was soon sent to Newport News, Virginia, port of embarkation for Europe. A few days later I boarded the S.S. General Meigs, a troop ship going to Naples. I hated sleeping below decks, fearful that a German torpedo would find my bunk against the bulkhead.

I soon found a spot on one of the upper decks where gay soldiers and sailors gathered in the darkness of the blackout. Some of them sat around talking and gossiping, and in the far corners I could hear the moaning and groaning of others in sexual encounters that were far less secretive than anything I expected. I was erotically intrigued, but didn't dare watch or participate. Here I met a group of gay soldiers, some of whom became my friends. They accepted me. But although I liked most of them and enjoyed their campy banter and flamboyant gestures, I still kept myself apart.

Charles, one of the gay soldiers, was a tall, skinny, redheaded kid, not good-looking but enormously funny, which made up for his looks. He had a Modern Library edition of Dorothy Parker stories, which we all read aloud together, taking the parts of her characters. One story caught our fancy and became our favorite. It was called "From the Diary of a New York Lady: During Days of Horror, Despair and World Change." It was about a campy spoiled woman who went to the same kind of parties with the same kind of people every night. Miss Rose, her manicurist, came each day to do her nails, and invariably our lady would inveigh against her for some mistake or another, "Damn Miss Rose . . . I could spit." Each time we read that line, we laughed and whooped and thought it brilliant. We adopted the campy repartee of Dorothy Parker's story as our trademark in our conversation and our letters.

When we landed in Naples, we saw that the harbor had been bombed and several sunken ships stood between us and the shore. A narrow catwalk had been precariously erected over them to a dock, and we had to walk across on the catwalk to get ashore. I started out in line with the other soldiers, but soon found I couldn't carry my heavy duffle bag any longer. I thought of tossing it in the harbor, but then a lieutenant came up, wriggling past the other soldiers. He looked at me in disbelief and said, "Soldier, move the fuck on." "I can't, sir." "What are you talking about?" "I can't. It's too heavy." The lieutenant said nothing more. He picked up my bag and carried it to shore, throwing it down on the dock with a "fucking asshole." Clearly my ability as a GI hadn't improved on the trip over.

As a member of the Young Communist League at the time, I sought out the local Communist party leaders, who were delighted to see an American comrade. We met at a bar in Bagnoli, a workers' suburb of Naples. We sang *Avanti Popoli* and other workers' songs and talked of revolution. It was a marvelous time. I asked my Italian comrades if there was anything I could do for them. They asked for food. I talked some kitchen help into saving food that was not eaten, explaining that it was for the hungry; I did not explain that it was for the communist hungry.

I also found gay soldiers in Italy. Word got around that it was my twenty-first birthday, and Charles, my friend from the boat, organized a party for me. He staged it on the roof of a bombed-out orphanage in

Bagnoli, where we were billited with seven or eight gay friends. The stars were out, and there was a magnificent view of the city and sea from our rooftop island. Charles toasted me with a GI boot full of wine—his satin slipper. We all locked arms, and sang Andrews Sisters songs. Then Charles took center stage and twirled a long string of beads madly around his neck in a crazy dance. That night we nearly floated away on cheap Italian wine.

Those good times ended soon when I was shipped out of Naples on some kind of Arab troop ship. Our destination was Casablanca, and I imagined myself to be Charles Boyer as Pepe Le Moko in the film *Algiers*. The Casbah beckoned!

We arrived in Casablanca, stayed overnight at the air base there (no Casbah), and next day were put in a boxcar straight out of World War I, a "forty and eight," built to carry forty men or eight horses in each car. It was ghastly. We crossed the whole of North Africa like cattle. It took four days, with me most of the time perched precariously on the roof of the boxcar, my gas mask tied to a wheel up there so I wouldn't fall off—a nightmare of broiling days and freezing nights.

At Cairo, I was assigned to Sheppard Field, on the outskirts of the city. At a bar in Cairo, I made two new friends from the British camp right next to us. One was a tall and wonderful looking blonde called Lofty because of his height. His best buddy (and I expect his lover, although that was never mentioned) was a cockney Jewish bandleader from London who became rather famous after the war. The three of us had a wonderful time in Cairo visiting the Mena House Hotel near the Pyramids, where we used the pool, and an ice cream parlor called Groppi's where we hung out. As nonofficers, we were not permitted to visit the famous bar at Shepard's Hotel.

On base I lived in a transient tent with nine other men. It was impossible to make friends, because soldiers kept rotating in and out the tent every day. We spent our time waiting for orders to go somewhere else. To pass the hours, I carried on an intensive V-Mail correspondence with some of my friends from the troop ship—including Charles. He and I started with "Darling" and ended each of our campy letters with "Damn Miss Rose. I could spit."

Then one day, a jeep stopped in front of my tent, and two MP's got out.

"Is there a Private Liebman here?" one of them asked.

"That's me," I said, and began to worry. Had something happened to my father? To my mother? What possible other reason could they have for asking to see me? My tent mates were equally curious but far less alarmed.

I rode in the backseat of the jeep to our squadron headquarters. "Captain Ripley (the CO), wants to see you," a noncommissioned officer outside the building said. I went in to an office where about ten or fifteen men were typing, filing, or just hanging around. Captain Ripley, a short, fat, and very redfaced Texan, was seated behind his desk on a raised platform. I saluted and said, "Private Liebman reporting, Sir."

I felt every eye on me. Obviously, the other men already knew what was up. I still didn't have a clue. Ripley shuffled his papers and picked up a V-Mail letter. My heart sank, and a premonition of doom came over me. What could I have written? I didn't remember anything bad.

"Did you-all write this?" he asked. He made me walk to him to look at the letter. It was the letter I had written the day before to Charles at his new base in Tripoli. Of course, it was written in the style of Dorothy Parker. All mail was censored, but I saw no reason to worry when I wrote it.

"Yes sir," I said, "I wrote it."

"Do you suck cock?" Captain Ripley asked, his face reddening in fury, playing to the audience of soldiers in the squadron headquarters.

"No, sir," I said. Desolation and terror engulfed me. My face was crimson, my knees wobbled.

"It's obvious to me, soldier," he said, "that you are a cocksucker, and that you like it, like all the other New York Jew faggots."

I thought that I would die on the spot, and prayed that I would. I was standing at attention and didn't know what to do or what to say or where to look. I felt tears coming up, and I knew that if I shed even one, I could never forgive myself.

"What do you say, faggot?" he said.

My mind raced like a roller coaster. "I would like to see a chaplain, sir," I said. That was something my tormentor could not refuse. It was a request that he was obliged to grant.

Two MP's drove me to the Chapel and took me in to see a Catholic chaplain, whose name I can't remember. What was I to tell him? I could not repeat what Captain Ripley said—not to a priest.

"What's wrong, son?" the priest asked.

"Could I see a rabbi, sir? I'm a Jew—I mean a Hebrew."

One of the MP's told him what was up. I began to tremble without control. I was left alone with the chaplain. He never answered my question about a rabbi. It really didn't matter. I just wanted some help.

"I hope this isn't true," he said.

"No, sir," I said.

"Because," he said, "you know it's a terrible, terrible sin."

"Yes, sir," I said.

"It's a mortal sin."

"Yes, sir," I said, not knowing quite what a mortal sin was, but it sounded terrible.

"What do you want me to do?" he asked.

"I don't know," I said.

"I think you should see one of those psychiatrists at the hospital. They should know how to deal with this," he said.

With that, he filled out some papers, and the MP's took me directly to the Thirty-eighth General Hospital about five miles away. I was left alone in a small room, and I waited for someone to tell me what to do next. My uniform was soaked with sweat. I was as miserable and alone as I have ever been in my life. A nurse finally came in and took me to see a Major Flummerfelt. All I can remember about him was that he came from Philadelphia and that he was very kind and compassionate and had deep circles under his eyes. This was about two hours after my confrontation with Captain Ripley.

I sat across the desk from him. "Are you a homosexual, Private?" he asked.

"Yes, I guess I am," I said. He asked me some more questions, and then he said, "Marvin, I have three options. I can send you back to your squadron, or I can recommend that you be transferred to the base in Bahrain, or I can recommend you for discharge."

I couldn't choose. I asked, "What do you think I should do?" At that point, I would do anything this kind man would ask of me or suggest.

"Well," he said, "if you go back to Ripley, your life will be hell.

Bahrain Island is not a pleasant place to be. It's about 140 degrees in the shade, and the GI's there are usually incorrigibles and misfits. I can recommend you for discharge, but it will be a blue one."

"You mean I can get out," I said.

"Yes," he said, "but remember, it won't be an honorable discharge." He tried to explain what a blue discharge meant. He said it was a "general" discharge, and he knew just about as much as I did about its possible impact on my future civilian life.

"I'll take the discharge," I said, and instantly a weight seemed to fall off me. I could escape this terrible situation and get away from Ripley and from the nothingness of my Air Corps career. Another jeep came and took me to the hospital's Section 8 ward for soldiers with psychiatric problems, a long barracks with cots running down each side and barbed wire surrounding it on all sides. I signed in with the nurse, was assigned a bed and, as I entered the ward, realized that I was in the midst of forty-some lunatics.

All the other patients had mental problems of one kind or another, either real or counterfeit. My terror returned. I was absolutely certain that I would be killed before the night was up. I turned in my uniform for pajamas and a maroon robe and straw slippers. I had no razor or comb or brush, or anything like that. All my stuff was in the tent. I felt really naked and alone sitting on my bunk terrified by everyone around me. All eyes were on me. I was the new one. I was scared.

That night, after falling asleep, I was awakened by a great crash on my bed. I opened my eyes, and I saw a man who thought he was Superman leaping from my cot to the next one, and then on to the next, waking people up as he went. A great hue and cry arose, with people screaming and weeping. Suddenly, in the midst of the wails and moans and shrieks —with nurses and orderlies rushing about trying to calm people—I began to cry, without shame, hugging myself and rocking. That was the last time I ever cried.

With the outside world cut off, I began to make friends with some of the other soldiers in our Section 8 ward and felt, in a strange way, very much like each one of them. One day, we were allowed to go to the PX surrounded by MP's: Forty crazy soldiers shuffling through the dusty sand in their maroon robes to get a warm Coca-Cola. A nightmare had come true. I didn't think anything worse could happen. But I was wrong.

After about a week, I had a hearing before three officers. They asked whether I was a homosexual, and I said yes. They asked whether I ever did anything with other soldiers on the base, and I said no. They asked me when I decided to become a homosexual, and I said, I didn't decide, I just was. They asked if any other soldiers I knew were homosexual, and I lied saying that I didn't know any. Then, they told me to leave.

The next morning, I was informed that I had been given a general discharge, but was to wait for final orders. They also told me that I would be sent back to my former post and would stay there until the orders arrived.

I was taken back to my old tent by the MPs. Some of the soldiers there knew me, and there were three or four new soldiers. They all stared at me and wouldn't speak. Nobody, but nobody, would speak to me.

That evening, the usual formation was held when the flag was lowered. The whole squadron lined up, and I was there with my tent mates not knowing quite what to do. The flag was lowered. I heard Captain Ripley bellow out, "Private Liebman, get your ass up here." He was with several other officers in front of the line of soldiers.

I marched out, wondering what horrors awaited me.

"I would like you men to see how a New York Jew faggot drills," Captain Ripley said. He then started barking orders at me and made me march in front of the whole squadron. As usual, I didn't know my left from my right, and so caused a great deal of merriment among the hundred or so guys watching.

Instead of being amused at his own joke, Ripley seemed to get angrier and angrier, and his orders came faster and faster. I was just about ready to die. For the rest of my stay, every morning and every night, Ripley had me march. I obeyed his orders, and with each step I lost more of my self-worth. I became numb. It was as if I had left my body and could stand outside myself, watching this miserable soldier stagger through his drill orders in the desert heat. Ripley stopped only when the heat got to him and to the others.

I became a pariah, bitterly lonely and desperately unhappy. I was shunned by everyone. Not one single word of greeting or compassion or understanding or even desultory conversation was uttered. I was also upset that I had been publicly called "Jew." This increased my differentness—a Jew faggot. The linkage was devastating to me; it was my first awareness of the terrible linkage of bigotry—Jew, faggot, nigger, spick, dyke, anyone different. And, boy, did I feel different. Could I be the only Jew faggot in the world to be so singled out? Finally, I was given my travel orders, taken to the transport plane like a prisoner, and put on board for home.

I don't remember how long it took, but I do remember that there were no seats, and everyone—I don't know how many—was on the floor with packs, duffle bags, and personal belongings next to them. We were all lying leg to leg, head to head, back to back, sleeping or just thinking. A man near me was asleep, and I felt a terrible compulsion to let my fingers rest lightly on his leg and march up his thigh and toward his crotch. I don't know what came over me, except that I knew that if they say I am, I must be, and I will be. My fingers moved with a life of their own. What do I want? What am I trying to achieve? I didn't have an answer before the soldier awakened with an angry shout, and I quickly withdrew my hand. Happily, the plane was so crowded that he didn't know just where the touch had come from. My heart was pounding.

The plane landed in Miami, and I began one of those terrible wartime train rides to Fort Dix, New Jersey, the separation center. I was there overnight, and the next day all of us who were to be discharged were lined up in the cold November air. The officer had a sheaf of papers, and he called out names one at a time. There were a hundred or more of us. One by one, each man went up to receive a white sheet of paper—an honorable discharge—proud and practically skipping away, each one of them like a high school senior on graduation day.

There were four of us left. My name was called, and I went up to receive a blue piece of paper. A military policeman came over, telling me to follow him.

I was told to take off my uniform and was given a shiny black suit and a sport shirt. I was permitted to keep my Army shoes and my dog tags. That's all. This treatment was the rule for all soldiers with blue discharges.

I left Fort Dix with a blue sheet of paper that read, "Discharged . . .

for habits and traits of character not beneficial to the Armed Forces of the United States." Wearing my black suit, I had a deep feeling of absolute desolation and emptiness. There seemed to be nothing left of me. I took a bus to New York and arrived in the city in the early evening. With the final pay they had given me, I bought a cheap raincoat to protect me from the snow and bitter cold. Then I rented a room at a sleazy hotel on Times Square.

That night, depressed and alone, I paced the room trying to get hold of myself. "Fuck 'em," I finally said to myself. "If that's what they say I am, then that's what I'll be!" More out of anger than passion, I went out and cruised the streets. I picked up the first available sailor and brought him back to my hotel room. We never said a word.

The next morning, I telephoned home. My mother's shrieks of joy were followed by questions. "Where are you?" "When are you coming home?" I took the subway to Brooklyn and walked up Ninetieth Street in my shiny black suit and my tacky raincoat. When I came to the corner, I could see my mother waiting on the porch in the freezing cold, just as she had said good-bye less than two years earlier. She shouted, "Sonny, Sonny," and when my father came out of the house, they both came down to hug and kiss me. My sister was there and Mrs. Vavoulis (whose son never came home) and Mrs. Jacomochi and Mrs. Flannigan.

"Where is your uniform?" my father asked.

"I didn't want to see it anymore. I threw it away."

"How did you get out of the Army so early?" he asked.

"I had a slight heat stroke in Cairo, and I got a medical discharge."

No other questions were asked. The lying had begun.

Chapter 3

Bohemia

I STAYED HOME in Brooklyn for several weeks doing nothing, hiding out from anyone who might ask me questions. I didn't know yet how to cope with subterfuge—how to lie with a smile—but I was learning. I had to invent a new me to present to the world with all the lies in place. It was as if I were a playwright creating a character that would please everybody. Conversations with my parents and my sister were strained. I noticed that they were speaking in whispers as if there were someone sick in the house, and there probably was. I avoided seeing any of the relatives. I had no friends to talk to. I spent lots of time at the movies. I could hide there and perhaps find a sexual adventure, which gave me momentary pleasure but always made me feel worse afterward.

Slowly I began to work out my new role. I decided to pass in public as an honorably discharged veteran so I wouldn't stand out—or be found out—as the shamed creature I had become. I bought the eagle (honorable) discharge pin in an army-navy store on Forty-second Street and dutifully wore it in my lapel—upside down to show I was unemployed and looking for a job. I was not eligible for any of the benefits that saw other vets through the first days of civilian life. I had to sponge on my father. A Christmas job in Bloomingdale's helped somewhat.

In January 1945, I met Patsy at the Museum of Modern Art. We were both admiring Picasso's *Guernica* mural. She was with a young man who was cruising me. He came up to me and asked me what time it was. He was good-looking but very effeminate. I didn't like nellie men—afraid that they might be a mirror of the real me or what I might become. I was intrigued not by him but by the girl he was with. She wore a purple knitted hat, a green wool skirt, a multicolor silk scarf around her waist, and black stockings, a perfect bohemian. I fell in love with her at that instant.

We went for coffee. Patsy told me she was an artist and a student at Cooper Union. We went back to her small apartment on Jones Street in the Village. Her friend kept coming on to me, but I couldn't have been less interested. He finally disappeared, and Patsy and I talked and talked until midnight. Then we went to the Waldorf Cafeteria on Sixth Avenue and lingered over coffee for another three hours. She was open and frank about her life and her art, which she took seriously. I spoke about deep things but told her nothing about me—only about the character I had created for myself. I walked her home, and we promised to see each other later in the day. I took the subway home to Brooklyn.

I was in love—with a woman. I had never before experienced this feeling of total exultation.

We saw each other every day for the next two weeks. A week later we decided to get married. I met all her artist friends, and they approved of me. I thought they were great—free spirits as I wanted to be. I'm sure she wondered why we didn't sleep together. She probably attributed it to some bourgeois inhibition on my part. The truth was, I never thought of her body in any remotely erotic way. But I loved loving a woman so deeply. To have a permanent crush on a female affirmed my manliness, and I loved being a man.

We were married by the Reverend Elliot White, the Dean of Grace Church in New York and the religion columnist for the *Daily Worker,* in his apartment in Peter Cooper Village. After the ceremony, we went up to the cafeteria at 13 Astor Place. I was working for *Spotlight,* the publication of the American Youth for Democracy (AYD) the postwar successor to such communist fronts as the American Student Union and the American Youth Congress. The building at 13 Astor Place was owned by Local 65, and it was tenanted by almost every communist front in New York, including the teachers union. We had our wedding brunch there, with the best man, the maid of honor, and friends from the magazine. Then we went to our new apartment at 73 St. Mark's

Place (which we rented for fourteen dollars per month) to begin our honeymoon.

I had imagined that once I was married, I would be "cured," but I was now beginning to get nervous. Maybe it wasn't that simple. She fell on the bed. She called me to her, and we started kissing. Then she undressed and put a pillow under the small of her back and spread her legs. I had never seen a completely naked woman before. I was still dressed. She waited expectantly, looking at me with the eyes I loved so much. Very gingerly, I got undressed and put myself on top of her. Nothing, nothing whatsoever. So I made some lame excuse, and we cuddled and loved each other, but nothing happened, no erection, no matter how I tried. That was my marriage afternoon.

For the first time I had my own home, and a wife and new family—Patsy's bohemian friends. We furnished our apartment in what we thought was the bohemian style: Patsy's unframed canvases on all the walls, big pillows scattered everywhere, a plant or two, no chairs, tables, or bed other than the paisley-covered mattress on the floor. My marriage didn't please my mother, and our way of life shocked her. She made a duty visit once but never came again. Sitting on the floor was too much for a portly woman like her.

About a month after our marriage, *Spotlight* closed down—it had lost its wartime paper allocation—and I was out of a job. I found work at Hearn's Department store on Fourteenth Street, then at Wanamakers on Astor Place, and at night would work in a new restaurant at 17 Barrow Street that was run by a lesbian friend. It used to be the home of a Russian-communist restaurant called the Skazka. The jobs never lasted more than a couple of weeks. I was too busy "living" and "writing" to worry about work or the rent or anything equally mundane and "bourgeois." Somehow, we got along.

One day, Patsy became really exasperated. The rent was due, and we didn't have a dime. I walked up and down Broadway looking for jobs. I was the provider, after all. There were a lot of "Help Wanted" signs. The war was still on. I saw a sign saying, "Wanted, Young Man in Plastics Industry—Big Future!" I went in, and they hired me on the spot. They asked me to report next morning at 7:00 A.M. 7:00 A.M.!

I arrived on time, the job was walking distance from St. Mark's Place.

They told me to take off my shirt. In my undershirt I went into a long dark room with a primitive assembly line lit with dim naked bulbs. Old men and women sat on either side of the moving belt. Plastic figures of Jesus Christ came in a parade along the belt. I was handed a drill and told to drill holes in each figure's eye sockets and then screw in two florescent eyes. The Italian woman next to me—dressed appropriately in black—then crucified Him. The first head came off. The next split in half. The third one shattered, and I dropped the eyes on the dusty floor. But on the fourth, I placed the eyes perfectly. The woman sat there watching my ineptness, impatient to crucify. That job lasted about three hours. Well, said Patsy, at least it dealt with sculpture, sort of.

Most of my new friends were Patsy's schoolmates. We'd drink lots of wine, mostly zinfandel, and talk. The "art" crowd couldn't care less about politics. Although politics was still important to me, I grew more interested in art. But various events caused a political turning point in my life. The war was coming to an end. The Communist party was in chaos and divided between the Browderites, who favored cooperation with the capitalist world, and the Stalinists, who favored a return to conflict with the capitalists immediately after victory. The Stalinists prevailed. My hero, Earl Browder, national chairman of the party, was expelled. I quit the party.

Browder was the victim of a purge by the party leadership of members who cooperated too closely with the capitalists during the war. The war was ended, and the United States and the Soviet Union were enemies again. This purge disillusioned me. Until then, nearly all my friends—except those I knew through Patsy—had been party members. Now I was ostracized by all party members; I had lost that family and had to look elsewhere for friends. My leaving the party in no way lessened my belief in Marxism, however. I had become an anti-Stalinist, not an anticommunist.

Neither Patsy nor I ever discussed our sex life—or lack of it—with anyone, not even with each other. Except for that, I thought we had the perfect relationship. But our celibate existence was especially difficult for Patsy. Among our circle of "free-spirited" friends was another married couple who didn't have sex with each other. He was gay; she was a lesbian. Like many gay men and lesbians in those days, they got married to please their families. To the melody of "Old Smokey," He used to sing in a high, sweet voice:

Fairies get married, and dykes do it too.
That's why, my darling, I'm married to you.

My marriage would have been simpler if Patsy had been a lesbian. It would have been perfect.

One night Patsy started weeping. She said, "I'm leaving." "Where are you going?" I asked her. She said, "I don't know, I really don't have any place to go." She put on her babushka and her only coat and went out into the pouring rain. I was angry with myself. I knew that this was about my sexual problem, but I was afraid to face it like a man. I was hiding from myself. About an hour later, she came back, sopping wet, shivering, weeping, very sad, and said, "I really have no place to go." "Why are you going? I love you, I love you," and I did. She said, "I know you do, but you can't let me love you," and she began to weep again.

It took me a long time to realize what she meant. It was easy for me to love, but it was nearly impossible for me to let myself be loved. I wanted to tell her that I was gay, but I couldn't say the word. We decided we should get an annulment.

Our marriage was annulled in June 1945, less than six months after the wedding. I left the apartment, and my sister got me a job at a summer camp in Wilmington, Vermont, as the dramatics counselor. I recuperated there with middle-class Jewish kids and young middle-class Jewish counselors. That summer at the camp I felt loved and admired by everyone. They treated me like a hero returned from the wars, an honorably discharged veteran. I was now being paid to teach other people how to play roles, something I had been learning from personal experience.

I spent the next year back in the Village playing, writing, drinking, and just hanging out. I found an odd job here and there to supplement whatever money I could beg or borrow from my family. The Village seemed suddenly existentialist—too deep, too serious, rather sad and boring. My new friends were involved with their own self-magnified problems, their own anxieties. Harry Hershkowitz was putting out *Death* magazine and writing a novel on the walls of his cold-water flat.

Donald Justice was writing poetry. A few of them were experimenting with marijuana, which was just beginning to be used outside the jazz community.

I, too, experimented with new options. I puffed "shit" (as marijuana was called then). I tried out new political ideas, including Trotskyism and socialism. I talked endlessly about death and the new existentialism. We all moved around a lot from apartment to apartment, sometimes leaving a place just before the rent was due. They were hardly glamorous —scruffy, dingy hovels with cockroaches—but we were all artists every one. I fancied myself a writer and would spend much of my day (when I wasn't sleeping off the night before) writing, mostly short stories about sad young men.

Our crowd spent long nights drinking in the MacDougal Tavern, listening raptly to such local celebrities as the poet Maxwell Bodenheim, and Joe Gould, who was writing a novel in "penguin language," which only he could decipher. We went to the Waldorf Cafeteria on Sixth Avenue after the bars closed. There I met Isaac Rosenfeld, Dwight Macdonald, Ned Rorem, and Jimmy Baldwin, with whom I became good friends for a while. I liked Jimmy, especially because he was the ugliest young black man I have ever known, and when he drank he cried a lot. All of us were very sad in those days. We drank coffee until six in the morning, anything to avoid going home alone again.

During this whole period, none of my friends knew of my sexual interests. I kept hidden from them my encounters in movie houses, in the park, or in whatever seedy apartment I happened to be living in at the time. A few lesbians were my pals, but I was far too inhibited to discuss my sex life with girls. So I kept secret the gay part of my life.

I had a lot of friends but no real family; I lived in lots of places but had no real home; I had sex but no one to love. Nothing in my new life seemed to fill the vacuum I was carrying around inside me. The artists, existentialists, and bohemians couldn't give me the shared sense of purpose and mission that I lost when I quit the Communist party. I was desperately looking for something to give my life purpose and meaning as the Communist party had done.

Chapter 4

Palestine

I SAW AN advertisement in the *New York Post* placed by a group called the American League for a Free Palestine (ALFP). It talked about "Hebrew" freedom fighters struggling against the British "occupying forces" for a homeland in Palestine. Among the sponsors of the group were many show-biz celebrities, including Ben Hecht, Milton Berle, Rosalind Russell, Stella Adler, Canada Lee, Charles MacArthur, and Will Rogers, Jr. It all sounded good to me—the theater, the movies, courageous Jews fighting British imperialism. I could join the fight, reaffirm my Jewishness, and maintain my leftist credentials. It was a perfect antidote to my now-empty life in Greenwich Village.

I volunteered my services to ALFP. At first I was an office boy/gofer. But they began to pay some attention to me when I came up with a fund-raising idea that I still think is good. It was a black brochure with a jagged cutout that revealed inside a gauze bandage with red ink on it that looked like blood. Above and below the cutout, in white letters printed on the black paper, were the words HEBREW BLOOD. This really startled people when they opened the envelopes, before they saw the pitch for money.

As contributions poured in, I became the boy hero of the ALFP. Peter Bergson, the Palestinian Jew who ran the outfit, and the nephew of the chief rabbi of Jerusalem, took notice of me. His approval thrilled me. I had discovered two things: that I could make a contribution behind the scenes, and that I was good at fund-raising.

A major ALFP project was to buy and outfit a ship to transport refugee Jews from the displaced persons camps in Europe to Palestine. The British had declared an embargo on Jewish immigration, so the ship would have to break through the British blockade. There were a number of refugee ships at that time in the Mediterranean (as later depicted in the book and film *Exodus*). All these were run and financed by the World Jewish Congress (WJC) and operated by the Haganah, the military arm of the Jewish Agency, then the unofficial government of Jewish Palestine. The Haganah kept the ships and their movements quiet, for obvious reasons.

The ALFP was considered to be outside the mainstream by the various groups and organizations within the American Jewish community. These were mostly allied with the WJC, the major international organization dedicated to the creation of a Jewish homeland in Palestine. The WJC was philosophically tied to the political ideals of social democracy and worked closely with British authorities, in the firm belief that Palestine would soon be turned over to them under the terms of the Balfour Declaration. In recognition of this cooperation, the British permitted the Jewish Agency, an arm of the WJC, to govern the Jewish population of Palestine.

The Revisionists, the far right in the Zionist political spectrum, broke away from the WJC, trusting neither the British nor the WJC leadership. The Revisionists wanted immediate action, with no concessions to the British or Arabs. They organized their own army, the Irgun Zvai Leumi under Menachem Begin, which carried out various military actions against the British "occupying forces" in Palestine.

It was to help finance the Irgun's activities that Peter Bergson was dispatched to the United States to organize the American League for a Free Palestine. The ALFP sought to focus attention on the refugee situation. They started a fund-raising campaign to buy and equip their own ship. This campaign caused a serious rift with the Haganah and the WJC in Palestine and in the United States. Mainstream Jewish organizations deemed the Irgun "terrorist" and the ALFP a divisive group.

Neither I nor most of ALFP contributors were aware of this rift, of the nuances of Zionist politics, or even of the existence of other refugee ships sailing the Mediterranean. The ALFP purposely kept us in the dark. The other potential crew members and I—most of us left-wing or at least liberal—had no inkling that we were proposing to enlist in what was secretly a right-wing endeavor.

The *Ben Hecht*, named after the author-screenwriter who was ALFP's chairman, embarked from a dock in Staten Island in late December 1946. Although the existence of the ship had been publicized, the exact date of its departure was kept "secret" (although just about every Jew in New York knew about it). My mother, father, and sister came to see me get on the boat, but could not stay to see it sail.

The ship was a private yacht, built in the Kiel shipyards some years previously, about two hundred feet long. It was originally named the *Abril*, and we flew a Panamanian flag. Among the twenty-two crew members were a few paid professionals, such as the captain and the engineers; some dedicated members of the Betar (the youth group of the Zionist Revisionists); and adventurers, including myself and some professional merchant seamen who had volunteered or been recruited. Merchant seamen are a breed apart, all of them poets, many of them vociferous readers, and, almost to a man, dropouts. They did their job on whatever ship they worked, and, when they went ashore, headed for the nearest women and booze. They were heavy drinkers and played hard. I enjoyed their company, especially one called "Heavy"—because of his girth—who was jolly and particularly kind to me.

I had begged, pleaded, and cajoled those involved to let me join the ship's crew so I could write the story of this heroic venture. So, except for Wally Litwin, the photographer, I was one of the only nonprofessional seaman aboard the vessel. I was given the job of purser, the person who is meant to keep the ship's records and supplies in order.

The voyage was particularly stormy, with constant rain and sleet, especially whenever I had to stand watch on the outside bridge. Most of my watches were taken by friends because I was constantly seasick. I usually stayed in the bunk of my purser's cabin, which was littered with chocolate bars, shaving cream, soda pop, razors, toothpaste, condoms, and everything else a good seaman might need. The room was a total mess, and so was I.

Our first landfall was Ponta Delgada in the Azores. My relief at seeing land knew no bounds. The ship anchored, and I couldn't wait to get off. My mind was racing—could I get a plane to take me to France to meet the ship when it arrived? I would do anything to get off and stay off. My shipmates, of course, were all hale and hearty. This was their chance to get broads, to get their rocks off. After all, they had had no women for twelve whole days. I made the appropriate sounds signifying that my rocks, too, had to get off and quickly. But it was not my rocks it was me. I wanted to get off—the ship, that is—and onto solid ground.

Heavy went ashore first. He was the main operator/hustler of the crew. He immediately went to work getting the broads. Within the hour, most of us went to a house called the Casa Nova, where we were greeted by nine bedraggled women, all of them in slips or negligees, all of them puffing on cigarettes. They were obviously recruited on the spot for our pleasure. Money changed hands, and the liquor began to flow. Tinny music was playing on an old Victrola. One by one, the men left with the women, and those who were left waited for the first group to finish.

I was absolutely terrified. What could I do, how would I manage it? The thought of being with any of those terrible women, any woman, filled me with dismay and horror. I was sure they were all deeply infected with syphilis, gonorrhea, or even, my God, leprosy.

Finally, I was left alone in the room with one tall, angular, not very attractive woman. She sat herself down on my lap in just a slip. Oh, horror of horrors! In those days I affected a cigarette holder. She took the cigarette holder from my mouth and stuck it in her mouth and started puffing away. Syphilis!

She started humming nervously, wondering what was happening. I recognized the tune. It sounded a lot like "Bei Mir Bist Du Schön," made popular by the Andrews Sisters during the war, an old Yiddish theater song. I said to her, "Bei Mir Bist Du Schön." She said, "Ya," and I figured she spoke nothing but Portuguese. Then she looked at me and she said, *"Du bist Yiddish?"* "Yes," I said, and she embraced me with such warmth and vigor that I thought I might smother. She then told me her story in Yiddish. She came from Vilna and was forced by the Nazis to serve as a prostitute for their troops. After the war, she wandered toward the West and, through some bad fortune, ended up in this ghastly little town in the Azores. She was slowly making her way to the Bronx to live with her Aunt Sadie and Uncle Max on the Grand Concourse. Did I know them? No, I didn't. Was I going back to the Bronx, to America soon? Yes, I was. Would I take them a letter? Yes. "Please," she said, "don't tell them what I do." I assured her I wouldn't.

We spent the next hour or so drinking glasses of tea. She babbled away about her adventures, and I built up my role on this famous boat that was going to rescue all the Jews left in Europe. I was an absolute hero to her. When the rest of the guys dragged themselves out of the seedy bedrooms, I was wide awake and happily drinking tea with this woman who obviously adored me. As we left, she embraced me and said in English, "Do not pay, do not pay." My reputation on the ship went up a few notches.

After two days in the Azores, the ship stopped at a port just outside Marseilles, Port du Bouc, where it was to be gutted and refitted with bunks for six hundred Jewish refugees. This would take about a month. I was in charge of paying the crew.

The night after we arrived, all of us went to Marseilles to the British American Bar. This was a major seamen's hangout on the fringe of the waterfront and the Old City, which had been leveled by the Nazis and was still in ruins. There were a number of people dancing, mostly sailors in civilian clothes, and a number of single women sitting at tables alone. In those days, European dance music was sort of tinny-romantic. One by one, my crew mates joined the women. What to do? Seated in the far corner, wearing a turban, was a young girl who looked remarkably like the child film star Margaret O'Brien. I figured she might be harmless, so I approached her. "Hello," I said. "'Allo, Johnny." (Prostitutes called everybody Johnny.) She said, "Ask me where I come from." "Where do you come from?" "I come from 'ollywood," and she licked her lips lasciviously as she pronounced the word.

I laughed dutifully, and I said, "Oh, I come from Hollywood, too." She brightened immediately. "Do you know Clark Gable, do you know Shirley Temple," pronouncing the last names in the French way, "Clock Gobbla," and "Shirlee Tampla." She told me her name was Peewee (because she was so small), and I learned later that her real name was Jannette Verdi. She and two of her friends—Susie and Maguy—made themselves at home on the boat for the next several weeks and never stopped eating our ample stores, mostly sardines.

Peewee took to me even though she knew that I was a "pede," the French diminutive for *pederaste*. She figured that out, she said, the moment I said hello to her. She tried several times to teach me how to have intercourse, but it didn't work. She laughed merrily and said it really didn't matter. One time we tried it in the absent Captain's bunk while a drunken party was going on in the galley, but it just wouldn't work.

One day, as a lark, Peewee and I—and a fourteen-year-old Algerian pimp named Mohammed—went to Monte Carlo on the Blue Train. It was about a two-hour trip. Mohammed took to me, and we played protégé/mentor, but I never knew who was who. I bought Mohammed some yellow shoes with very thick gum soles to give him some height. He was inordinately proud of them. Peewee and Mohammed and I were standing in the great lobby of the Casino just looking around when two elderly English ladies, wearing the usual crushed hats, asked me, "Excuse me, sir," pointing to Mohammed, "Is that the Prince of Monaco?" I answered, "No, Madam, it is His Highness's playmate," and the two old girls left quite happy at having gotten so close to royalty.

In Marseille I met the "heavies" who were handling the refitting for the Irgun. Monsieur "Palest" (a nom de guerre from the word Palestine) looked like Sydney Greenstreet, and his aide, Gershon Hakim, looked like Peter Lorre. Since my job as purser was to pick up the money for the crew and to make sure the accounts balanced, Palest's cloak-and-dagger style, and the pistol he carried, made me especially careful. He was later killed when the second and last Irgun ship, the *Altalenia*, was destroyed by the Haganah just off Tel Aviv.

Three weeks later, the ship was ready to leave. The Irgun had rounded up some six hundred Revisionist Jewish refugees and brought them to the boat. But some of the refugees refused to board on the Sabbath. After many entreaties, they did, with the promise that we would not move until Saturday night.

When the engines revved up during the day, no one asked to debark. With the passengers standing on deck, the Panamanian flag was brought down, the Star of David was hoisted, and everyone spontaneously started to sing "Hatikvah," the anthem of the Jewish state. But before the middle of the song, the ship ran aground and the engines stopped! After four more tries and four more singings of "Hatikvah" the *Ben Hecht* took off.

The "passengers" were separated from the crew so we could get on with our work. Nevertheless, I did get close to some of them. I had a few favorites, and, when I could, I smuggled out to them cans of sardines and other food from the galley. Most of them looked stuffed—not from eating, but because they wore everything they owned. If a woman had three dresses and two sweaters, she would wear them all; a man, three pairs of trousers and two jackets.

About four days out, two British destroyers came into view and ordered us to stop. When we didn't, they pinned us between them and took over the boat. There was some panic, but most of all we were heartbroken. The crew was ordered to the bridge, and the ship was taken over—as the ALFP organizers might have expected—by a British commander and crew. Because I wanted to stay with the refugees to report on what happened to them, I pretended to be one of them, changing my role from "writer" to "undercover journalist."

We arrived in Haifa harbor at about 8:00 at night. All the passengers lined the deck, which by then was encircled by barbed wire. There were tears as they looked at the sparkling magical lights of Haifa, this precious land that they had striven so hard to reach. As I stood against the rail, I actually felt a terrible grief. I was one of them, longing for a home I couldn't have.

The next morning we were taken off the *Ben Hecht* one by one and transferred to a British naval ferry that was to take us to the island of Cyprus. There we were to be put in a British detention camp with other refugees who didn't get through the blockade. The word got around: "Don't go easily. Give them trouble!" The women started shrieking, the men shouted curses, and I, who wanted nothing more than to walk off like a civilized human being, had to be carried off shouting feebly in Yiddish, "Pigs, pigs!" Once on the ferry, we were detained in a large hold for several hours as the *Ben Hecht* left Haifa, and then we were allowed on deck.

That night we were sleeping on the deck, shoulder to shoulder, hip to hip, men, women, and children. Half-asleep, I was remembering the Air Force plane that had taken me back to the States after being thrown out of the Army. Suddenly I was startled by a hand creeping up my thigh.

I tried to move it away, thinking it was there casually, but the hand was insistent. I turned my head and saw a man with the most mournful, staring eyes. Out of compassion for him, and for all of us on that ship that night, including myself, I did nothing and let him fondle me.

At Cyprus, we were loaded onto British Army trucks, and taken to a camp outside of Nicosia. On the way, we passed a German POW camp, and the Germans hooted and shouted insults at us: "Wilkommen, Juden! Welcome, Jews! Welcome to the camps again!" I was frightened and angry, because they were correct. Was there no escape for the Jews from the camps? Would it be one camp after another?

I spent about fifteen days in this camp, housed in one of the many Quonset huts with the other refugees, pretending to be one of them. The camp was run by Jews working with a representative of the Jewish Agency, who as the months wore on would send the refugees, group by group, to Palestine while others arrived to replace them. I heard through the grapevine that my fellow crew members were taken from Haifa to the infamous Acre prison, run by the British in Jerusalem, and then sent back to the United States. Everyone around me, of course, knew that I was an American, and they went out of their way to protect me and make me more comfortable. They kept saying to each other, "The American is not used to such things!" and indeed I wasn't.

We got up in the morning to get our tea in metal mugs and a hunk of black bread. For lunch, we lined up again and got more tea and bread. In the evening, they gave us soup or weak stew, bread, and tea. We weren't starving, but there was really never enough to eat. From time to time, we would get fresh oranges from the Cypriots. There was a lot of bartering being done in the camps.

The Quonset huts had about twenty cots on each side, about forty people to a hut. Family groups would try to put blankets up between their bunks. There we spent our days talking, which was difficult for me because hardly anyone spoke English. But with my meager Yiddish and their meager English, we found ways to communicate. In the evenings, we would go to a little theater to see a show put on by refugees or to hear other refugees give lectures on literature, history, Zionism, politics, and many other subjects. The camps, I discovered, had a rich cultural life.

My favorite times were around the campfire. The women would sing the saddest possible songs, old Yiddish folk songs that I remembered from my mother and new songs about the camps. After the singing, the young people would dance the hora and other Israeli dances with great merriment around the fire.

I loved the people with whom I shared the Quonset hut. They had lost everything and everyone and had nothing left but memories, most of them too terrible to recall: There was Miriam, the schoolteacher, who had survived by being an official prostitute for Nazi troops. Herr Hutz, the head of a slaughtered family whom he imagined were still with him and with whom he conversed endlessly in Yiddish. The Rabbi, with his beard gray and growing back after the Nazis had plucked it by the handful from his face—not speaking, just staring from his cot day and night. Frau Blumkin, the upper-class lady from Vienna who had survived the past seven years through sheer chutzpah and fury at being thrown in with such riff-raff by barbarians. The young lovers, Channah and Motel, beautiful and alive, planning their lives in Eretz Israel.

Finally there was David, the communist. He had worked with the Resistance in Poland and was out to turn Palestine into a communist state. A dedicated Marxist, he was delighted that I had been in the party in the United States. Afraid to disappoint him, I didn't let him know that I had quit.

These people looked after me as if I were their youngest son—even Frau Blumkin. I was the outsider, the "Americaner," the savior who failed but was still worthy of help.

The British pretty much left us to our own devices. The camp was surrounded with high barbed-wire fences and guard posts—towers with armed British soldiers guarding them. The British didn't want to be there any more than we did.

One day, David told me to come with him—there was going to be a riot. Why riot? "Why not?" he said. I went to another part of the camp, and there was a great crowd, mostly young people, chanting "Let us out, Let us out! Send us home, send us home! We want to go to Palestine, we want to go to Eretz Israel." And the crowd grew bigger and bigger. When they started approaching the gates, the British threw tear gas bombs. Many of the young people picked up the bombs, which must have been fiery hot, and threw them back at the British. I couldn't shame myself in front of David, so I stood with him, watching. Happily a bomb didn't fall near me, so my courage wasn't tested. That was my first riot.

I learned a lot about Zionism through these people—their will to live, and their longing for a home. Most of them were alone, having lost wives, husbands, children, mothers, fathers, but they were willing to start anew. I felt proud that I had something to do with trying to help them get to Eretz Israel, their home in a world where they had no place else to go. I had never known this kind of personal pride in the Army Air Corps. Now I was a soldier participating in the history of my people, men, women and children who were my family, not just images and newsreels.

A few weeks later, I met a young French journalist who had arrived, also passing as a refugee, to report on life in the camps. When she heard about me, she came over to talk to me, and we became friends. A few days later, she and I went together to the head of the Jewish Agency at the camp. She introduced us as two journalists (which made me proud) and said that we had no desire to go to Palestine and wanted to get out. He invited us to lunch at his house, served us sour cream, radishes, and cucumbers—a real treat!—and then arranged for us to leave. The Agency sent her back to France and gave me enough money to go to Athens, where I wanted to join the communist rebels in the Greek civil war.

I spent a couple of days in Athens. I went to the Acropolis, which I had always wanted to see. Riding in a horse and buggy up that winding road that rose above the city, I found, instead of the glory of Greece, people lying on the side of the road dead from starvation. Even the Acropolis was not a refuge from the chaos of war. Walking through the city streets, I realized that it was dangerous to talk to strangers, and no one spoke English anyway. My plan to join the communist rebels turned out to be hopelessly romantic.

I cabled my family to tell them I was alive and needed money immediately. The money they wired got me from Athens to Marseilles. There I went directly to see Peewee and the girls at the British American bar. They greeted me as a returning hero and raised the money to send me to Paris. Arriving there by train, I went to the office of the Irgun, where I saw my old friend M. Palest and others who debriefed me, put me up at the Meurice Hotel, and gave me some spending money.

I spent about four days in Paris, mostly with my young French journalist friend. She showed me around the city and took me to meet her family. In their home, I began to realize that the Jews in Cyprus, in Paris, and back home in Brooklyn were like members of one enormous family—the same customs, same way of communicating, same spirit, or as the Russians would say, the same soul.

One morning I decided to visit André Gide. I had a fantasy of moving in with him as his young companion and getting to meet all the French literati: Jean Cocteau, Edith Piaf, Jean Renoir, and all the others. My friend Harry Hershkowitz, publisher of *Death Magazine* back in Greenwich Village, had claimed to be Gide's friend. "Do you really know André Gide?" I had asked him. "Of course," he assured me, and gave me his address in Paris. So I bravely found my way to André Gide's residence. As I walked up the stairs to his apartment, I wondered what in the world I would say. I pulled the bell and waited, rehearsing all the French I knew. The door opened, and there was André Gide, whose face I recognized from photographs I had seen. "Monsieur Gide," I said. "*Oui*," he said quizzically. Then he looked closely at me. "You are American," he said. "Yes, sir," I said. "Ah, you admire my work?" "Oh, I do very much, sir." "Thank you," he said, and shut the door. Thus began and ended my life with André Gide.

When I returned home to New York, I wrote a series of four articles on my experiences in the Cyprus camp, which were published in *p.m.* (a liberal New York daily), much to the chagrin of I. F. Stone. One of their top columnists, he had been in Cyprus at the same time I was, but couldn't get British permission to visit the camps. I had scooped the famous I. F. Stone!

My family greeted me as a conquering hero, as did the friends and supporters of the ALFP. On April 21, 1947, just about four months after the *Ben Hecht* had left Staten Island (although it seemed like a lifetime), I was asked to speak at a banquet given in honor of the ship's crew at the Hotel Astor's Grand Ballroom. I was thrilled to be in the company of the other speakers that night: Ben Hecht, Milton Berle, and Rosalind Russell. My sister, who attended the dinner, later told me how proud my father was when he heard me speak. This was one of my only successes he lived to see.

My homecoming was different from the one three years earlier. I was proud of what I had done, and my family was proud of me. There were no lies, no subterfuge, no charade. I was a hero, not only to them, but also to myself.

Chapter 5

To Hollywood

SOON AFTER THE state of Israel was declared on May 14, 1948, I landed a job in New York City with the United Jewish Appeal (UJA). It was there that my professional fund-raising career began.

The UJA's 1948 goal for funds to send to the new Jewish state was an unprecedented $200 million, an amount that nevertheless was raised by the end of the year. The UJA enrolled all new staff members in an intensive two-week school. It was run by tough old-time fund-raisers for Jewish causes. They taught us all the techniques, from the primitive direct mail packages of the time (I realized then how innovative my "Hebrew Blood" mailing had been) to the UJA trick of "calling names" —asking people to announce their gifts publicly and, if they were not considered generous enough, to shame them into giving more.

After our graduation, I was assigned to UJA's West Coast headquarters in Los Angeles and given a one-way train ticket to California. I couldn't have been more pleased at the thought of going to Hollywood, the show biz, movie, and glamour capital of the world.

On my way across country that July, I made a detour to Philadelphia (arriving on my twenty-fifth birthday). It was an important turning point in my political development. I attended the Progressive party's national convention, which brought together three thousand delegates and alternates from all over the country. These were my people— communist and noncommunist alike, dedicated to all that I thought was good and true and beautiful. The convention seemed the epitome of the progressive and labor movement of the postwar years, a real chance to change the face of America.

The Progressive party was an amalgam of two communist front groups—the National Citizens Political Action Committee and the Independent Citizens Committee of the Arts, Sciences, and Professions. Together they organized the Progressive Citizens of America, which, in turn, called a convention to establish the Progressive political party and to nominate presidential and congressional candidates.

Two years previously, these two groups, together with New York's American Labor and Liberal parties, organized a September 1946 rally at Madison Square Garden. Former vice president and then secretary of commerce Henry A. Wallace delivered a highly controversial foreign policy speech that was pro-Soviet and bitterly critical of Truman's foreign policy. President Truman was furious.

Wallace had started his national political career as secretary of agriculture in Franklin D. Roosevelt's cabinet. In July 1940 he was nominated as FDR's vice president and elected. In the 1944 campaign he was dropped by FDR in favor of Harry S Truman. But Wallace became Roosevelt's secretary of commerce, a post he held under Truman until his Madison Square Garden speech.

Wallace then became the unwitting front man for communist activities in the United States. The Philadelphia convention was totally controlled by Communist party *apparatchiks*. The delegates nominated Wallace as their presidential candidate and Senator Glenn Taylor, a Democrat from Idaho, as his running mate.

I wasn't a delegate, but I wanted to participate in the convention. So I offered my services to the staff of Calvin B. "Beanie" Baldwin, of the Congress of Industrial Organizations (CIO) political action committee.

The Wallace campaign was the last attempt by the Communist party to organize a popular front in the United States. It almost worked, but it was defeated by the stupidity and arrogance of the communists who were unwilling to compromise. Anything remotely anti-Soviet was booed and hissed. Even a minor resolution by the Vermont delegation—stating that no blanket endorsement of the foreign policy of *any* nation should be given—was shouted down. They even opposed liberal Congresswoman Helen Gahagan Douglas in California and fielded a candidate against her.

She had voted for the Marshall Plan, and that was enough to damn her.

Although Baldwin knew I was no longer a party member, he assigned me—along with a number of communist volunteers—to put out any liberal or anticommunist fires. I was very much involved in quashing the so-called Vermont Resolution. The arrogance of the communists was beginning to make me rethink my relationship with them. But I played along. I thought I had no place else to go.

At the convention I met Jerry Fielding, a delegate from Hollywood who was a young and attractive musical arranger, composer, and conductor. We agreed to travel on to California together, and spent the next three days on the train drinking and talking endlessly about politics and "life." I became very attached to Jerry (another unrequited love). In Los Angeles I met his wife, Ann, and became friends with both of them.

I hadn't been to California since my service in Fresno during the war. I fell in love with the state, especially Los Angeles. As Ronald Reagan once said, "If the pilgrims had landed in California, the rest of the country would never have been discovered."

The United Jewish Appeal office on Wilshire Boulevard assigned me to be advance man for Eddie Cantor, the famous stage, screen, and radio comedian. Cantor and I were sent out to work the small and medium-size towns throughout the state—Elsinore, Eureka, Ventura, San Luis Obispo, Santa Rosa—an endless series of boring provincial places.

I arrived in town a day or two before Cantor to set things up. The local chairman gave me the names of all the potential contributors in town as well as information on their net worth, maximum contribution expected, and whatever personal details we could get on their children, spouses, brothers, sisters, family illnesses, and celebrations. I put it all on three-by-five cards. This was our ammunition.

Then Eddie Cantor would arrive, and we'd go to work. Eddie, as he insisted I call him, was a high-strung man when he wasn't "on." But the instant he appeared before any audience of people—from a small living room to a temple auditorium or a huge theater—he became the consummate performer, completely at ease. He told jokes. He sang and danced. He reminisced. He clapped his hands. He did his shtick.

Alone with me, he was impossible. His temper tantrums terrified me. Although he was totally devoted to Israel and raised as much money as possible, he was primarily dedicated to his own ego. He was driven to do better than anyone else, to raise more money, to set a record.

A typical fund-raising event would take place in a businessmen's club, a synagogue auditorium, or the living room of the wealthiest Jew in town. As often as possible, wives would be invited so they could shame their husbands as required. Eddie would stand up in front of the room facing the assemblage. He'd sing a song, tell a few jokes. The crowd—especially the women—was absolutely thrilled to be in the presence of this great star. The men were less thrilled because they knew what it would cost them.

Then Eddie would take out the dreaded cards and read a name. "Sol, Sol Ludwig, how are you, Sol? How's Bessie? (his wife). I hear that Johnny (his son) is going to Stanford. Great! I'm glad that you can afford it. Ha, ha ha. So, Sol, what about it? The dress store did very well last year, I hear. How much are you going to give?"

Poor Sol would mumble some figure, and Eddie would say, "What? A little louder! I didn't hear!"

Sol would meekly say, "Two thousand dollars?"

"Sol, you must be kidding," and he would go into a pitch about the growing dress business, what was needed in Israel, and shaming Sol into raising the gift to at least four thousand, if not more.

When Eddie had got everything he could out of Sol, he'd go on to the next name on the list. It was a dreadful but very effective way to raise money. Once the pitch started, the audiences were petrified, waiting for the next name to be called. But their desire to see the great Eddie Cantor kept them coming.

Our total take from a two-week tour of the smaller communities in California was a remarkable $700,000. I learned a lot about fund-raising from that experience, especially the techniques of personal solicitation and how to use group psychology, including the desire to give money as a way of showing off.

I quit the UJA to volunteer my services full time to the last months of the Henry Wallace presidential campaign. I worked out of San Francisco, raising money in most of the towns I had been to with Eddie Cantor. The Wallace headquarters gave me just enough money to meet my expenses. I returned to New York to cast my vote.

Wallace got about 1.3 million votes, most through the New York American Labor party. He received no electoral votes. His campaign was a dismal failure; I was bitterly disappointed. I still wanted to have a cause, and leaders I could respect. But neither Henry Wallace nor the Communist party could fill the bill.

I needed a job. Looking around for work, I realized that my only real asset was my Palestine/Irgun/UJA experience, and so I looked in the classifieds for something that might fit. There was an ad from an organization called the Aguduth Israel. I went up to a seedy office in the West Forties for an interview.

The Aguduth Israel was an orthodox organization in the business of "rescuing" Jewish children from Polish convents. The line was that Jewish mothers, to save their children from the Nazis, had left them in convents, where they were raised in the Christian faith. It was time to get these children back to Israel. How many, if any, children in convents were actually saved I don't know. But the Aguduth Israel, if they hired you, assigned you to a certain territory and allowed you to "sell" the children for three hundred dollars a child—one hundred would go to you, and two hundred would go to the Aguduth Israel. This struck me as bizarre, but I needed the money.

I was hired, and ordered to buy a hat, because all religious Jews had to keep their heads covered with hats or yarmulkes. I agreed, although I had never worn a hat before or since. I was given a partner named Ezra, and we were told to go to Boston. Because I was more "modern" than Ezra—who wouldn't handle money on the Sabbath—I was given the advance of a hundred dollars to cover our expenses until we sold our first child.

Ezra irritated me. He would eat no food other than fruit, which he carried in a brown paper bag. At his insistence, we took a bus to Boston (I would have taken the more expensive train, of course). We checked into a terrible cheap hotel near the bus station. Ezra went out to meet the local rabbi and set things up. It was a beautiful day, so I took a walk. The thought of sharing the same room with Ezra that night or selling Jewish children even at a profit of a hundred dollars each for us (and only half for me) was more than I could bear.

I went back to the hotel room, which already smelled strongly of fruit, left my hat and fifty dollars for Ezra on the bed, and absconded with the rest. I went across the river to Cambridge, where I stayed happily for the next five months and never saw Ezra again.

In Cambridge, I discovered an academic oasis different from any I had known. I found young men who were clean, fresh, and innocent, bright students from Harvard, MIT, and the Putney School in Vermont. To them, I was exciting and worldly-wise, an eccentric, bohemian nonconformist who had traveled the world and had adventures and experiences to talk about.

In Cambridge, I was a "floater"— one of the writers, poets, and others who audited classes and hung around the universities. I became friends with a number of students at the Harvard Law School; I also made friends with a group of Harvard freshman. Among them was Owen Lattimore's son, David; Lattimore was to play a part in my later life. Dick Button was a fellow freshman and roomed just across the hall. Button was a celebrity; he had just won the Olympic figure skating championship. David and his friends were graduates of the Putney School in Vermont, which I visited a number of times, becoming enchanted with its idyllic location, its faculty, its progressive education, and its wonderfully attractive students.

I took a room in a house at 35 Concord Avenue that also had students from the MIT architecture school, poets, writers, and other floaters like me. I spent long hours with them drinking wine and talking. I wrote and wrote short stories. It was like being back in the Village but cleaner and prettier—both the place and the people.

My ex-wife, Patsy, came down from Vermont to visit me for a couple of weeks. She was living with her father at Goddard College while recuperating from a stay at Pilgrim State Hospital in New York after a breakdown. We had a great time—even went to the Dartmouth Winter Carnival weekend as the guest of a student friend of mine. I still loved Patsy. Now that there were no sexual expectations between us, I discovered that we got along terrifically well. I felt protective of her. I enjoyed introducing "my ex-wife" to my new student friends. Everyone adored her and she was good for promoting my heterosexual image.

I was deeply attracted to these students, but never let them know I was gay nor pursued sexual relationships with them. Instead, every couple of nights, and in secret, I would go to the Silver Dollar and other gay bars in Boston. Sometimes, I would unexpectedly meet a student in a gay bar or in the park. We would then studiously ignore each other if we happened to meet again in public. I worked hard to keep these two worlds from overlapping.

I was always broke. Working from time to time at the Harvard Co-op didn't give me enough money to get by. But I found other ways to survive. I supplemented my nonincome by stealing textbooks from the Co-op—taking them out under my jacket or sweater—and selling them to the used book dealers down the street. David and his Harvard friends would sneak me into their freshman dining room fairly often, and that's how I had enough to eat.

I stayed in Cambridge until February 1949, when I ran out of money. With money I borrowed from my sister I came back to New York and rented for $125 a month a yellow brick house on Third Street and Second Avenue in the East Village. The top three floors of the house had nine rooms, one kitchen, and one bathroom. The basement was already rented by an artist who was happily reclusive and had nothing to do with me. My basic plan was to get free housing by living in one room and then renting out all the others. I started with the very largest room, but ultimately, as my house filled up with people, I ended up in the smallest room in the attic. I was living rent-free but not very comfortably.

My housemates and I decided to organize ourselves into something like a commune to share the work and food. After about two weeks with twelve people sharing one bath, one kitchen, and one toilet, I would open the refrigerator door and see little notes on eggs, on bacon, on bread, saying, THIS IS MINE! DO NOT TOUCH!! DO NOT TOUCH!; or WHAT HAPPENED TO THE MILK THAT WAS HERE?!!! In order to get the phone company to install a pay telephone in the hall, I had to use the name Marvin Liebman Community Center. For six years, until 1955, the Marvin Liebman Community Center was listed in the Manhattan telephone book.

Among my housemates were two men who were lovers and believers in Reichian therapy. Reich was a psychologist who developed the Orgone theory, and the boys built an Orgone Box of their own and would sit in it for hours. The Orgone Box was like an outhouse lined with steel wool, copper wires, and God knows what and they would sit while their orgones reflected against the box and back into them. It was weird. They were very private about their therapy and were interesting only when they both tried to get in the box at one time.

I occupied most of my time writing short stories and a novel. I lived on handouts from friends and from my parents and sister and the few odd jobs I was able to get and willing to take—as busboy in restaurants and as stock boy in department stores.

I had a strange experience one night. It was November, but it was unusually balmy and springlike. I walked from Second Avenue over to the West Village. I looked at the boys and men passing, all the couples holding hands, and I felt terribly, terribly alone. Somehow the hours passed.

At about 2:00 A.M., I went to Washington Square to cruise, looking for something or someone. I saw the shadow shape of a sailor standing just away from me under a streetlight. I paused about ten feet in front of him, and I lit a cigarette. The sailor didn't move. I fantasized about this wonderful, handsome, and kind young man who would be my beloved forever. I smoked another cigarette and finally a third, but he did not move. I then summoned all my courage and approached the sailor. It wasn't a man at all. It was a tree! I was cruising shadows!

I became frightened, and I started running out of the Square, which, by that hour, was filled with homeless people going through the trash cans. I ran past New York University, down Eighth Street just past Cooper Union, and I saw a man approaching me dressed in white like a ghost. As he came closer, I saw that he had blood all over him. I was terrified and just about out of my mind. I ran as fast as I could. (Later I realized he was probably a butcher coming from work early in the morning.) I finally reached the house on Third Street and frantically inserted my key in the lock. The key bent. The door wouldn't open. I banged hysterically at the front door until I was let in.

That incident led to a terrible bout of depression. I was going through something that I couldn't understand. I had reached an age when I knew I should be making a living. But instead I felt lonely, useless, and empty. I didn't like myself or my life at all. Bohemianism appealed to me less and less.

It was a cold winter. There was a homeless shelter for men on Third Street and the Bowery, just down the block. Twice, one of us came out in the morning to find a man frozen to death. It was a hard winter for me and the Bowery derelicts. I wondered if I was that different from them, if I would end up like them.

Patsy came in from Goddard College to spend Christmas of 1949 with me. Her visit was a bright spot that pulled me temporarily out of my depression. During a brunch I put together for her, she gave me one of her paintings as a Christmas present. Among the guests were three of her ex-lovers (whose names I have forgotten) and, of course, I was her ex-husband. The painting looked rather like a red island in a churning sea of green. Could it be Manhattan? Knowing I could get away with it, I said, "It's wonderful, darling, but what is it?" She knew that I never understood her art. She said, "Why, it's a penis, of course." Her three ex-lovers and I exchanged glances. Whose penis was it? I knew it wasn't mine.

My parents had become seriously alarmed at my depression and my inability to find work. Through our family doctor, Leo Ginsberg, they met a man who worked for the American Fund for Israel Institutions (AFII). The man with the AFII wanted to send me to Los Angeles to organize a local chapter for them. I lied and said I knew everything about Los Angeles and charity groups and Jewish organizations. I used my United Jewish Appeal work to back me up. They hired me and gave me a ticket to Los Angeles. My mission was to set up a local organization for the Fund. I arrived in Los Angeles in January 1950, and I went immediately to my old pals, Jerry and Ann Fielding. Jerry was then the musical director of the Groucho Marx TV show.

Jerry and Ann helped me find an apartment in Hollywood on Gardner Street just off Sunset Boulevard. Outside the pink-and-green stucco building was the place where the trolleys turned around. I had two floors —a large living room, a large kitchen, and an upstairs bedroom. It was much grander than my small attic room in the East Village and only $95 a month. With the help of the Fielding's friends (most of them communists or fellow travelers), I was able to furnish the place. Everybody donated something. They were like members of a big family who made me feel at home once again.

My new friends were involved in defending the Hollywood Ten

through the National Council on the Arts, Sciences, and Professions. Since the Philadelphia convention, the communist-run Council had fared poorly in the Progressive party campaign, so its members now put all their effort into raising money for legal defense of the Hollywood Ten —film industry men who had been ordered to testify before the House Un-American Activities Committee. HUAC was investigating commu- nist influence in Hollywood. The Ten refused to testify on Fifth Amend- ment grounds and ultimately served time in jail for contempt of Congress.

Out of its offices at the Crossroad of the World, a cul-de-sac off Hollywood Boulevard, we hung out together, raising money, doing good communist things, and feeling very close to one another. I was accepted as a former communist who was still sympathetic. I set up fund-raisers for the Hollywood Ten—including one where Lena Horne sang and one hosted by Charlie Chaplin. I was never invited to any Communist party meetings, nor would any of my friends let me know of their communist activities. This arrangement was how communists and fellow travelers operated in Hollywood. I was used to this type of relationship as a gay man moving among people who never discussed my homosexuality.

In Hollywood I was welcomed into a small gay crowd. I met them through Betty Berzon, who ran an avant garde book store on Las Palmas Avenue just off Hollywood Boulevard called Berzon Books. Betty's store became a hangout for many Hollywood intellectuals and bohemians. Betty, who was about twenty-one years old, was trying to come to terms with being a lesbian, and many of her friends were gay or lesbian, too. She served coffee, had poetry readings, showed avant garde films, and had a spectacular opening party at which Edith and Osbert Sitwell were guests of honor. Anais Nin did several readings.

On Christmas Eve, Betty sent me a sailor as a present. My doorbell rang, and there stood this gorgeous young sailor. "Merry Christmas!" he said. "I'm new in town. I just went to Betty Berzon's bookstore, and she said I would be interested in meeting you." So he stayed for over three hours. Then, we went out afterward to party with Betty and her lover.

The world of my left-wing activist friends was completely separate from my gay and lesbian friends. They had little interest in politics, and my political friends did not know that I was gay. Once in a while, I tried to get the Berzon group and the Fielding group together, but it never really worked except occasionally at a party that I gave at my apartment on Gardner Street.

For a big party, someone said we should have a "lion," a celebrity. I tried to get Marlon Brando, but he couldn't make it. Folksinger Josh White was able to come, and my guests were delighted as they sat on the floor around him while he sang and played his guitar. Suddenly, one woman shouted out, to everyone's horror, "Josh, why did you do it?"—he had testified before a congressional committee and named names. He looked at her and said, "You might have, too. You're white, and you don't know what it means to be a colored entertainer who would starve without work. I can't see any of you organizing a benefit for *me*."

One evening, a painter friend of mine, Max Band—who had become a member of the AFII advisory board—and his wife and I went out for a pastrami sandwich at the Gotham Cafe, a Jewish deli in the Hollywood Roosevelt Hotel. As we sat down, Max saw his old friend Charlie Chaplin at a table with about ten other people.

"Max," Chaplin called out. "Come over and sit with us."

We sat down. Chaplin, of course, was the center of attention.

"They never let me make the pictures I want," he was saying, "like this!" and he jumped up to demonstrate, to everyone's rapt attention, miming every movement and gesture.

"Charlie comes into this cafe and sits down. He lights a cigarette and calls the waiter. He has only enough money for a cup of coffee. He orders the coffee, smokes the cigarette and looks around. At the end of the room is a black curtain and in front of it sits a party of Wall Street types at a long table. They're fat, wear silk top hats, smoke big cigars and have money bags in front of them. They talk Wall Street talk—millions, billions, war, munitions. The curtain slowly rises. Charlie sees two feet, crossed, a big nail sticking through them, bleeding.

"'Hey!' Charlie calls to the waiter, 'There's a man nailed to the wall.'

"But the waiter pays no attention. The curtain rises completely, and Charlie sees Jesus Christ on the cross with tears rolling down his cheeks.

"'Hey!' Charlie yells at Wall Street. 'There's a crying, bleeding man nailed to the wall behind you.'

"Wall Street says, 'Fuck you!' and tells the waiter to throw Charlie out.

And he does."

And with that, Chaplin grabbed the seat of his own pants and propelled himself from the table. I was transfixed, as were all the others, sitting over our half-eaten sandwiches.

"But," Chaplin added, shrugging his shoulders, "they won't let me make pictures like that."

My reason for being in Los Angeles, of course, was not to become a progressive activist or to meet the stars but to set up the local chapter of the American Fund for Israel Institutions. The AFII was paying my salary, and I had to do something for them.

I began by enlisting Mildred Allenberg to be chair of the new group. Mildred was a rich, charitable activist in Jewish causes, and she leaped at the chance to be head of a new organization in Hollywood, especially one that was involved with the major cultural activities in Israel, including orchestras, theaters, and museums. She was well positioned for her new role because her husband was Bert Allenberg of the then-prestigious Berg-Allenberg Agency, which represented many of the top film industry people. Mildred and I soon became friends.

Next I found an office, which we shared with an old man, Louis Shmuckler. Shmuckler had come to Los Angeles from New York with his daughter and son-in-law. He had worked in the Yiddish theater most of his life with Maurice Schwartz, Jacob Addler, and all the other greats. His daughter was Helen Beverly, who had been a leading Yiddish actress and was now married to Lee J. Cobb, the stage and screen actor who brilliantly originated the role of Willy Loman in Arthur Miller's *The Death of a Salesman*. Helen supported Lou, and he spent his time trying to raise money to start a Yiddish newspaper in Los Angeles. He was a charming man who lured me away from my work each day with wonderful stories about the Yiddish theater.

In between listening to Shmuckler's stories, working with the Hollywood Ten and hanging out in Betty's bookstore, I organized a prestigious group of Los Angeles musicians, artists, screen writers, actors, and intellectuals to serve as the advisory board for the Fund. But I did far better at organizing the Board than I did in raising money. I really didn't pay too much attention to that important but less interesting task. Because the people at the main office in New York were delighted with the prestigious names I was assembling, they cut me a lot of slack, though only a small salary.

One day Mildred Allenberg called me and said, "Darling, come up to the pool. I have a wonderful girl for you to meet." She was always doing that. She loved me and tried to save me from what she called "those trashy Reds you hang out with." I was really not very interested in meeting anybody, certainly not a girl. But she continued sotto voce. "Also, I think she's Jewish. Even though she's in the Industry, she's not trashy like the rest. Very nice!"

"Why do you think she's Jewish?" I asked.

"Well," said Mildred, "her father is a dentist or something, in Chicago, so she must be."

I went over to Mildred's pool and met the young actress—Nancy Davis. She wasn't Jewish. But she ultimately became Nancy Reagan, which would have been almost as good in Mildred's eyes. I went out with her twice, each time to Barney's Beanery in Hollywood. She was rather square and not very interested in politics, although she really tried. I felt a bit sorry for her. She wanted so much to be liked by everyone, even by me. I didn't see her again until almost twenty-five years later at the Buckleys' home in Connecticut.

Later that year, I quit the AFII to work full time raising money for the Hollywood Ten. I was paid little in my new job, but it was the work I most wanted to do. By April 1951, I was totally broke. My electricity, gas, and telephone were turned off. One morning, when I was still sleeping, there was a great knocking and banging on the door. It was a bill collector. I had to sneak out the back window and climb down the fire escape. I had a car, a Studebaker, which my father had helped me get. On that, too, I owed a lot of money, and I had to park it in a different place every night to avoid the repo men.

It was clear that I had to leave Los Angeles, and soon. Two nights later I made my escape with an acquaintance, Joe Singleton, who was looking for a ride to New York. We had a gas credit card and thirty-two dollars between us. We pooled our meager resources and drove twenty-four hours a day, sharing shifts, because we couldn't afford to stop anywhere. By the time we were getting out of Texas, which seemed endless, I couldn't stand him any longer—he drove me crazy humming "Ah, Sweet

Mystery of Life" as we drove—and he couldn't stand me either.

Finally, in desperation, I said, "Joe, let's stop at some motel, take a shower, and get some sleep."

We stopped at a cheap motel and took two cabins. The proprietor asked, "Would you like your rooms with facilities or without?" Being used to the better things of life, I said, "With facilities, of course." Joe said he would have his without.

I got into the cabin and took a shower, which must have lasted about twenty minutes. When I opened the door, there on my bed was a naked woman wearing black stockings. I slammed the door and looked for another door, figuring I had made a mistake, but there was no other way out. So, I peered out and said, "Miss, you must have the wrong cabin."

She asked, "Didn't you order me?" She was the facilities!

I told her there must have been a mistake, and she was quite distressed: "What's the matter, you queer or something?" I didn't have the courage to nod in agreement.

We finally reached New York just in time for me to march in the May Day parade of 1951. As I walked with all the others, I realized that I had become bored by the slogans, by the songs, and most of all, by the desperate earnestness. It was also difficult for me to accept the latest party pronouncement: South Korea had invaded the peace-loving North, which had called on its "agrarian reformer" Chinese neighbors for help in fighting the South Korean and American fascist hordes. It was like Finland invading the USSR in 1939 all over again. I was disillusioned with all of it. It didn't make sense any longer. This was my last May Day parade.

Chapter 6

Anticommunism

I WENT TO MY parents' home in Brooklyn. I knew that at age twenty-seven I had to stop playing at being a revolutionary and get down to real life—making a living.

Just before I left Los Angeles, the woman who headed the office of Americans for Democratic Action (the major liberal organization of its day) suggested I look up Harold L. Oram when I got back to New York because he might have a real job for me. She said that even though he was a "social democrat", he was a nice man.

I telephoned Oram. He told me to come up to his office at 8 West Fortieth Street. He was head of his own fund-raising/public relations firm, which bore his name, and specialized in public interest organizations with a non-communist but liberal point of view. He started his career just before World War II, working to help loyalist refugees from Franco's Spain. He also worked with Christopher Emmet's Christian Committee Against Nazi Germany, and they became good friends. (Emmet was to come into my life some months later.) During World War II, Oram served in the Army Transportation Corps. When I first met him, he was already successful. Among his clients were the International Rescue Committee, the American Association for the United Nations, the Legal Defense Fund of the National Association for the Advancement of Colored People, and several other charitable liberal organizations. He employed about twelve people, account executives and support staff. It was with Harold Oram that I did my fund-raising apprenticeship.

Initially, I found him rather unattractive and brusque. He asked me a lot of questions about my life and experience. He asked me what I had done "professionally." Ashamed at having so little to show at my age, I lied and exaggerated to sell myself to him. I inflated my fund-raising experience with the American League for a Free Palestine, the United Jewish Appeal, the American Fund for Israel Institutions, the Wallace presidential campaign, the Hollywood Ten, and even the Aguduth Israel. I also told him I had a B.A. from Harvard and that I was honorably discharged from the Army Air Corps.

As half of me babbled on, more and more desperate to impress him and to get the job, my other half seemed to be observing me operating. It was a strange sensation, this being divided and still functioning. My pattern of lying, of hiding the things I knew to be the truth, was beginning to become an integral part of me. Sure, I had developed a style. Everyone with whom I worked liked me, even respected me. But my restlessness had become chronic. I couldn't stay in one place for too long.

I did not lie about my past membership in the Communist party. Impressed that I had confided in him, Oram said that my communist past didn't matter so long as I didn't consider myself a Stalinist any longer.

To the non-communist and anticommunist world in those days, being a member of the Party was a terrible thing indeed. It was as bad as being a Nazi. But it was not so bad, so evil, so awful—or so I was convinced—as being a homosexual. If one was publicly branded as "queer," there was nothing further to expect for the rest of your life except being the sad and scorned "bachelor," or lying and hiding—or suicide. I chose the middle course.

I won over Harold Oram. "Come back after Labor Day," he said, "and we will see if we can find something for you. I just may be able to turn you from an agitator into a fund-raiser."

We shook hands. I was disappointed that I wasn't offered a job then and there. I really wanted to work, and I liked Oram. I wanted to work for *him*, to make *him* proud of me. This affection is a feeling I had for most of the men with whom I worked over the years. It was as if they stood in for my father as men whose pride and admiration I could win by doing what I wanted to do.

Oram had no job after Labor Day, but he got me a temporary job with New York's Liberal party, which was fielding Rudolph Halley as a candidate for President of the New York City Council in a special election later that fall.

The Liberal party was the political arm of two major New York labor unions—the International Ladies' Garment Workers Union (ILGWU) and the Amalgamated Hatters Union, run respectively by David Dubinsky and Alec Rose. They were only a bit to the right of the communist-controlled American Labor party. The Liberal party had rejected Stalinism in favor of social democracy. These groups shared control of the New York City Democratic party with the corruption-ridden Tammany Hall. I felt a little guilty working for the liberals rather than a "progressive" group, but at that stage of my life, a job was a job.

Rudolph Halley had been the counsel and the real star of the widely publicized Kefauver committee of the United States Senate. Senator Estes Kefauver (D., Tenn.) held hearings on organized crime in 1950 that were the first to be nationally televised and brought him and Halley instant fame. Halley's trademarks were his tough questions and his black horn-rimmed glasses. He became the darling of the national press and the Liberal party. Dubinsky and Rose dreamed of starting him in New York City politics, then sending him on to the state house in Albany and ultimately into the White House.

I had no particular admiration for either Halley or the Liberal party, but I didn't have any real animosity against them either. Harold called the political director of the Liberal party, and I was put on the payroll at $65 per week. I was assigned to maintain the contributors lists and to draft fund-raising letters. Halley's campaign headquarters was in the Algonquin Hotel, with its Round Table where some of the great wits and pundits of the 1920s and 1930s regularly dined, including Dorothy Parker, who got me into all that trouble with the Air Corps. The Algonquin made my work seem glamorous indeed.

To allay my guilt at working for the Liberal party, I gave the local chapter of the Progressive party a mimeographed copy of the names and addresses of the major Liberal party contributors. This list was passed over surreptitiously in the lobby of the Algonquin Hotel over coffee at one of the small round tables.

This was when I first became aware of the great importance of lists—

names of contributors. Some people give money. Most do not. An individual who had made a financial contribution to anything at any time could, in most cases, be counted on to make another contribution. Therefore, his or her name became enormously valuable. If one didn't have a list of former financial contributors, one might just as well solicit the names in a telephone book. In the future, I learned to guard my own lists very carefully.

The actual work in my new job was boring, especially keeping the lists in alphabetical order. I drafted dozens of letters, but none was accepted. Finally, after about two weeks, Alec Rose, the chairman of the Party that year, approved one of my letters. Because of my inexperience, Rose said this first letter should be a standardized "Dear Friend" letter. The process used for this was cheaper than the more personalized technique of typing each name by hand and reproducing the body of each letter individually on the duplicate typing machines used in those days.

I was put in charge of this mailing—my first large direct mail operation. Wanting to make it a huge success, I came up with two ideas to personalize the envelopes at no extra cost. I had the addresses handwritten by volunteers who worked in the office; that way, I knew the recipient would pay special attention to the envelope. I also had a volunteer affix a first class stamp rather than using a Pitney-Bowes postage imprint. Through the years, I have always used these personalizing techniques, even with large mailings. They have proved more successful than using labels or metered postage.

I paid close attention to other details of the operation as well. I went over the letter again and again, checking each paragraph, sentence, and comma for mistakes. Halley's signature, printed in blue, gave the form letter a final personal touch. At last, the letter went out to a list of seventeen thousand smaller contributors to the Liberal party. I added my own name and address to the list so I could see when the letters arrived and how they looked, a quality check I have used on every mailing I have done since then.

When I returned home to Brooklyn and saw the beautiful envelope hand addressed with a real stamp awaiting me, I was thrilled. I carefully opened the envelope so as not to rip it, thinking that this will be a souvenir for the rest of my life—my first real professional mailing. It looked splendid, especially the blue signature of Rudolph Halley. I read the text over, savoring my stirring words.

What? It couldn't be!

The idiot printer had left out the *r* in the word *Friend!*

My God!! FIEND!

Seventeen thousand earnest liberals in New York had received a letter from Rudolph Halley that very day beginning "Dear Fiend."

Alec Rose and Rudolph Halley were not amused. In spite of Harold Oram's pleas on my behalf, and my own abject apologies, I was fired from the Liberal party campaign to elect Rudolph Halley president of the New York City Council.

My sense of humor saved me from total despair. The mistake really was funny. Even Oram thought so. He offered me another temporary assignment with one of his clients at the time, the International Rescue Committee. The IRC, a liberal, social democratic, anti-Stalinist organization, was helping refugees from communist Eastern Europe who were fleeing into West Germany, Austria, and other Western European countries by the tens of thousands.

Harold suggested that I go to California to help organize fund-raising meetings in San Francisco and Los Angeles for Elinor Lipper, whose book about her eleven years in Soviet prison camps had just been published. She had come from Europe to the United States to help raise money for the International Rescue Committee.

I told Harold that although I needed a job badly, I couldn't possibly work with anyone who said she spent eleven years, or even one year, in a Soviet slave labor camp. There were no slave labor camps in the USSR. The woman was obviously a fraud.

Harold then did something for which I will always be grateful. Instead of shrugging his shoulders, he said, "Meet her. Talk to her. She's staying at the Algonquin. I'll set it up." He arranged for me to have tea with Elinor Lipper in the Algonquin lobby that afternoon.

I arrived at the hotel and looked around, hoping to identify her from her photograph on the book jacket. I recognized her across the room, sitting alone at one of the small round tables—her hair short, her eyes so large that you could dive into them and drown.

I approached her. "Miss Lipper?"

She turned toward me and smiled. Only three times in my life has anyone had such an instant impact on me. My wife Patsy and Bill Buckley were the other two.

Elinor Lipper told me her story. She was born in Brussels in 1912. Her parents were German Jews. In 1931, after living an upper middle-class life in Belgium and Holland, she went to Berlin to study medicine, where she joined the German Communist party. After the rise of Hitler, she fled to Italy. In 1935, she became a Swiss citizen through a marriage arranged by her family. In 1937, she went to the Soviet Union to make a new life. She found work in a publishing company that specialized in foreign books. But two months later she was arrested and sentenced to forced labor on suspicion of counterrevolutionary activities. After eleven years of Siberian slavery, she was released in the summer of 1948 with the aid of Swiss authorities.

In 1949 she wrote a book, published in Germany, on the slave labor camps in the Soviet Union. "From that region," she wrote, "I have brought back with me the silence of the Siberian graveyards, the deathly silence of those who have frozen, starved, or been beaten to death. This book is an attempt to make that silence speak."

She told me about the eleven years she spent in the most primitive conditions in Kolyma in Siberia. She revealed that much of the Soviet economy was based on slave labor, particularly mining and timber in the far north. To provide this labor pool, the Soviet authorities arbitrarily arrested innocent people from every segment of Soviet society, convicted them, and sent them to Siberia. They were thus able to instill terror into all Soviet citizens and, at the same time, continue to maintain the slave labor pool in spite of an attrition rate of almost 70 percent each year. Simple and effective.

Because of her medical background, Elinor was assigned to various primitive hospitals. Her skills made her valuable to camp authorities, and so she survived. She was lucky. Most other prisoners died, but there were always plenty to replace the dead. It was a life without hope, without love. The living dead. The Great Gulag of the Soviet Union.

During the war, a rumor swept Elinor's camp that the president of the United States was coming. Everything was scrubbed; new blankets were issued; the watch towers were even taken down. Kolyma now became a vast Potemkin village. But it wasn't the President who came. It was the vice president, Henry A. Wallace. The inmates were gathered together to greet him. Wallace smiled and waved. He was told that this was a camp for incorrigible prisoners who were mentally ill.

Suddenly, a woman ran from the ranks and threw herself at Wallace's feet. She screamed in Russian how the prisoners were being treated, how they were dying, how they were innocent, as innocent as the snow at his feet. "Please," she sobbed, "please help us."

She was taken away, of course, while Wallace's translator told him that she was mentally ill and he could not understand what she was saying.

Two hours passed while Elinor spoke and I listened in silence.

"Why were you a communist?" she asked. "Why do you still have emotional ties with the Soviet Union?"

"Because I believe in peace and goodwill to all men," I answered. "I believe that Negroes and artists should be free, and that there should be an economic system where workers and farmers benefit from their labor." My words sounded strange as I spoke these meaningless platitudes.

"I believe that too, God knows," she said. "But, my dear, you must accept the fact that the Soviet Union is the antithesis of all that. The Soviet Union has betrayed socialism. It has drowned the idea in blood. A believer in socialism cannot believe in the Soviet Union. For it is impossible to defend the slaughter of millions of innocent human beings and to claim, at the same time, to be striving to benefit suffering humanity. It is just not possible."

Her story overwhelmed me. I felt totally betrayed. What was worse, because I had believed in the Soviet Union, I felt personally responsible for what had happened to her. The change seemed quick, but it was really the culmination of five years of internal intellectual conflict that I had hidden from myself. This catharsis, there in the lobby of the Algonquin Hotel, was a turning point in my life.

I went to San Francisco ahead of Elinor to prepare for her West Coast tour. I set up a large rally that was attended by the mayor and many dignitaries. Lipper impressed the crowd with her moving and powerful story. The IRC raised a good amount of money.

Next, I went to Los Angeles, where, in addition to the formal fund-raising meetings, I arranged for Elinor to meet my Hollywood crowd in the Malibu home of Bette Davis, who was then married to my friend Gary Merrill. My friends came to see me, to hear this woman to whom I had obviously sold out, and of course to meet Bette Davis. The house faced the ocean, and everything was rather chic and elegant. The Hollywood guests sat on the floor and listened to this woman talk about the horror of her life. Yet, almost to a person, they disbelieved her. How could she have been in a slave labor camp when her complexion was so good, when she was so pretty? Miss Davis sat grumpily behind the bar, smoking one cigarette after the other, obviously bored by the entire proceedings.

One of the women there seemed to speak for all when she said, "If this is true, and if I believe it, then what is left for me, what else am I to think?" And so they knowingly clung to their illusions rather than believe this woman and be left with nothing. The response of my friends saddened me. I saw my former self in them, with all the desperate illusions I had before that moment in the Algonquin Hotel.

When we returned to New York in January 1952, I arranged for Elinor, at her request, to meet Henry Wallace. I got his number through directory assistance, and he answered the phone himself. I was amazed that it was so easy to get hold of a former vice president of the United States. I told him about Elinor and said she wanted to meet with him. He invited us to his farm in South Salem, New York. She told him what actually had happened that day in Siberia. As she spoke, his face paled. "I didn't know," he said. "I didn't know—please believe me—I just didn't know."

I saw in him the sense of betrayal that was engulfing many of us who had worked with the communists. Later that year, Wallace published his mea culpa and repudiated his past cooperation with the communists. I subsequently discovered that Wallace's translator that day in Siberia had been the same Owen Lattimore who was my friend David's father. Now Lattimore was under attack by Senator Joseph McCarthy for his "close association with the international communist conspiracy." I had been sympathetic to Lattimore's plight, but when I found out what he had said in Siberia, I felt betrayed by him, too.

After she completed her tour of the United States, Lipper returned home to Switzerland. While attending an anticommunist conference in Berlin in 1955, she disappeared, and it was rumored that she had been kidnapped by the Soviets, as so many others were.

I went back to Harold Oram. He still did not have an "account" for me, but he obviously wanted to keep me around. He made a proposition. "There's a Chinese general—at least he calls himself a general—named Ernest K. Moy. He has an idea of helping Chinese refugees, and he's come to me for help. According to Moy, there are tens of thousands of refugees flooding Hong Kong, including intellectuals, professionals, and artists. Many are graduates of American universities. Moy wants to help them out. Speak to him. I'll pay you fifty dollars a week for the next four weeks as walking around money. If you can turn this into an account or a paying proposition, I'll give you another fifty dollars a week retroactively and put you on the payroll at a hundred per week." I was grateful and excited. Was this to be the beginning?

I met Ernest Moy, a slight man who certainly did not look like a general. But then, no general I ever met out of uniform looked like a general. He was full of vim and vigor, a real operator. He reiterated what he had told Harold. He believed that these people were the treasures of China and must be helped. He thought a fund-raising drive could be organized to support them by appealing to the alumni of the refugees' alma maters in the United States. Many wealthy Chinese families had sent their children to American universities and colleges for their higher education before the war. Madame Chiang Kai-shek and her brothers and sisters were educated in the United States.

I prepared an outline of the steps I thought were needed to organize mobilization of American aid for Chinese intellectual refugees in Hong Kong. The format I created was based largely on my knowledge of how the Left organized and also my brief introduction to how Oram organized such groups. It is a perfectly simple pattern, which I used many times in my future work:

1. Enlist an individual of prestigious and, if possible, nonpartisan national reputation to take the lead.

2. Organize a list of prominent figures, representing all walks of life, who might conceivably be interested in the specific project even though they may differ on other matters.

3. Draft a letter for the leader to sign and a statement enunciating the purposes of the group and invite the list to endorse the statement and serve as "members" or on an "Advisory Board" or as "sponsors" of the project. These letters should be as personalized as possible, including getting the signer to indicate first names of those he knows personally. I have found that there are about a thousand celebrities in the world, and they all know each other.

4. When sufficient acceptances have come in, print a letterhead and elect or appoint officers. If necessary, incorporate the new organization. Enlist a well-known business leader to serve as treasurer and to do the corporate fund-raising. Then print the statement and its endorsees as either a full page advertisement and/or a mailing piece to solicit money.

5. Appoint or elect the individual who took the lead chairman or president. Set up an executive committee to really do the work or to rubber stamp what you are doing, and take some title for yourself, such as secretary.

You're off and running! If you're around long enough, you can develop a "stable" of VIPs who trust you because of past experience, and you can set up an important looking letterhead in a matter of days.

At the height of my professional activities in the years that followed, I was sometimes compared (by both friend and foe) to the German communist activist in the 1920s and 1930s Willi Munzenberg. He was a master at organizing the various groups that helped make up the Popular Front of the 1930s. His organizational techniques were the essence of the propaganda so admired by the Marxists and the Fascists of the time. There would be Doctors and Lawyers Against . . . or Artists and Workers for . . . The trick was to get respectable names on the letterhead while, at the same time, keeping control in communist hands. Willi Munzenberg was murdered at Stalin's orders in the South of France in 1940.

Oram was impressed with my plan. Looking for a prominent figure to be spokesman for the fund-raising organization, I asked around and found that Congressman Walter H. Judd, the Republican from Minnesota, was a great advocate of Taiwan and a staunch anticommunist. He was an outstanding legislator, a brilliant orator and anticommunist crusader. If he agreed to work with us, Judd would fill the bill.

A physician and missionary from Minnesota, Walter Judd first went to China in 1925 ministering to the sick and preaching the gospel. After the Japanese invasion of China, Judd traveled throughout the United States speaking before any group that would listen—churches, campuses, civic organizations—denouncing the Japanese attack and urging U.S. support for the Chinese resistance. He was elected to Congress in 1943, and from there, especially after the communist takeover on the mainland in 1949, continued his efforts to free China.

When he was young, Judd was given radiation treatment for acne and had a badly scarred face, but his brilliance made people ignore this almost instantly. Miriam Judd, his wife, described Walter, who could speak for hours on end, as a man who, if you asked him the time, would give you the history of clock making.

Oram made arrangements for us to meet Judd just after Christmas 1951. That meeting in the Commodore Hotel in New York was portentous for me: I started my first organization, and Walter Judd became one of my foremost teachers, mentors, colleagues, and friends in the years to come.

Judd agreed to join the project, but could not actively run the group. If we could find a full-time executive officer, he would go ahead as we planned and sign the letter of invitation to potential "members."

Harold thought I was too inexperienced to be executive officer, and I guess I was at that time. So Harold hired Christopher Emmet to help organize the group.

Although Emmet was an American, he came off as a typical, eccentric English don. He was tall and gangly, mustached, fumbling and nervous. He came from an old New York family that had married into the Astors; they still had some money (but not much) and kept the old estate on the Hudson River occupied by Emmet's even more eccentric mother. Christopher lived in an enormous family co-op apartment on Lexington Avenue and Sixty-ninth Street that was littered with old newspapers, books, manuscripts, and magazines. It was crowded and dusty and dark.

Prior to World War II, Emmet had organized the Christian Committee Against Nazi Germany. He felt it important for the world to know that it wasn't only Jews who were opposed to Nazism. He was a staunch anticommunist as well. He told me once, "It is not enough to hate one kind of tyranny. An honest man must hate all tyranny, no matter what—right, left, and even tyranny masquerading as democracy."

Emmet was always in need of money, and that's the reason Harold took him on to help. But within a few months, he dropped out to work on projects closer to his European interests, and later founded two important groups; American Friends of the Captive Nations and the American Council on Germany. When he left, I took over the executive responsibilities of Aid Refugee Chinese Intellectuals (ARCI) temporarily.

We worked quickly to get ARCI going. Oram personally advanced the funds needed to pay for the mailings, for an office at 537 Fifth Avenue, and other preliminary expenses. Oram regularly advanced his own money to help new organizations get started, a practice I continued over the years.

ARCI had its first formal meeting on January 30, 1952, at which Judd appointed an executive committee. Among the members of this "working group" were Mrs. Maurice (Beth) T. Moore, the sister of Henry Luce; E. C. K. (Kip) Finch, a top aide to Henry Luce; Mansfield Freeman, an officer in one of the major Hong Kong business organizations, C. V. Starr & Company; and Lyman Hoover, who had worked in various refugee causes since World War II. We agreed to incorporate ARCI under the awkward name Aide Refugee Chinese Intellectuals, Inc., known forever more as ARCI.

Events moved with a speed that caught me by surprise. Looking back, I see that it was government support, including that from the CIA, that helped things move along at such a rapid pace. ARCI received tax-exempt status from the Internal Revenue Service in only three days. This was arranged by Arthur Ringland of the State Department. He also arranged for ARCI to join the State Department's Advisory Committee on Voluntary Foreign Aid, enabling us to receive the government refugee relief money that was so plentiful in the years following World War II. Within the week, the Free Asia Committee (a CIA front) contributed five thousand dollars for immediate expenses and pledges of twenty-five thousand dollars each were received from the Eli Lilly and Kresge foundations. Similar pledges soon came from the Rockefeller and Ford foundations. Much of the CIA funding in those days was channeled through cooperating foundations.

Although we started ARCI as a nongovernment, humanitarian organization, it was taken over by the CIA in a classic operation. The public was supporting us to aid the refugees; the CIA used us as a front to expand their intelligence network in Hong Kong. That is why they were so helpful in getting ARCI started. It wasn't until several months later that I became aware of their involvement, and nobody else in the leadership of ARCI—certainly not Walter Judd—had a clue. Oram might have known, but we never discussed it.

In February of 1952, ARCI sent a two-man survey mission to Hong Kong: a Catholic priest, Father Frederick A. McGuire (whose sister, coincidentally, was one of my grammar school teachers at PS 185), and James Ivy. McGuire was head of the Department of Foreign Missions of the National Catholic Welfare Conference in Washington and had completed thirteen years of missionary service in mainland China. Ivy was the associate director of the Committee for a Free Asia. The two men returned and confirmed the enormity of the growing refugee problem in Hong Kong.

Prior to World War II, the relatively sleepy British colony of Hong Kong had a population of 600,000. By the end of 1951, this population had increased by 400 percent to nearly 2,500,000 with the influx of refugees from Red China. Included in this group were well over 20,000 individuals who could have been described as University-educated "intellectuals": artists, doctors, engineers, and other professionals. About 7,000 in this group were alumni of American colleges and universities. There had been a great outpouring of American aid for European refugees from the displaced persons camps and to the tens of thousands from Eastern Europe. ARCI was the first American group to focus attention on the Chinese refugees.

Within weeks, we opened an office in Hong Kong and over 12,000 ARCI questionnaires were completed by desperate refugee scholars, scientists, and professionals who qualified for ARCI aid. Most were unemployed and living in substandard conditions. Although the British administration was faced with growing numbers of refugees, they did not want to provoke their Red Chinese neighbors into imposing sanctions or invading Hong Kong. As a result, the British were wary of any organization that would focus more attention on the refugees. ARCI therefore stressed that its primary purpose was to "resettle" the refugees and get them out of Hong Kong. It also emphasized its nonpartisan nature—neither pro-communist nor pro-Taiwan.

Initially, Judd sent out his own letters of invitation to some of his friends and colleagues—philanthropists, professionals, and businessmen who had worked with the Christian missionary organizations in China.

These people were being denied access to mainland China by the communist government. Their interest in ARCI, however, was not political, although most were anticommunist, but based on their desire to continue their charitable work by aiding Chinese refugees. Because they deeply mistrusted any government involvement—either from "Free China" or the CIA—they liked the idea that ARCI was completely a "citizens" organization.

Oram's strategy was to bring these early supporters into as broad a spectrum of other supporters as possible. I watched him carefully as he did this. It was his basic premise that an organization must be bipartisan, with as many representatives of the opposition as possible on the list.

We set up an Educators Advisory Board that included the presidents of some of the most prestigious universities and colleges in the United States, including Massachusetts Institute of Technology, Wesleyan, Georgetown, New York, and Columbia universities and the state universities of Indiana, Colorado, Florida, Minnesota, Texas, California, and Pennsylvania.

The members listed on the official ARCI letterhead also included Senators Paul Douglas, Alexander Smith, and Robert Taft; Generals George C. Marshall, A. C. Wedemeyer, William D. Donovan, and Claire L. Chennault; Admirals Chester W. Nimitz and Leland P. Lovette; Ambassador Joseph C. Grew; publisher Henry R. Luce; author Louis Bromfield; Rev. Henry Sloane Coffin; and many other government officials and intellectuals of the time.

Over the next twenty years, whenever I organized a "conservative" or "anticommunist" group, I followed Oram's example and tried to include as many "liberals" as I could on the letterhead to create the broadest possible base of support. I did this by concentrating on the "rifle" rather than the "shotgun" approach, that is, keeping the focus of the group as narrow as possible so that people with strong differences on other issues could agree to support it. In the early days of ARCI, this meant focusing on the plight of intellectuals, a cause that appealed to other intellectuals whatever their political stripe.

The next weeks were frantic, and I enjoyed the tension and excitement. At the office on Fifth Avenue the only staff people were Emmet, his secretary, and me. The office served mainly as a mail drop for receiving contributions and to provide a desk and telephone for Emmet. When the mail came each day, I took the contributions to Oram's office on Fortieth Street to be processed. Most of the contributions came in printed, postage-paid envelopes. I loved to open these envelopes with Oram's clerical staff. It was like a game of chance to see who could come up with the largest single contribution. "Here's two hundred fifty dollars," someone would call out, or, "My God, it's a thousand," or, if they hit the jackpot, "Five thousand dollars!"

In those precomputer days, Oram had developed his techniques into a science. His walls were lined with metal shelves and drawers holding thousands of three-by-five cards, each one hand-typed with a name and address and other pertinent information.

Each card also had affixed to it different-colored small metal flags to indicate to which groups the contribution was made. The cards were arranged in four categories: $25 or under (the largest group), $26 to $99, $100 to $499, and over $500. Each contributor received a hand-typed receipt, with the duplicate carbon copy alphabetized and filed as a backup. The system was efficient, except that sometimes the flags would fall off the cards. Almost everything was done by hand—time consuming, but it worked.

Whenever a large mailing went out, we used the services of a mailing house that had more sophisticated equipment. Even in those early days of direct mail fund-raising, a good firm could get twenty-five thousand "packages" out in a week—letters typed, enclosure and contribution envelope printed, mailing envelopes addressed, postage affixed, and all dropped at the post office. But they were never quick enough for me; I was an impatient man and always wanted the idea to become reality immediately.

I kept my eyes open, absorbing everything. I felt very constrained by both Emmet and Oram, to whom I was accountable. I wanted to deal directly with the principals and not have to go through a committee or anybody else. It was then that I learned that I worked best when I was in control of an organization, although working behind the scenes rather than out front on stage. I liked a one-man operation with a rubber stamp board. I arranged to be elected secretary of ARCI, a position that gave me some power and control while the executive secretary dealt with the public. It also made me a peer of the other officers and executive committee. I took on this title in many of the organizations I later founded.

After much preliminary work, ARCI was publicly launched at a gala dinner at the Plaza Hotel in New York City on April 28, 1952. Here again, Harold Oram outdid himself in organizing a prestigious committee of American and international intellectuals to give ARCI the aura of an intellectual committee. He included their names in a full-page ad he placed in the *New York Times* to solicit funds. They included poets Conrad Aiken and Siegfried Sassoon, author McGeorge Bundy, cellist Pablo Casals, novelist John Dos Passos, psychologist Carl Jung, architect Walter Gropius, philosopher Bertrand Russell, Norman Thomas, the American Socialist party leader, author Rebecca West, historian Arthur Schlesinger, physicist Robert Oppenheimer, playwright Thornton Wilder, ten Nobel Prize winners, and over fifty other VIPs.

This was a perfect example of how people who disagreed with each other on many issues could agree on an issue—the need to help Chinese refugee intellectuals who had fled Red China—if it was framed in the narrowest of terms.

Dean Rusk, former assistant secretary of state for Far Eastern affairs, gave the keynote address, which took an anticommunist, pro-intellectual stand and was reported the next morning in the *New York Times* and syndicated throughout the country. He told the assembled supporters that it was important to preserve refugee intellectuals "in communities outside the borders of China who could be available to the Chinese people when freedom returns to that unhappy land." The *New York Herald Tribune*, in a Sunday editorial featuring the new organization, described ARCI as having "a distinguished sponsorship representing virtually every shade of non-Communist opinion in many lands." It praised ARCI's efforts to extend to China the "same generosity, wisdom and energy which have been devoted to the refugee intellectuals of Europe."

At the dinner, and with the press coverage and contributions that followed, I saw the genius behind Oram's strategies and how effectively they worked. ARCI was now fully launched and under way.

The major work of ARCI that year, and in the years to follow, was resettlement of refugees. In 1952 we set up offices in Hong Kong and Taiwan and carried out the regular work of any refugee organization.

As the organization grew, tensions and conflicts surfaced, especially between the "philanthropist" sponsors and the more "activist" anticommunists. The philanthropy faction, which included Judd, Emmet, Oram, and most of the directors, controlled the organization. Behind the scenes, I was slowly becoming the force behind the activist faction. My allies were few, but important with Charles Edison as the leading figure.

One of the early internal conflicts was won by the philanthropy faction. It centered on Ernest Moy, who had come up with the original idea for ARCI. Moy was just too anticommunist to be able to deal with the old China hands. Contrary to Moy's positions, Judd and the other nonactivist sponsors thought it was vital to keep ARCI a nonpolitical, American, and strictly philanthropic operation. They opposed any ties to the Taiwanese and demanded no public opposition to Red China. And so Moy was quietly dropped from the organization he was instrumental in founding. Some years later, the general committed suicide in Taiwan.

As each day went by, my own anticommunist convictions were becoming stronger. The change that had begun with the Elinor Lipper experience was still developing. Through my work, I became aware of the horrors that the communist regimes visited on their people in the USSR and in China. I read everything I could on China, on Chiang Kai-shek, on the Chinese revolution, on Sun Yat-Sen, whatever I could find. And I wanted to do something about it. My juices were flowing; I wanted to become an activist again.

The more anticommunist I became, the more I tried to politicize the efforts of ARCI. There were powerful opportunities in the organization to educate the public on what the Chinese communists were doing, and to use the refugee intellectuals to help fight the communists on the mainland through agitation and propaganda. This put me on a collision course with the non-activist faction in a battle for what I believed was the soul of the organization.

My chief "activist" ally on the board of directors was Charles Edison. He had been head of United China Relief during World War II and was therefore considered an "old China hand" by Walter Judd. I met Edison at the second meeting of the initial organizational stages of ARCI. I had looked forward to meeting this man with the famous last name. He had been governor of New Jersey, and I always called him by that title. As time went on and we became close friends, he asked me to call him Charles. I never could; it was always "Governor."

Edison took to me almost immediately. Although we were worlds apart in background and age (he must have been fifty-five or so), he felt we had lots in common because I reminded him of himself when he was a young man. When I met him he had snow white hair and a twinkle in his eyes. I could make him laugh easily. For a man of his reputation and wealth, he was extremely diffident and shy—except with me. "I can be myself with you, young feller," he would say, but I was never really sure that he knew just who "myself" was. He was a father figure for whom I felt great affection.

Edison was the oldest son of Thomas Alva Edison, the great American inventor. He lived in the shadow of his father, who hoped his son would follow in his footsteps. Charles spent a little over a year at the Massachusetts Institute of Technology, but he wasn't remotely interested. He left school and took a year off to travel out West, spending time in San Francisco. In 1914 he discovered Greenwich Village and stayed there for three years—a period he called the best years of his life. He was particularly interested in my stories of Greenwich Village, and he told me many about his own Village days.

His father had given him a property on the corner of Fifth Avenue and Eighth Street, where he turned a whole floor into the tiny "Thimble Theater," which put on experimental plays. Young Charles at the time was writing and publishing poetry under the pseudonym Tom Sleeper.

One night, Charles and a group of friends went to a local cafe called Marie's Crisis. On each of the tables was a wine bottle with a candle in it. As the candlewax dripped down the side of the bottle and the candle went out, the management put in a new candle, letting the drippings remain.

One of the women at the table, Edna, gazed intently at the waxy wine bottle with the candle burning on top and asked young Edison for a pen. Then she wrote on the menu,

> My candle burns at both ends, it will not last the night.
> But O my foes and O my friends, it gives a lovely light.

When the Governor told me this story, I doubted its authenticity. Whereupon he went over to his files and took out the old menu. On it were inscribed the two lines, plus the words "To my dear friend Charlie, Edna Millay."

It was during his Greenwich Village days that Charles met his wife, Carolyn, to whom he was totally devoted. Her attitude toward me over the years, however, was deeply condescending, at best. I thought she was an insufferable snob, and I couldn't bear her phony airs or her bigotry.

Edison was a fighter and loved a good battle. And a battle was coming. He became my prime ally against the non-activists as I began my campaign to politicize ARCI.

After Emmet left the organization, the job of executive director was taken over by B. A. Garside, who was deeply involved in most China philanthropic organizations in the United States. Although he was anticommunist, he was opposed to anything that might politicize ARCI. He became another of my stumbling blocks.

I began to develop my strategy. I thought I might increase the power of the activist faction by consolidating those in the organization whose views were similar to mine. I did this by organizing the "Literature" project in Hong Kong in October of 1952. The anticommunist refugee writers would form a group to write and publish anticommunist material to use on the mainland against the Red Chinese regime and in other Chinese communities in Asia. Our work would help counter the communist propaganda from mainland China that was flooding Southeast Asia and also provide an income for the refugee writers.

We solicited financial support for this relatively activist project, which masqueraded as another refugee relief effort. And once again the CIA got into the act. Money meant control.

The Committee for a Free Asia was developing a literary program similar to ours. The CIA at that time was more interested in establishing a political "third force" in China's political spectrum than in the straight anticommunist effort that I advocated. The third force they imagined would be Chinese who were neither procommunist nor pro-Taiwan who would develop a new political philosophy that might rule China. But this third force never existed; it was merely a CIA fantasy and a way for some Chinese to, in effect, rip off the naive CIA money men. The CIA kept promoting this phony third force idea for years, refusing to admit their error in judgement.

Just weeks after the Free Chinese Literature Program was announced, I received a telephone call from a John Osher of the Committee for a Free Asia. We arranged to meet for coffee at a nearby cafeteria. Osher was secretive and had a habit of whispering, like a secret agent in a Hollywood spy film. He said that even though his group was planning their own literature project in Hong Kong, they still wanted to be of assistance to ours. But because of "political considerations," their help would have to be kept off the record, hidden especially from the ARCI board. He said he was sure "I would understand," assuming that I, unlike the members of the ARCI opposition, would not balk at receiving CIA money and would keep it secret. He asked me if I would personally deliver their contribution to Hong Kong.

I had no idea why they chose me to do this, but I jumped at the chance to go to Hong Kong. I had never been to the Far East, and this was a great opportunity. I was also intrigued by the secrecy, flattered that he picked me, and pleased that I would be responsible for bringing in such a contribution, even if it was government money. The thought of such an adventure thrilled me.

But just to be safe, and contrary to Osher's instructions, I sought confidential advice from Father McGuire, who had gone to Hong Kong as part of ARCI's early survey mission. I liked Father McGuire, and I trusted him as a priest to keep my secret. I wanted to find out whether it was appropriate for me to go and whether he knew anything about Osher, and I wanted to let somebody know what I was doing in case anything happened to me. McGuire knew of Osher and assumed he worked with the CIA. He said to go ahead because there was nothing I could lose, and I would get a free trip to Hong Kong. I didn't tell anyone else where I was going.

Osher gave me the round-trip ticket to Hong Kong on Northwest Airlines, $500 in cash for expense money, and a briefcase that contained $25,000 in U.S. currency. He told me that I would be met by an "associate," Paul Frillman, and to be sure that Frillman had proper identification. I was excited and scared to death. The CIA! Cash! What if I lost the money? Would they kill me?

The flight left the next day. The prop plane was routed through Seattle, Honolulu, Toyko, and then on to Hong Kong. I clutched the briefcase tightly throughout the endless journey, never letting it out of my hand except when I sat on it. We landed in Tokyo, and I waited in the airport for my connecting plane to Hong Kong, still clutching my briefcase in sweaty hands. By that time I was wondering even more why I was assigned to deliver the funds; why couldn't they be transferred from the Hong Kong office of the Committee for Free Asia to our people? Why me? It smelled fishy. But I was on my way.

I was met at the Hong Kong airport about noon by Frillman, who worked with the United States Information Service. They took me to the Peninsula Hotel, where I checked in, and then to a meeting with the heads of five refugee "colleges" that were set up in Hong Kong by former Chinese scholars and teachers.

Our literature project was run under the aegis of this refugee college project. One of my plans was to consolidate these small and struggling institutions into one large anticommunist university in Hong Kong. At the meeting I turned the money over, as directed by Frillman, to the Chinese "president" of the Hwa-kui College of Engineering and Commerce. He didn't open the briefcase but thanked me politely. We then spent about an hour talking in generalities. After many more thanks, the meeting was over. And that was it. I realized that I had been nothing more than a courier. I still didn't know why they had chosen me.

With my mission accomplished and with nothing else to do, I explored the city. A young Chinese student and writer who worked with the ARCI literature project offered to show me some of the sights in the brief time I had left. He was very friendly, and he spoke English.

My guide took me to some antique stores and for a ride on the ferry, and gave me a grand tour of that wonderful city. Hong Kong has a unique smell—the smell of China. We went to a seafood restaurant on a great junk where the fish were taken from tanks on the side and prepared in dozens of different ways—all delicious. I became more and more enamored of the city, the Chinese, the ambiance and—the more we drank of the very potent Chinese brandy—my escort. Finally, absolutely exhausted, and just a little drunk, we both went back to my room at the Peninsula Hotel. "Would you like a Chinese massage?" he asked.

"What's a Chinese massage?"

"Lie down, relax, and I'll show you," he said.

For the next two hours, I enjoyed what is probably the best sexual encounter I have ever had. It was about 3:00 A.M. when he left with mutual promises to write, to keep in constant touch. I don't even remember his name.

Was this a CIA setup? Were they trying to get the goods on me to use against me if they needed to discredit me sometime in the future? I didn't know. In any case, they never did. And it was so much fun, I didn't care. I was a little worried that Oram or Judd would find out, but they didn't even know about the trip. I returned home.

Despite the $25,000—or maybe because of it—the ARCI literary project in Hong Kong did not last long. Subtle pressure was exerted by the State Department that if we wanted to continue getting money from their Advisory Committee on Voluntary Foreign Aid, we had to stick with relief work and not get involved in anything remotely political. They considered the literary project to be political. So the ARCI executive committee closed it down, creating a vacuum that the CIA filled with their own third force literary project through the Committee for a Free Asia.

My career was beginning to take off. Thanks to the high-paying ARCI account and my other work, Oram appointed me vice president of Harold L. Oram, Inc., and raised my salary.

Nevertheless, I was extremely frustrated by the path ARCI was taking. I believed that there was a good chance to bring down the Red Chinese regime by fomenting strife on the mainland and encouraging an invasion of free Chinese forces from Taiwan under Chiang Kai-shek. The weapons were agitation and propaganda, and the shock troops were the millions of refugees in Hong Kong, the overseas Chinese communities throughout the world, and the will and commitment of Chiang Kai-shek and his army.

I decided to make my case to the powers in ARCI and drafted a passionate memorandum. I cleared it first with Charles Edison and received his enthusiastic support. I did not discuss it with Harold Oram, because he was on the side of the nonactivist faction.

I tried to persuade the strictly philanthropic majority in the organization that they should change ARCI into an activist, anticommunist political organization. I argued that the resettlement and literary projects were meant to help the refugees but were not ends in themselves. They were the means toward mobilizing action against the Chinese Communist regime. My memorandum recommended that ARCI should "form a political action committee to carry on extensive lobbying in Washington and the United Nations and plan and execute political projects in cooperation with our registrants." I asked the committee to "re-examine where we are going and, once this is decided, go ahead full steam with as few compromises as possible along the way."

Oram was angry about the memo. I had gone over his head to change the organization into something he didn't support. But he needed me, so there was little he could do. I was learning how to maneuver as an activist within the organization.

The executive committee did re-examine where we were going and decided not only to reject my recommendations but to rededicate themselves to purely philanthropic activities. It became clear that I was not going to get any political mileage out of ARCI. The more U.S. government money was contributed to its work—through various relief agencies—the more cautious the "old China hands" became. I had to make a choice between staying on or finding another vehicle for my activism.

I decided to move on, although in name I remained secretary of ARCI until the end of 1968, when I left for England. In 1970, eighteen years after it was organized, ARCI was formally dissolved.

Despite my disillusionment with its lack of political commitment, I am proud of what ARCI was able to accomplish. It had assisted fourteen thousand college graduates and their families to resettle in Taiwan; brought twenty-five hundred to the United States; helped over a thousand to resettle in other parts of the world; and helped more than fifteen thousand other Chinese intellectuals rebuild their lives and careers in

Hong Kong, where they chose to remain. Nearly thirty-five thousand of China's finest and their families found new lives in freedom. I believe that what we accomplished is a shining example of the best of American philanthropy.

Throughout my career, I received considerable satisfaction from the knowledge that the various groups and committees I worked with provided hope to people living in the darkness of communism—the hope for ultimate freedom, and the knowledge that others really cared about their plight.

At ARCI, I completed my basic training in how to set up and run fund-raising organizations. It was also where I fought my first anticommunist political battles. Now, I was ready to strike out on my own.

Chapter 7

Committee of One Million

WHEN I REALIZED that Aid Refugee Chinese Intellectuals would never become the activist group I wanted, I set about organizing one of my own: the Committee of One Million. It became the bedrock of my activism for the next fifteen years, and one of the most successful and long-lived, anticommunist conservative organizations in modern politics.

As the armistice talks ending the Korean War concluded in the summer of 1953, the issue of whether the Communist Chinese regime should be recognized as the legitimate government of China—and admitted to the United Nations—was coming rapidly to the fore.

There was only one UN "China seat" and the Free Chinese occupied it. To Communist China, admission to the UN meant worldwide acknowledgment of the legitimacy of its regime. To anticommunists, keeping Red China out of the UN was an opportunity to deny the communists that legitimacy.

Most of Europe, including Great Britain, and many Asian and African countries favored admission. A growing number of prominent liberal American individuals and groups were also arguing for China's admission.

Just after Labor Day, 1953, I called a small meeting at New York's University Club. Christopher Emmet, Walter Judd, Charles Edison, and I, along with other activists from ARCI, discussed how best to combat the pro-Red China sentiment that seemed to be taking hold of

American intellectuals. Judd made a good point: if we (the "responsible" anticommunists) didn't do something quickly, Joe McCarthy would run with the ball and just about assure Red China of a UN seat. Already McCarthy was seeking out alleged subversives in the government responsible for the "loss" of China.

My idea was to adapt the successful 1950 communist-organized Stockholm peace petition technique by circulating a petition against UN admission for Red China in the United States. The others liked the idea, and I went to work. Three of us, Judd and I and Count Nicholas de Rochefort (who had testified before Judd's House Subcommittee on the Far East and Pacific and who held ideas similar to ours), drafted the text of a petition listing eight reasons for opposing the admission of Communist China to the United Nations. This petition became an important historical document. It ultimately garnered over one million signatures—hence the Committee of One Million—and served as the philosophical basis of the committee's work for the next fifteen years. (See Appendix B for text of petition.)

Then I started to build the organization. I still leaned heavily on Oram, but I was beginning to have my own ideas and way of operating, based largely on what I had learned from him. Part of the style I had developed was to keep out of the limelight and let other more prestigious people carry out my plans. This technique not only proved effective, it gave me an invigorating sense of power over events.

Walter Judd (my stern father/conscience) and Charles Edison (my mischievous father/buddy) were my key players. They enlisted other steering committee members as initial signers of the petition; including Senators John J. Sparkman (Democrat, Alabama) and H. Alexander Smith (Republican, New Jersey), and Congressman John W. McCormack (Democrat, Massachusetts), former Ambassador Joseph C. Grew, and former President Herbert Hoover.

The plan was to send the petition with this small group of VIP signatures to a broader VIP list—Democrats and Republicans, liberals and conservatives—and get them to sign it. We would use these names to give the petition legitimacy when we published it in a newspaper ad, so that we could solicit even more signatures and funds for our campaign.

The initial cost of the mailing was advanced by Oram. The envelopes were personally addressed, and the seven signatures were printed in different colored inks so that they looked personally signed. The letter was a far cry from my "Dear Fiend" days. It went out October 2, 1953.

Two hundred ten of the recipients responded positively, including 49 members of Congress (23 of whom were Democrats), 12 governors, 20 retired generals and admirals, 14 prominent religious leaders, 22 nationally known scientists and educators, and 33 business leaders. The others included retired diplomats, publishers, journalists, labor leaders, and representatives from the arts, entertainment, and sports. If there had been time, we could have enlisted twice as many signatures through follow-up correspondence, but the initial response was enormously gratifying to all concerned. Judd was particularly pleased to see former General of the Armies and Secretary of State George C. Marshall sign up. Judd had always thought Marshall rather "soft" on communism.

A little over two weeks after the letter was dispatched, on October 22, 1953, the petition was personally presented to President Dwight D. Eisenhower in the White House.

Our appointment was scheduled for 9:30 A.M. All the signers of the October 2 letter—except for Hoover—were there. We arrived at 9:00 A.M. and were ushered into the Cabinet Room just outside the Oval Office. Everyone, even the four politicians, appeared nervous. This was my first experience of how awesome was the presidency of the United States. I was nervous, too, even though I had no plans to go with the others to see the president.

A presidential aide came in at 9:30 sharp to lead the group into the Oval Office. Judd took my arm and said, "Come with us. This may be a once-in-a-lifetime opportunity. You won't want to miss it."

The six men sat down. I stood by the door, trying to disappear into the woodwork. President Eisenhower—"Ike" himself—favored me with one of his dazzling smiles and pointed to the chair next to his desk. "Sit here, young fellow," he said. For the rest of the meeting I sat at the president's side.

Judd explained our purpose. Eisenhower was interested, and asked a lot of questions. Judd was pleased that the president saw us for ten minutes longer than scheduled. Immediately after that meeting, Judd wrote a thank you note, and Eisenhower responded with a written letter expressing his agreement that "existing international facts . . . preclude the seating of the Chinese Communist regime to represent China in the UN." Victory!

The publicity engendered by the petition and its presentation to the president, coupled with my lobbying, took our activity one step further. Walter Judd announced the formation of a Committee *for* One Million (Against the Admission of Communist China to the United Nations). We would circulate the same petition to individual Americans throughout the country and enlist at least one million signatures.

The committee's office at 36 West Forty-fourth Street opened on October 26, 1953. Edison put up the first month's rent. The Steering Committee consisted of the petition's original signatories: Sparkman, Smith, Judd, McCormack, and Ambassador Grew (Hoover retired from any further leadership position). Former U.S. Senator and our first Ambassador to the UN Warren R. Austin became Honorary Chairman, Charles Edison was Treasurer, and I, of course, was Secretary.

I now had my own office. I was the boss and in total control, along with my new friend, Charles Edison. On November 23, I drafted (and Edison signed as Treasurer of the Committee) an agreement with my boss, Harold Oram, that paid his firm three thousand dollars a month for fund-raising and public relations services. This, and the three thousand per month the firm was getting from ARCI, made me a hot property at Oram. I was beginning to feel powerful and independent.

In 1954, we entered stage two of our plan: the national petition drive. In January Governor Edison convinced his good friend Herbert Hoover to do us just one more favor—to issue a public appeal urging Americans to sign the committee's petition. He agreed. Then we mobilized the mayors of nearly every major city in the United States to issue a proclamation supporting the petition drive on February 22.

The resulting national publicity was tremendous. The Scripps-Howard newspapers pledged their editorial support to the campaign, as did William Randolph Hearst, who printed an editorial and coupon in all his papers for the petition. The *New York Times* followed up with favorable editorials and numerous additional stories about the petition campaign. The American Legion and the AFL-CIO came on board. It was a tidal wave.

Thousands of signatures poured into the committee's office. Suzanne LaFollette (a journalist soon to become a founding editor of *National Review*) and Nora De Toledano (wife of Ralph and a great friend of Vice President Richard Nixon's secretary, Rose Mary Woods, and in daily telephone contact with her) were in charge of counting the signatures as they came in. Later, Nora went on the payroll and took over the press responsibilities. One of our volunteers was a young actress, Barbara Baxley, instructed by her agent to volunteer so as to avoid the blacklist. And so, for a few days, my favorite fields mixed—show biz and politics. But I felt sorry for Barbara—and ashamed for myself—that she felt it necessary to "purge" herself by working with an anticommunist organization. She had no politics whatsoever.

On July 7, 1954, less than four months later, the receipt of the one millionth signature to the petition was officially announced by Governor Edison.

As vice president of Harold L. Oram, Inc., I also had other duties. Early in 1955 Oram called me into his office. "I received a letter from that kid who wrote *God and Man at Yale*. He's starting some kind of magazine and needs to raise money. Go and see him. He probably wrote to a number of fund-raisers, but there might be something in it for us."

I had heard of the book and its *enfant terrible* author, William F. Buckley, Jr., but I hadn't read it nor did I have any special desire to do so. I went reluctantly to his office on East Thirty-seventh Street, which was the headquarters of the Buckley family oil business, the Catawba Corporation. What did I know about raising money for a magazine? What would be my pitch to this upstart Yalie?

I was ushered in to a small room crowded with books and papers and just about everything else. A tall young man came from behind a messy desk, hand outstretched, to greet me. We talked for about an hour. I was impressed by his ideas for a publication that would articulate his conservative ideas. But, most of all, I was deeply impressed by him. I never thought that he could get his magazine off the ground, because there didn't seem to be enough of an audience for it. I offered a few not very constructive ideas, and left, vowing that I should see him again.

I reported back to Oram that the idea wouldn't fly and that there was nothing in it for the firm. It wasn't until four more years had passed, after *National Review* was off and running, that Bill and I became close friends and colleagues.

Once the Committee of One Million had reached its goal of one million signatures on its petition, the steering committee prepared to disband, despite my arguments for continuing. My arguments ran directly counter to my long-held belief that when an organization has accomplished (or failed to accomplish) what it set out to do, it was time to shut it down.

But this committee was different. I felt there was a real need for a responsible, bipartisan organization dedicated to the advancement of the anticommunist cause. And Red China was a good hook on which to hang such an organization. I, of course, was the best man to lead it. It provided a base for many other activist ad hoc groups. I thought it might be the exception that proved my rule, and I was right.

I lobbied the steering committee to no avail, and it disbanded. A few months later, in February 1955, I decided to try again. I organized a meeting of former members of the committee at the Washington, D.C., home of Ambassador Joseph Grew to consider the revival of the Committee *for* One Million as the Committee *of* One Million. I drafted a memorandum that I mailed to everyone to read and discuss at the meeting. It discussed the accomplishments of the original committee from October 1953 to May 1954. Since then, sentiment was growing for accommodation with the Red Chinese—in Britain, France, and among many groups in the United States. "We believe it is not entirely a coincidence," I wrote, "that these dangerous developments have coincided with the end of our committee's activity."

The others at the meeting were persuaded and agreed to follow my lead in setting up a more permanent group.

On March 4, 1955, I mailed out an appeal—signed by Judd and Edison—to the VIPs on our earlier letterhead calling for the reorganization of the committee under the name "Committee *of* One Million." On April 12, 1955, we took out full-page advertisements in the *New York Times* and *Los Angeles Examiner* to announce the new committee. Most of our former endorsers—and a few new ones—were listed in the ads.

In the midst of this activity, my father died of a heart attack. The gap between us could now never close.

The new committee soon went into action. Our goal was to influence public opinion through the media, publishing our own newsletters and booklets and using radio spots and newspaper ads, and engaging in behind-the-scenes lobbying to promote and build our campaign. Each time an opposing point of view was raised, we responded immediately with a press conference and/or press statement and/or a full-page ad signed by VIPs from as wide a political spectrum as possible. What resulted was an ongoing "battle of the full-page ads."

By then I had learned a political rule of thumb: perception is more important than reality. The perception that we were a powerful lobbying group speaking for one million Americans was far more important than the reality. What it came down to was one individual—me—with a circle of influential allies who could get all these VIPs to sign the public statements we wrote on behalf of the "millions," thus creating the illusion of an enormous people's movement. It was a technique I first learned from Marxist propagandists. And it worked.

In January 1956, we announced the publication of a newsletter on China. Circulation reached thirty-five thousand. We produced and distributed LP records of prominent Americans, doing public service spots of one, three and fifteen-minutes, which were played by hundreds of radio stations. In September we published a booklet by Ambassador Grew entitled *Invasion Alert*, which was translated, in whole or in part, into eighteen languages and received international publicity and circulation. I was beginning to establish liaison with anticommunist groups abroad.

These were heady days. I was high on my growing independence at Harold L. Oram, Inc., the quick success of my own organization, and my desire to play an important role in overthrowing communism. The smell of victory was in the air.

Chapter 8

Hungary

BY THAT TIME, I was chain-smoking four packs a day. I should have learned something from my father's death, but I kept puffing away. Then something happened that, for a moment, made my dream of a popular uprising against communism come true—not in Asia, but in Eastern Europe.

On October 23, 1956, Hungarians rioted in Budapest against Soviet occupation. The world was electrified, and I was ecstatic. Four days later, the Red Army left Budapest. Freedom was in the air. It was a victory for all free men. But on October 30, the Red Army returned in full force, and for the next ten days the fighting raged. It ended in the defeat of the anticommunist forces and victory for the USSR. Over 160,000 refugees fled to Austria, creating an enormous problem for the West. Harold Oram and the International Rescue Committee were very active in helping the refugees. There was really very little I could do, but I sure was not going to stay out of this fight.

I became involved in two ways: I started mobilizing an army of liberation; I helped in publicizing the constant picket line around the Soviet UN delegation building at Sixty-ninth Street and Park Avenue.

The picket line was relatively simple. There were plenty of Hungarians in New York, and they were furious. It was also rather easy at first to get Hungarian-born celebrities to join the line and thus get publicity for the cause. I ran through all the Gabor girls, from Zsa Zsa to Mother Jolie. Bela Lugosi, the famous Dracula, was on the West Coast.

Who else Hungarian could get the attention of the news photographers?

What about Ilona Massey, who starred with Nelson Eddy in *Bala-laika*, the gorgeous blonde Hungarian with the black beauty spot. Was she still alive? I asked around and I was finally able to arrange for her to meet me just outside Hunter College across the street from the headquarters of the Soviet delegation to the UN. It was freezing cold. We were to meet at 6:00 P.M. I informed the press that the famous star Miss Ilona Massey would picket to protest the brutal Soviet invasion of her country.

At 6:00 P.M. sharp an enormous limousine pulled up. I peered inside and there was the ice goddess, beauty spot and all. Ilona Massey sparkled! She was dazzling! She wore a black sable shako hat and a sable coat, long diamond earrings, and a diamond choker; her lashes were coated in sparkle dust, as was her hair and even her lips. She was gorgeous! Radiant! Glamorous! Ilona Massey, the film star! The Gabors were peasants in comparison, which was exactly as Miss Massey would have wanted it.

But for a picket line? Protest? Angry? Not really! After a brief introduction, she noticed my rather crestfallen look.

"Is not good?" she asked.

"Well, Miss Massey, you look marvelous, but this is a demonstration for the young Hungarian students, boys and girls who are being crushed by Soviet tanks," I said lamely. "Something less glamorous, perhaps."

"Oh," she said reflectively. "Are the boys here?" (She meant photographers.)

"Yes, we have the *Daily News*," I said.

"OK, I fix," she said.

And with that, in seconds, all the makeup was removed, including the eye lashes and the glitz. Earrings off; diamonds off; hat off; hair mussed, but only just a bit; beauty mark in place. Perfect!

"Get camera ready, quickly. It's very cold, no?" she said.

I got the cameraman, and Ilona Massey got out of the car, a gorgeous blonde in a plain black dress, no makeup, nothing, but still dazzling.

"Ready?" she asked.

"OK," said the photographer. She threw her face and arms to the sky and shrieked, "Butchers! Murderers! You kill my people! Monsters! Free Hungary!"

"Is OK?" she asked. A crowd was gathering. "Just one more time, Miss Massey," said the photographer.

She did her act again, screaming even louder, "Butchers! Murderers! You kill my people! Monsters! Free Hungary!" She was freezing by now. She got back in the limo, pulled out her compact and repaired everything: put on her jewels, put on her furs, and turned to the crowd, smiling with the perfect and very white teeth.

"Was OK?" she asked me.

"It was terrific, thank you," I replied.

She gave me that wonderful smile that had smiled on Nelson Eddy, and drove off.

The next morning the front page of the *Daily News*, the whole page, carried her ravaged face and the legend "FORMER MOVIE STAR, ILONA MASSEY, AT ANTI-RED PICKET LINE." A real triumph except I would guess she didn't appreciate the use of the word "former."

My army of liberation took more effort. At the beginning of the revolution, Bill Buckley had an idea. In the *National Review* he suggested that President Eisenhower take the presidential plane to Rome, pick up the pope, and then fly to Budapest and tell the Russians to "just cut it out"! Not a bad idea. Neither the president nor the pope wanted to play, however, and that idea was scrapped.

I received a telephone call from a Princeton College junior who asked if he could get some of his classmates to join the picket line. I invited him and a couple of his friends to my office to discuss it that very afternoon. We quickly came up with our scheme: We would organize a Volunteer Brigade of Ivy League students to march into Hungary unarmed and do what their president would not do—declare solidarity with the Hungarian students, and tell the Russians to get out.

It was a terrific idea. It couldn't miss. The Russians wouldn't dare fire on them. After all, they were Ivy League, and if there was any trouble, their rich and powerful parents would make the U.S. government take immediate action.

I told the boys I would call them, and then got in touch with Governor Edison. At the same time, the young Princetonians started telephoning friends at Harvard, Yale, and Columbia. The next night, five of them, representing four different colleges, came to Suite 38A in the Waldorf

Towers, where they met with Governor Edison. He was as impressed by them as I was. As we discussed strategy with the Governor, I vowed that I would go with them. I would lead my own army, at last. Edison told me to find out about chartering a plane from Canada. He would get the money together to cover the cost of the plane and whatever other expenses were necessary. I started to worry about who would lead the troops—Edison or me.

I now had transport. All we needed were more troops. The original group worked out of my office telephoning students all over the East Coast. Three days later, we had our first meeting at my apartment on Fifty-eighth Street. I had four cases of cold beer, plenty of pretzels, potato chips, and peanuts. Judy Sheftel, my neighbor down the hall, was assigned to make coffee and keep bringing it in.

There were thirty-one young men sitting around my floor and on the couch and chairs. I was in heaven. It was wonderful. Each one was better looking than the next. Some of the kids brought maps, and we planned strategy. We would fly the chartered plane to Vienna and hire buses to take us to the border and over, if possible. If we couldn't drive across the border, we would get off and start walking toward Budapest. By this time, I had humbly accepted leadership and became the Generalissimo. The Hungarian revolution would be saved by my army of rosy-cheeked Ivy Leaguers. My apartment had become the headquarters of the Army of Liberation.

Fortunately, all the boys had valid passports. The initial group, which had become a committee of correspondence, had enlisted close to ninety-five young men, representing Princeton, Yale, Harvard, Columbia, Brown, Dartmouth, and even Duke University. I was already mentally assigning rank: the most attractive boys would be captains and majors; the rest would be lieutenants. There would only be officers in my army, no enlisted men.

Then, disaster struck! Midterms! My mobilization collapsed. The boys went back to school to take their exams, dreaming of what might have been. The revolution in Hungary had been crushed—by the Soviet tanks and by Ivy League midterm exams.

My neighbor Judy—who later married and divorced Jules Feiffer, the cartoonist and playwright—was a close friend. She was one of the most beautiful girls in town, a Jewish Holly Golightly, and lived on the two-apartment third floor of this wonderful brownstone just off Fifth Avenue. My bay window overlooked the Plaza fountain, and all for ninety-five dollars a month. In those days, we both entertained gentleman callers. So, to protect ourselves from unruly guests, we fixed up a bell system: a bell near her bed, a wire down the hall, a bell near my bed. Several times her bell pealed and woke me. Following instructions, I'd rush down the hall and bang on the door, shouting as loud as I could, "Judy, Judy," until she opened the door and her terrified guest departed.

One night, I picked up a young naval officer in a jazz/dance-girl bar in Times Square. He was good-looking and seemed pleasant enough. The bar closed at 2:00 A.M., and I asked whether he'd "like to come back to my place for a nightcap?"

"Sure," he said. "Good idea."

I was ready for the big seduction scene. He was quite drunk, and I was feeling no pain. It should be easy. We got back to the apartment, and I started to fix the drinks. I told him to take off his uniform jacket and "relax."

When I turned around, he was facing me with an opened switchblade knife in his hands. "I know why you brought me here," he said.

"To have a drink. If you don't want one, please feel free to go now," I said, really scared.

"I'm going to have to hurt you," he said, and I knew I had found a real psycho.

I slid over to the bell and pressed it as hard as I could. Oh God, I hope she's home! Oh God, let her be home!

He started to slowly approach me, smiling, brandishing his knife. This is it, I thought. Was I really going to die?

Then there was an enormous banging on the door, and Judy's voice shrieking, "What are you doing with my husband? Stay away from my husband!"

Husband?!?!

My navy officer was disconcerted (who wouldn't be), and I opened the door and Judy rushed in looking like the wrath of God in her pajamas and with disheveled hair. At that moment she was the most beautiful girl in town.

She screamed, "Get out, get out!"

And my navy man ran for his life. We slammed the door and fell into each other's arms. Judy looked over my shoulder and whispered, "My God, he forgot his cap." Sure enough, the officer's cap with the gold braid was on the table. We were both terrified that he might come back for it, so Judy spent the night sleeping on the couch. In the morning, it took a lot of courage to open the door, but he was gone. I kept the hat for a couple of years as some sort of memento and warning.

Chapter 9

World Travels

IN AUGUST OF 1957, as a representative of the Committee of One Million, I went on a Far East tour to establish ties with anticommunist organizations overseas. I was invited by the Chinese to attend a meeting of the Asian Peoples Anti-Communist League (APACL) in Taiwan as an official observer for both ARCI and the Committee. For a relatively small additional cost, I convinced my hosts to turn the airline ticket into a globe-circling trip. I wanted to take a break from my high-pressure job and see the world, and also to establish communication between anticommunist groups in Asia and in the West.

Ultimately, my purpose was to set up a worldwide anticommunist revolution by establishing an organization to coordinate and mobilize international activity that would combat the Moscow-based International Comintern (which coordinated activities of all communist parties and their fronts in the world). It would be a kind of "anti-Comintern" with me pulling the strings.

My Chinese hosts made arrangements for me to meet with anticommunist groups in all the countries along the "Rice Circuit" (as the Eastern rim of Asia was called in the State Department). The Free Chinese were heavily involved in much of the anticommunist activity in Asia, and other American anticommunist activists also gave me names and addresses of people to contact.

I arrived in Tokyo to be met, not by anticommunist leaders, but by my Uncle Harry and Aunt Fanny! He was working there at an American

army base. In between meetings with a few anticommunist groups in
Japan, I spent most of my time with my uncle and aunt from Brooklyn.
They took me from The Imperial Hotel to their home near the army
base, where Aunt Fanny served me homemade gefilte fish.

From Tokyo I went to Seoul, South Korea, where I met a number of
anticommunist groups who were eager to go along with my plan. At that
time, the leading anticommunist countries in Asia—and those that
funded most of the anticommunist activities throughout the world—
were Korea, Taiwan, and Vietnam.

In Taipei I attended the Asian Peoples Anticommunist League conference. I did some major lobbying among the more than one hundred
delegates. Most—if not all—of their travel and living expenses had been
paid for by the Chinese. I made contacts with people representing
anticommunist "organizations" from throughout the world, knowing
that most of the groups were little more than letterheads. Ku Cheng-
kang, who was head of APACL, was enthusiastic about my idea of an
anti-Comintern, as was just about everyone else.

From there, I went on to Hong Kong, and saw firsthand what an
impact ARCI had made on the refugees there. I was invited to Rennie's
Mill Camp, on an island in Hong Kong Bay that was turned over by the
British to a group of several thousand refugees, mostly military. These
were the people who were most difficult to place. In most cases, their
training had been military. Many of the men worked as "coolies" in
Hong Kong and returned by launch at night to the island.

My escorts to the island arrived about 8:00 A.M., and we had tea.
Many of them seemed uneasy as we waited. I asked one man what the
trouble was, and he said they were worried because the day before, a
launch had gone out to the island with some anticommunist leaders from
Hong Kong and both the launch and its passengers had disappeared.
A Red Chinese "fishing boat," a disguised naval vessel, had probably
picked them up and transported them to the mainland. I realized that
we, too, could be in danger.

We finally left in the pouring rain. As we approached the island, I
saw written on the cliffs in letters about five feet high WELCOME
MARVIN LIEBMAN, ARCI, THE COMMITTEE OF ONE
MILLION, WE THANK YOU TOO MUCH FOR YOUR HELP

TO WE REFUGEES. The whole community had turned out to meet me, literally thousands of people, many with banners thanking ARCI and the Committee of One Million. I was overwhelmed and very proud.

After a tour of the island, they held a mass "lunch" meeting in tents in the rain. There were the usual speeches, and the leader of the community said, "I want to thank you, Marvin Liebman, for the work you have done for us. There is one solution to the refugee problem, and that solution is for the refugees to go home. While we are here, we need the help of your great organization, Aid Refugee Chinese Intellectuals, to succor us. Just as important is the political job of the Committee of One Million to help us to go home, to get back to the mainland."

They were very poor, and the lunch was sparse in quality but not in quantity. I had already learned that it is very impolite not to eat everything that is put in front of you; food is a precious commodity in Asia. I was sitting on a rough dais with the leaders. Everyone else was sitting at long wooden tables. There were many dishes—all vegetables of one sort or another. Even though there was no meat, the idea was to set as many dishes before a guest as possible. I looked down at the latest dish before me, and I saw a very green and very fresh-looking vegetable of some sort or another, rather like an exotic asparagus. I picked it up with my chopsticks, and, to my horror, I saw it move—little legs scrambling in the air between my sticks. Oh my God, some new kind of delicacy! I had just about put it up to my mouth to bite off its head when my neighbor laughingly nudged me. My vegetable was a large praying mantis that had jumped on my plate from the muddy ground below.

I went to Saigon, then on to Bangkok, Thailand. On the morning of my arrival, I paid a courtesy call on U.S. Ambassador Max Bishop, a tough anticommunist. He asked me to join him for a walk in the garden, where he told me he was certain his office was bugged by one or another faction of the CIA, and that there was nothing much he could do about it.

It was from Bishop that I first became acquainted with the Byzantine convolutions of our intelligence agencies, their internal rivalries, and the total absence of liaison so that one agency had little idea of the activity of the other. Bishop asked whether I was going to Rangoon from Bangkok. I told him that I had planned to, but I couldn't get a visa from the pro-communist "neutral" Burmese, and so had scratched it from my itinerary. He said that he could arrange a visa for me and asked me to go and deliver something to a man named Thakin Ba Sein. Ba Sein was the major anticommunist opponent of Burma's leader, U Nu. He had contacts with the insurgents in the north and could possibly mount a coup. The CIA—and the American Embassy in Rangoon—were very pro-U Nu and did not look with favor on Thakin Ba Sein.

I was flattered and felt very much the secret agent. Bishop didn't give me any papers or secret capsules with microfilm. He said that all he wanted—and this was important—was for Ba Sein to get the message that he, Bishop, and his "friends," would arrange for the support he had requested. What this support was, I didn't know.

"That's all?" I asked. How easy.

"Just that," said Bishop. "I just want you to get this word to him in a personal and quick way."

Bishop thanked me and invited me to a party one of the royal princes was giving that night.

I was thrilled.

Bishop told me the difference between ordinary Highnesses and Royal Highnesses. We were going to see a Royal Highness. I borrowed a black tie and white dinner jacket from a young man at the embassy who had caught my eye and went in the embassy car to the palace of our host. Bishop told me that I would be on my own because he had a lot of handshaking and moving around to do.

It was a perfect Bangkok night—a full moon, stars, warm, fragrant. When we approached the palace, I could see light coming through the stone walls. They were translucent. Alabaster? I went down the receiving line with Bishop. The prince was a short, portly man wearing Thai dress, and the princess was tall for a Siamese, wearing an elegant Western gown and a diamond tiara. She looked like Bill Buckley's wife, Pat.

I entered a large room. Western music was playing softly from the back. There were a great number of small round tables covered with pink tablecloths. Dozens of servants in Thai costume held candelabra to provide light. At one end of the room was an enormous buffet table, laden with every conceivable kind of food, including an enormous bowl filled with caviar. Servants proffered trays of champagne or orange juice. I took the champagne and looked for a place to sit. There was a table with three young people, two men and a woman. I asked if I could join them and sat down. One of the men was from the French Embassy, another from the Australian, and the woman was from a Western newspaper. We chatted amiably, and I lost shyness with each glass of champagne. The Frenchman volunteered that our hostess was a fraud. "She is really Chinese," he said, "not Thai at all!"

Out of a corner of my eye, I saw the princess—followed by a servant holding a candelabra aloft—wandering among the tables as any good hostess would. As she arrived at our table, she said, "Ooo la la, may I sit down for a moment? These shoes are killing me."

She affected a vague French accent and prefaced everything with, "Ooo la la." She was older than she first appeared. A seat was brought for her, and she sat herself down with the servant standing behind her like a statue.

"Ooo la la," she said to me, "and who are you, young man?"

She couldn't care less. Her eyes were darting around the room. I told her my name. "Ooo la la, I read about you in the newspaper today," she said.

I said, "Thank you," although I can't imagine why I should be thanking her for reading about me. It wasn't much of a story anyhow. She took a little more interest in me.

"And where in your divine country do you come from, young man?"

"New York City," I said.

"Ooo la la, his Royal Highness and I adore New York! It's so amusing! We go there every other year at least, incognito, of course. We stay at the Plaza Hotel. Do you know it?"

"I live just across the street from the Plaza, your Royal Highness, on Fifty-eighth Street," I said.

"Ooo la la, that is so interesting, so amusing. Tell me, have you seen *My Fair Lady*?"

"Not only have I seen it, I have the LP recording with me, and you shall have it in the morning," I replied. For some reason, I had brought along five recordings of *My Fair Lady*, the hottest thing around, to present to my new friends. Happily, I had one left for the princess.

"Ooo la la, how kind of you. That is so sweet. Thank you." She was really pleased. "The last time His Royal Highness and I were in your

wonderful New York City, we went for a weekend to such an amusing place—what was it called? Apple Blossom? No. Peach Tree? What
was it?"

I got the message quickly. "Could it be Cherry Grove, your Royal
Highness?" I asked.

"Ooo la la," she said, "that's it! It was so funny, so very amusing! You
know of it?" she inquired.

Cherry Grove was and is the homosexual summer community on Fire
Island. It was very wild in those days. I had rented summer houses with
friends at both Ocean Bay Park and Fire Island Pines, each community
adjoining Cherry Grove. On Saturday nights, we would usually walk
along the beach to Duffy's, the only bar and dance hall at the Grove at that
time. When Duffy's closed, I would then go to the infamous "meat rack"
—where men cruised to pick each other up—just under the boardwalk
and along the beach. I informed the princess that I summered close by,
and that I knew Cherry Grove very well.

"Ooo la la," she said in great excitement. "His Royal Highness will be
so very pleased to meet you." She clapped her hands and ordered the
servant, still holding the candelabra, to fetch the prince. His Royal
Highness waddled up, a seat was plunked under his posterior as if by
magic, and she spoke to him in Siamese.

He clutched my hand and said, "My dear boy, tell me, was that
charming dance hall badly damaged by the fire?"

There had been a minor fire at Duffy's just about a week before I left.

"No," I told him. "It will be fine. It's probably repaired now."

"Thank God!" said the prince, "Oh, thank God!" and he pressed my
hand in his and rubbed his knee against mine.

"Ooo la la," said the princess.

Small world!

The following year, at the APACL Conference in Seoul in 1958, I
was introduced to Syngman Rhee, the president of Korea. Rhee was
a wonderful old man, a strong anticommunist, who had helped liberate
his country from the Japanese.

A young aide to Henry Luce, who was there to observe for TIME-
LIFE, was a fellow delegate. He was an earnest young man, indeed.
He asked whether he could join me in my audience with President

Rhee. There was "something important" he had to communicate. I figured it must be some message from his powerful publisher boss, and arranged it.

We were both ushered in to see the grand old man, who was sitting in an easy chair with his pet white Pekingese cradled in his lap. After a few pleasantries, I started to tell him of my anti-Comintern ideas. Rhee was enthusiastic. I should "count on Korea for whatever cooperation was necessary." He said he would assign George Paik, president of Chosen University, as his liaison with me. This was far more than I had hoped for. I thanked him profusely.

Rhee then turned his hooded eyes to my companion. What did he think?

"Well, Mr. President," said Bourne, "don't you think it would be possible to bring North Korea closer—to make it more friendly— through an exchange of artists and cultural events. Dancers, theatre, opera, all of that." His earnestness almost brought tears to my eyes.

"War," said Rhee, "war."

"I beg your pardon, sir," said the young man meekly.

"WAR," thundered Rhee, standing up and dropping the dog to the floor. "War will bring the North closer. WAR. WAR." The old boy was now screaming. My friend stood ashen-faced, and I was taken aback, too.

That was the end of the audience. We were led out, leaving President Rhee still sputtering.

At the last APACL conference I ever attended in Taipei in 1967, I saw Chiang Kai-shek for the last time. I first met him in 1957. I was on a receiving line to shake hands with Mme. Chiang Kai-shek. Walter Judd was just behind me as I whispered to Mme. Chiang that it was Dr. Judd's 69th birthday the next day.

"Walter," she said in her perfect, slightly southern-accented, English, "Please come tonight and take pot-luck with the President and me, and you too, Marvin. Oh, please, this is an important birthday because on our calendar you are actually seventy years old. We would both be so honored to have you join us."

Of course, Judd and I accepted with alacrity. There were only Chiang, Mme. Chiang, Samson Shen (the President's young interpreter who now serves as Foreign Minister), Judd, and me sitting around the table. The "pot luck" was a banquet, but I hardly touched the food. I was too excited to eat. Later, Judd told me he had never seen the Generalissimo so animated or in such good spirits. I remember only two incidents.

Chiang Kai-shek told this story, which I here paraphrase:

"When I was quite small, my father was the Village elder. A Western missionary had come to the village. He was from Scotland, and had red hair and a hearing aid in the form of a large horn. Everyone in the village remarked on this strange object the missionary carried about with him. They had no idea that he was deaf. My father invited him over for tea, as was the custom, even though the women of the household were horrified at having a 'foreign devil' with his undoubtedly foul odor in the house.

"The missionary spoke Chinese and so he and my father were able to converse quite amiably. But my father was confused as to why the missionary kept putting this large object next to his mouth. So, to be polite, he carefully spat into it three times," and with this Chiang laughed heartily.

The other incident I remember (which I also paraphrase) was when Judd raised his glass in a toast and said in Chinese something like, "Next year we will drink together on the Mainland." This was the usual toast, rather like the Jewish Passover toast, "Next year in Jerusalem."

Chiang said, "No, Walter. I don't think so. I think I will be on this island until I die. I would like to go home again, and I know I could if you in the West were wise enough to do what is required. China, or what is called China, was never a single nation and is not one now, in spite of the Communist terror used to make it one. It is many nations, like the Soviet Union, which will ultimately break up into these separate countries. To start with, China can be divided into three separate areas. I will govern the area around Canton, which I consider to be the heart of China. The Japanese can develop Manchuria until it is ready to set off on its own. And let the Communists keep the North until they are deposed by the people. In that way, China can never be a threat to any other nation. But, I don't think this will happen, my old friend."

Judd told me that that was the first time he had ever heard Chiang speak like that, and he thought that I was a witness to a historic statement.

Back now, to 1957. I left Bangkok for Rangoon. When I got off the plane late at night, I was met by several uniformed Burmese. They took me to a room at the airport, searched me, confiscated all my traveler's checks, took my passport, and left me whatever cash I had. Someone must have told them to be on the alert. Although I was told by Bishop that I wouldn't get much "joy" from it, I asked to see somebody from the American Embassy. I didn't want to give up my passport. I was told that everything would be looked after, and I would have the passport returned "in due course." There was no reason to concern the Embassy.

I was concerned, but I didn't know what else to do except leave. I went into the waiting room, where I was met by a number of Burmese all dressed in long sarongs. One was Thakin Ba Sein, who was with his wife and some of his colleagues. They had waited all that time for me, and I was really appreciative. It was like seeing family—even though his wife was puffing on a cigar, which was the custom there.

I told them about my passport, and they said not to worry, all would be OK. I had not made any hotel reservation, so Ba Sein took me to his home. After I gave him the message, which delighted him, he took me to a room where there was no bed, only a mat on the floor. I stayed in Ba Sein's house for two nights.

He arranged for me to make two speeches—one to the Chinese community and another, at night, to about four hundred Burmese priests. That was difficult. All of them had shaved heads and were dressed in saffron-colored robes, and they just stared. There was a translator, but there was no reaction whatever from the audience. Ba Sein said I did very well.

When I was ready to leave, Ba Sein gave me an envelope to deliver to "a man who would meet me at the airport in Karachi." I didn't have any trouble getting it out of the country. Ba Sein seemed to know more about my movements than I did. My passport miraculously appeared at the airport, but no traveler's checks. I left my new friends, and I found that I was really fond of these people who were so kind to me.

I flew from Rangoon to Karachi, where I was met by a nervous Pakistani and handed him the envelope. I went on to New Delhi, then flew to Istanbul, where I stayed two nights at the new Hilton Hotel. The next morning, from my balcony I saw the magnificent Bosphorus, where Asia and Europe come together.

I spent the day sightseeing, but by the time evening came I was bored and lonely. I knew no one. I went to the bar at the Hilton and sat alone at a small table. There were four American sailors drinking at the bar, good-looking and boisterous and getting quite drunk. My antenna went up, and in a few minutes we were all sitting at the same table, and I was buying the boys drinks. One of them, the one that I found the most attractive, was the lightweight boxing champion of the fleet.

We talked and laughed, and I dropped as many names as I could to impress them. They knew very few, but they were particularly impressed by my ability to pay for the drinks and then some sandwiches. I was having a good time, and I didn't know where all this would lead. I told them that I had a special bottle of Chinese brandy that had been given to me by the general in charge of the garrison at Quemoy. Should we continue drinking in my room? They readily accepted my invitation, and the five of us went up.

They were impressed with the view and the brandy. By chance, there were three American college girls in the room next to mine. There was great laughing and banter on the adjoining balconies between my group and theirs. It was turning into a very jolly evening. The boys and the girls were cute, and it was fun watching their little games. I was getting quite drunk on the Chinese brandy.

Three of the sailors took the three girls downstairs and left me with the boxer.

He said he was feeling "tired" and "drunk" and asked, "Could I lie down?"

"But, of course," I said.

So, for about an hour or more, the boxing champion of the American naval forces in Turkey and I enjoyed each other's company.

His mates returned and knocked at the door. I was alarmed, but they couldn't care less. The boxer was still in bed. "Boy, I must have fallen asleep. I don't remember a thing!" he said. That was a line I heard in many cities, in many countries. He got dressed, and the four of them left, vowing that we would all keep in touch with each other.

I went on to Rome, for fun, with no politics, and then to Vienna, Berlin, and Paris, where I stayed at the Meurice Hotel, the same one that I visited ten years earlier on my way back from Cyprus. Finally, I stopped in London and stayed in Chelsea at the house of a friend who was away in Portugal. Even though I knew nobody, I loved London, especially Chelsea. That night, walking down the King's Road, I came to the Royal Court Theatre. There was a crowd outside for the hit play *Look Back in Anger*. Taking a chance, I went to the box office, and, sure enough, there was a ticket available. I was privileged to see the beginning of the British "kitchen sink" theater period with this terrific play on my first night in London. I vowed that I would return someday.

After I got back to New York, I wrote a report for the steering committee on the situation in the seven Asian countries I visited: Japan, Korea, Taiwan, Hong Kong, Vietnam, Thailand, and Burma. My contacts there had expressed concern about America's will to combat communism in Asia and praised the committee's efforts to mobilize American and international opinion against communism.

Over the next few years, as pressures grew in some circles for trade with Red China, the Committee of One Million continued its campaign, responding with behind-the-scenes lobbying, public statements, and full-page ads. Until the mid-sixties, we had a string of victories in swaying public opinion to our side.

Years later, in 1964, despite our continuing efforts, the tide began to turn against us. The committee suffered a number of defeats. Among the most damaging were defections by members of Congress. In January, France decided to recognize Communist China. As a result, retired Senator Ralph Flanders, a long-time committee supporter, issued a statement that he was not "irrevocably committed for the indefinite future" to the nonrecognition of Red China.

The bipartisanship of the committee, meanwhile, had suffered from criticisms by liberal Senators Paul Douglas and Thomas J. Dodd. They complained of my close ties with conservative groups. In the early sixties I had been working closely with Bill Buckley and his *National Review* colleagues helping to organize a number of conservative organizations, including Young Americans for Freedom and the American Conservative Union. I also worked closely with the Goldwater presidential campaign in 1964. (See chapters Eleven and Twelve.)

The committee continued to lose supporters. Public opinion polls were beginning to go against us, giving liberal supporters a chance to jump ship. Senators Abraham Ribicoff (D., Conn.) and Jacob K. Javits (R., NY.) resigned from the committee. (Javits resigned every off year and, thinking better of it, joined again each election year.) Finally, Paul Douglas, who had done the most to maintain the committee's reputation as a bipartisan organization, lost his Senate seat in the 1966 elections and subsequently resigned from the committee. This was a loss we could not take.

By June of 1968, congressional supporters of the committee were down to forty-two Democrats and fifty-four Republicans in the House. It was urgent to get presidential candidate Richard Nixon to make a statement supporting the committee's position on Red China, especially because it was expected that Democratic candidate Hubert Humphrey would take a soft line on the issue. Nixon, however, refused. He did not want to take a hard-line stand on China during the campaign, and indeed had other ideas in mind, as subsequent events would prove.

In 1971, Red China was admitted to the United Nations. The representatives of the Republic of China, which had been a founding member of the UN and a permanent member of the Security Council, were *expelled*. They were the first and only nation to be thrown out, an international act of total hypocrisy. Soon after, the Nixon administration formally recognized China.

Nonetheless, the Committee of One Million was an extraordinary success. Against impossible odds, we helped to deny Communist China what it most wanted and needed: the Chinese seat in the United Nations. I was in London when the Reds were admitted to the UN. I remember feeling bitter but also proud that for fifteen years I had played a leading role in keeping the prize from them.

Chapter 10

Marvin Liebman Associates, Inc.

WHEN I RETURNED from my round-the-world trip in early September 1957, I was restive and looking for another life change. My trip had considerably broadened my horizons. I was already planning my anti-Comintern, and I was ready to do battle on all fronts. I was inhibited by Oram's shop and by my colleagues there. I was the "right-wing" member of the staff. Although they liked me, they all rather looked down their noses at my work. I really wanted out.

Harold Oram was under pressure from the American Association for the United Nations (AAUN), one of his major clients, to disassociate his firm from the Committee of One Million. The committee had criticized the AAUN because of its subtle pro-Red China stance. Eleanor Roosevelt, who was head of the AAUN, had complained to Harold about this. In October, bowing to these and other pressures, Oram announced that the firm must drop the committee as a client. I was to concentrate on enlisting new accounts and work on the AAUN account.

I drafted a confidential memorandum, which I sent to Walter Judd, Charles Edison, and Frederick C. McKee. Fred was a mild-mannered man who was president of the National Casket Company. He was the consummate mortician; always in a black suit and starched white shirt, he had a pale complexion with pursed lips. Under all his mildness, however, was a dedicated anticommunist who had been an activist in anti-Nazi and anticommunist groups since before World War II. One day I was attempting to make some light conversation with him. "Well, Fred," I said, "how's business?"

"Not very well now that it's summer," he replied, seriously. "Last winter was one of our best yet, what with the flu epidemic and all. People don't seem to pass so much in the summer."

I dropped the subject.

The gist of my memorandum was that the anticommunist/conservative movement was growing. The Left had plenty of professionals at their command: fund-raisers, public relations people, advertising agencies. Our side had no one but me. (I was not lacking in ego in those days.) Wouldn't it make sense to support an organization that would provide expertise to the growing movement at either reasonable cost or pro bono? I was prepared to fill the vacuum, but I needed help.

The three men discussed my idea by telephone, and Edison called me to his suite in the Waldorf Astoria Towers.

"Marvin," he said, "This is a capital idea, and I'm all for it. You know what I think of you, and . . ." Here he paused, rather embarrassed. "It's good for . . . people like you . . . It will make you happier . . . to be in business for yourself. You know what I mean."

I certainly did. Jews—even nice Jews like me—should be in business for themselves rather than work for someone else. I wasn't offended, I was deeply touched. The old man really cared for me.

I worked up a minimum budget—rent, equipment, minimum salaries for me and a secretary for a couple of months, deposits on telephones, etc. Edison guaranteed the money. It was about seven thousand dollars. He gave me this admonition. "Keep it simple. Don't buy a carpet for your office at first. I have seen too many young men with fancy offices go down the drain. You don't need a carpet to start off with." He seemed obsessed by carpeting.

I agreed, of course, but—passing a rug auction on Lexington Avenue that very day, I bought some used wall-to-wall carpeting, which I stored until I got an office. It was just too good a deal to miss.

I sublet a dentist's office at 17 Park Avenue at a good monthly rental. I advertised in the paper for a secretary. I went to the used office furniture store. I was ready to go.

Finally, I told Oram. He was furious. He had groomed me, he said, to take over the business and look after him in his old age. I was the best he had. How could I betray him like that?

He was truly disappointed and also really livid. Like all bosses—like me—he had always had the dream. You took one of the young men who worked for you, trained him, and gave him the business in due course so that he and the business you founded would take care of you in your golden years. It hardly ever happens.

I hired an English secretary, who was wonderful except that she was a disciple of Ayn Rand and refused to type the word *God*. In those days it was very prestigious to have a secretary with a British accent. We moved in to our new office on January 2, 1958, ready to take over the American Right. I decided that the name Marvin Liebman, Associates, Inc., sounded good and duly registered it.

Now that I was on my own, I could provide my professional know-how to the fast-growing anticommunist/conservative movement in America. All kinds of ideas were first tried out in my offices on Park Avenue, then Lexington Avenue, and finally at 79 Madison Avenue. Just a few streets down from my Madison Avenue office were the offices of the *National Review*. Together we became, for a number of years, the hub of anticommunist and conservative activism in America.

In addition to the carpeting I bought when I first moved into 17 Park Avenue, I brought a number of other valuable assets along. The most important was the trust and respect of Bill Buckley and his colleagues at *National Review*, Charles Edison, Walter Judd, Fred McKee, Eddie Rickenbacker, Christopher Emmet, Spruille Braden, and a host of others.

This "host of others" provided the base for all the various committees and organizations that I organized in Marvin Liebman Associates, Inc.'s busy ten years (and the five years I operated again when I returned from London in 1975). They included about a hundred prominent individuals representing just about every field of American endeavor: politics, business, finance, education, religion, the military, literature, show biz, and sports. These men and women trusted me to protect their names and permitted me to put them on the letterhead for any anticommunist and/or conservative cause that struck their fancy. I was therefore able to organize a committee, on almost anything, practically overnight. All I needed was Walter Judd, Eddie Rickenbacker, Charles Edison, or Bill Buckley to sign the letter or telegram of invitation asking them to join, and they did.

The other asset I started with was the contributor list of the Committee of One Million, which I finally obtained from the Oram office. There were about twenty thousand names and addresses on three-by-five cards. We also had an addressograph and a mimeograph machine—this was before copiers and computers. Utilizing the always shaky credit I had established with the telephone company, Western Union, American Express, printers, and mailing houses, I could start almost anything with no money at all—and usually did.

Once, when I was on the other side of the fund-raising solicitation, I was outsmarted myself. When Buckley first started fund-raising for *National Review*, I sent in a self-sacrificing contribution of $100. It was returned with a note from Bill saying something like, "We don't take money from colleagues, but thanks a lot anyway." I was relieved. I needed the money. But the following year, to continue to make a good impression, I sent a contribution of $250. This time, instead of returning my check, I received a form letter that said, "Dear Mr. Liebman: We thank you in all sincerity, for your handsome contribution . . ." It was signed by William F. Buckley, Jr., L. Brent Bozell, James Burnham, Willmoore Kendall, Frank S. Meyer, and William A. Rusher. Needless to say, I never again made a contribution I didn't mean.

Working out of my new office, I thought about building an international anticommunist organization starting with my Asian contacts. Two of these efforts are noteworthy: one a bitter failure, the other an overwhelming success.

In October 1957, I consulted with my friend T. F. Tsiang, the Chinese ambassador to the United Nations, and Ku Cheng-kang, the head of the Asian Peoples Anti-Communist League (APACL). We agreed to organize a preliminary, off-the-record international meeting for March 1958. There a small group from anticommunist groups in Asia, Europe, Latin America, and Africa would discuss the feasibility of forming a larger organization. I was asked to serve as coordinator. I put together a board of advisors and went to work.

We set up a joint bank account with seven thousand dollars from APACL (I put out feelers to the CIA to no avail). I made sure that the account required two signatures on each check. I was always careful to cover myself in any public financial matters. Whenever possible, I'd avoid signing checks. In any public interest group, the first place anyone looked when they wanted to embarrass you was not your sex life, it was financial affairs. I always tried to be above suspicion.

I didn't want this to be seen as an American operation, and I thought it would be best if it seemed to come from Latin America. I decided on Mexico City. I asked a man I met at the APACL meeting earlier in the year, Jorge Prieto Laurens, head of a Latin American group called the Inter-American Confederation for the Defense of the Continent (IACDC), to issue the invitations from his organization and handle the logistics from his headquarters in Mexico City. I sent him six thousand dollars from our account for expenses. I told him what groups to invite from Europe and Asia and asked him to name two Latin American organizations. There was no major anticommunist organization in the United States at that time except for the Committee of One Million, so I would represent the committee. I recommended that no more than twelve individuals and their staffs participate.

But then disaster struck. The moment Laurens got the money, he started to take over. I discovered too late that his international anticommunist connections were with the most extreme right-wing organizations, many anti-Semitic. His major benefactor was the Anti-Bolshevik Bloc of Nations (ABN), and they practically owned his group. Laurens was completely in their control. I had lost control to a bunch of jerks. I was furious with myself.

I contacted my board of advisors and asked them for help. Ku insisted I attend and make peace with Laurens. He offered to cover my expenses. After meeting with my colleagues, I decided to go to Mexico City to see if I could salvage anything of my original concept.

It was in Mexico that I first became the target of bigotry on the anticommunist Right. I realized that few of the delegates represented nothing more than letterhead groups. Many were part of the ABN apparatus and were public anti-Semites. Jaroslaw Stezko was the head of the group. He was reported to have been a Nazi collaborator in the Ukraine during World War II and may well have been indirectly responsible for the slaughter of my mother's family there.

Out of courtesy to Ku Cheng-kang, I went along with the meetings in the hope that perhaps the perception of an international anticommunist organization might overshadow the reality. The conference established the World Anticommunist Congress for Freedom and Liberation "to consolidate the anticommunist forces of people the world over and combine efforts to deal a blow to the aggression of the international communist movement and to guarantee the freedom of all nations and to promote universal human rights."

I was elected by unanimous vote, with the Anti-Bolshevik Bloc of Nations abstaining, Secretary General of the new organization. One of my first acts as secretary general was to demand membership fees, which caused mutterings of Yankee imperialism, particularly from my anti-Semitic ABN friends. Returning home, I established my Secretariat in my small headquarters at 17 Park Avenue. The "secret" files and documents of the new organization were kept in the bathtub.

For a few moments after I returned to New York, I really believed something could be done. Then, reality set in. My Chinese friends went for the perception, but I had finally accepted reality. There was no way I could deal with these people. On July 14, a little more than three months after Mexico City, I submitted my resignation as Secretary General, which I sent to all "members," and closed the books on the organization.

After my resignation went out, I received about twenty-five telephone calls that I assumed were from Stezko's people. The gist of these calls were, "You will die, Jew Bolshevik! You have sabotaged the great anticommunist cause! Death to the Jew Bolshevik!" I heard echoes of the Army officer's insults when I had been drummed out of the service. For a while, I was really frightened. I even went to the police station next to *National Review* to see if I could get a permit for a gun. They said I should get a shotgun and saw off the barrel.

The ABN was furious with me, as were their allies in various parts of the world. Ku Cheng-kang was angry for a while, but I was much too important to him for him to be angry for very long.

But that was the end—at least for a while—of my first empire!

About one year later, in March 1959, a Mr. Djab Naminov telephoned to say he wanted to speak to me—it was urgent. "Who is he?" I asked my secretary. "He says he's a Kalmuk." "What's a Kalmuk?" "I don't know." "Put him through." I was rather curious. My reputation was beginning to grow, and I was getting telephone calls from all sorts of people.

Naminov was calling from New Jersey, where he lived. He said that he and two of his colleagues were most anxious to speak with me about the problem in Tibet. I had been reading about the beginning of a Tibetan uprising against Red Chinese occupation, but there wasn't a lot of press coverage in the early days. Tibet was so remote and far away.

Naminov and his two friends appeared the next day, dressed in gray business suits. They said it was vital to do something for the Tibetan people. The Red Chinese were practicing genocide. Most important, the Dalai Lama, their spiritual leader, was a prisoner in the capital, Lhasa.

My visitors told me the story of the Kalmuks, the last survivors of Genghis Khan's hordes. Genghis Khan swept through Asia and into Europe, covering most of the area that was the USSR. He left behind soldiers and their families. They maintained their identity by not intermarrying with the native people. Just before World War II, the Kalmuks numbered about half a million. They were considered one of the "minorities" of the Soviet Union. As they were a nomadic people, they refused to fit into the Soviet system of collectivism.

When World War II started, the Kalmuks began their exodus from the Soviet Union toward Tibet. They were all Lamaist Buddhists and considered the Dalai Lama of Tibet a deity. After centuries in a foreign land, they wanted to go home, to be close to their God.

The sufferings of the Kalmuks on this great pilgrimage were enormous. Of the five hundred thousand who started over the Himalayas, only thirty thousand survived. They never got to Tibet. They were interned in India for most of the war. After the war, the various international refugee agencies declared the Kalmuks displaced persons. A few thousand were resettled in the United States—in New Jersey and Pennsylvania. The last of the hordes of Genghis Khan were now middle-class American businessmen.

It was difficult to think of what to do. There was no Tibetan constituency in the United States, no organizations that could lobby Congress to help Tibet. I said I would think about it and call them the next day. I felt sorry for them and resolved to try to do something. They had put their trust in my ability to help.

I telephoned my two major allies, Walter Judd and Charles Edison, to ask them what we could do about Tibet. Set up a committee, of course, and bring the situation to the attention of the public. Who knew anything about Tibet? The only authority I could think of was Lowell Thomas, the famous radio commentator, explorer, adventurer, and author.

Thomas was difficult to get hold of, and I wanted to get started right away. The Dalai Lama had escaped from Lhasa on March 17 and was now in India. I drew up my usual list of VIPs—expanded to include all the liberals I could think of—and convinced Walter Judd (representing ARCI), Joseph C. Grew (representing the Committee of One Million), and Magnus I. Gregorsen (representing the American Bureau for Medical Aid to China) to sign a telegram asking them to sponsor our effort.

Four days prior to that, and in order to give Naminov and his friends something to do, I suggested that they get members of the Kalmuk community—along with (and this was most important) robed Buddhist monks—to demonstrate at the United Nations and to call on the UN to take immediate action of one kind or another.

I planned the demonstration for Friday, March 27, just ten days after Naminov first came to my office. I sent out a press release and was ready to lead my troops. I arranged for them to present a petition to Andrew Cordier, the deputy secretary general of the United Nations, at 4:00 P.M. with the demonstration to begin at 1:30. Our mobilization point was just in front of the Carnegie Endowment for International Peace across the street from the UN building.

I was waiting there at noon when four buses pulled up, two from New Jersey and two from Philadelphia. All at once, as the buses came to a stop, the heavens opened. Out into the pouring rain came about three hundred Kalmuks—men, women, children, infants—and monks. The monks were dressed in their saffron-colored robes, with prayer wheels and all the other paraphernalia of Buddhism. The rest were dressed in native costumes. They looked splendid as they rushed from the buses into the Carnegie Endowment Building to take refuge from the torrential rains falling on New York.

But I couldn't have a demonstration with umbrellas, and besides, there weren't enough umbrellas to go around. I was really desperate. A demonstration was promised, however, and a demonstration we had. My troops came out into the rain with their costumes and robes sticking to their skins, wet black hair falling over their faces, infants wailing, felt slippers squishing—it was a mess. The petition was presented to Cordier, but nobody was paying any attention. I thought that the sight of Buddhist monks spinning their prayer wheels outside the UN would create some press. It didn't. The sopping remnants of Ghengis Khan's hordes went back to New Jersey and Pennsylvania.

The invitational telegram enlisted many liberals to this anticommunist cause. Among these liberal supporters were Roger Baldwin, founder of the American Civil Liberties Union; Justice William O. Douglas of the Supreme Court; Dr. Reinhold Niebuhr, the Protestant theologian; and most important of all, Norman Thomas, the American Socialist leader. Lowell Thomas served as chairman of this ad hoc emergency committee; Judd was vice-chairman. I appointed myself executive vice-chairman. Headquarters, of course, was my office.

On Monday, April 13, the American Emergency Committee for Tibetan Refugees was officially launched with a press conference and a cable of support to the Dalai Lama. Two days later, we asked Travis Fletcher, head of the Hong Kong ARCI office, to go to India to make as full a survey as possible of the refugee situation there. We were receiving reports of literally thousands of Tibetans going over the mountains into India to escape the savage Chinese suppression of their uprising.

I was too busy—and having too much fun organizing the group—to bother with thinking about fund-raising. I made peace with Harold Oram by hiring him to handle the fund-raising for the emergency committee.

We were all in the dark about the real situation in India until we received our first overseas telephone reports from Travis Fletcher on April 30. He had met with various Indian government officials and private Indian organizations and with Tibetan refugee leaders and made a firsthand survey of the fast-growing refugee camps in northern India. On May 4, Fletcher sent us a cable, which we of course later used for fund-raising purposes, to report that there were thousands of refugees, many seriously ill and in need of medical care and clothing, and that medical supplies were urgently needed.

One of our members was George Meany, president of the AFL/CIO, who assigned Harry Goldberg, head of their Department of International Affairs, as liaison with us. Goldberg was well connected abroad and through his contacts in India the Central Committee for Tibetan Relief was established in New Delhi under the chairmanship of J. B. Kripalani, a prominent Indian member of Parliament. Fletcher now had somebody with whom to deal.

Within days, over one million dollars in medical supplies and cash had been pledged by individuals, groups, and corporations in the United States. I was in seventh heaven. I felt as if I could move the world. From a wet demonstration just one month before, we had an important international committee.

India was in an awkward position. They were afraid to offend their powerful Communist Chinese neighbors in any way. Helping Tibetan refugees could be a source of friction. But there were thousands of Tibetan refugees in India in those first weeks, and something had to be done. Prime Minister Nehru agreed to accept private American aid only if it was absolutely nonpolitical. There must be no hint of any anticommunist motivation. It was a repeat of the Hong Kong/ARCI situation six years previously.

The Indian ambassador in Washington called Judd in for a private meeting. It was Nehru's wish, the ambassador confided, that Marvin Liebman not have any leadership responsibility. It seemed that my anticommunist activities had reached the attention of Nehru, and he wanted no part of me.

Poor Judd. He was torn between loyalty to me and his humanitarian desires to help the refugees. We all knew that this could not be done without the cooperation of the Indian government.

Of course, I complied. Though I was angry, I was also proud to be noticed. On May 15 we "reorganized" our committee to meet the demands of the Indian government. I resigned as executive vice-chairman. The office was moved from 17 Park Avenue to the Graybar Building just over Grand Central Station. I remained a member of the executive committee, but, in essence, I had given up all power to B. A. Garside and Harold Oram.

I really didn't object too strongly. As with all the groups I started, it was a lot more fun beginning them than running them. I had my triumph. Now I could leave it to the accountants and clerks. Nevertheless, I was still able to utilize the committee for various anticommunist statements and other activities over the next few years.

So, from mid-March to mid-May—a period of only two months—I had created, organized, and left the American Emergency Committee for Tibetan Refugees.

In mid-June, I visited India on my way back from an APACL conference. Through a CIA contact I arranged to be taken to see the Dalai Lama before visiting Travis Fletcher in New Delhi. It was profoundly moving to meet this young man who seemed to bear the sorrows of the world. His great sweetness made a lasting impression on me. We spoke for about two hours, and most of the conversation had little to do with communism. It was mostly about living and thinking and praying. I saw in him what I love most in the world—innocence. He said, sadly, "What a great loss for the world, what a sad absence it will be to lose its last museum piece, Tibet. A museum piece caught in time." I couldn't resist, however, imploring him to speak out, to call for world help for his people.

I don't know whether it was what I said, but five days later the Dalai Lama called a widely covered press conference appealing for world support for the freedom of his people. The press conference caused an uproar in India, increasing their fear that the Tibetan problem would be brought before the United Nations—something the Indians did not want.

Some four years later in January 1963, I came up with the idea of organizing an international tour by the Dalai Lama. I thought he could be used to focus world attention on the continuing menace of communism and on the fallacy of "coexistence." If free people throughout the world could see the Dalai Lama and hear his words, perhaps they might see their own ultimate fate unless action was taken.

I outlined such a tour to Lowell Thomas, and he was most enthusiastic. Our greatest problem was how the Dalai Lama should be presented. "If he agrees to put himself in our hands," I wrote to Thomas, "we must make every effort to see that he is presented in the most dignified and correct way possible. What must be taken into account at all times is that the Dalai Lama—both to himself and to his millions of followers—is a Deity. The Dalai Lama is more untouchable, if you will, than Pope John. This makes for extremely delicate and difficult arrangements."

After much negotiation and consultation, the tour fell through. The Dalai Lama was far less approachable in those days than he is now. The snag came in my plans for him to visit the United States and appear at a Madison Square Garden rally. In the ordinary course of events, a visiting head of state would go to Washington to be received by the president. In this case, because the visiting head of state was God, it was thought that the president should go and meet him. We could never overcome this protocol difficulty.

On April 13, 1970, eleven years after it began, the emergency committee was finally dissolved. "We have made a significant contribution to an admirable and courageous people at a time of great tragedy and suffering," Lowell Thomas wrote in a final letter to the committee. "We also participated in a memorable demonstration of international cooperation and goodwill in humanitarian services."

Once again, instead of fighting the communist oppressor, we took care of the oppressed. This was second-best to me, but at least something was accomplished, and some of the innocent were saved, even as the oppression continued in their homeland.

Chapter 11

New Organizations

*F*ROM THE TIME I QUIT the Communist party, I have been a firm believer in the importance of the individual over any state, political party, or religious hierarchy. To me, the individual is all, subservient only to God. With my belief in the individual comes a belief in the sanctity of privacy and the freedom of silence. At first, this belief was vital to my hiding as a homosexual. As I grew older, it became an integral part of what I believe—the right of privacy, to "do your own thing" as long as you don't hurt anyone else. The less regulation, the less interference in one's life by government—the better. It seemed to me that Bill Buckley's brand of conservativism, and his articulation of it, represented exactly what I had believed for so long.

Although we met early in 1955, when he was starting *National Review*, and saw each other many times in the four years that followed, Bill Buckley and I didn't become real friends until about 1959. Prior to that, I had become close friends with his brother-in-law and sister, Brent and Tish Bozell, and his sister Priscilla—the four of us once spent a hilarious week in Haiti. But it wasn't until Bill took me into his life that I really began to know him and his family—his wife, Pat, his nine siblings, and his mother, Aloise. They accepted me as one of the family, and with them I found my most enduring home yet.

It was early in our friendship when I had a rather drunken dinner with Buckley and Bozell. This was not difficult to do. The three of us were in our cups, and we felt a strong bond of amiable comradeship. "*Vieux*," Bill said to me—that's what he calls me most of the time—"we can really make a revolution in this country. I will make conservativism 'shoe' (the Yalie term for being accepted, as in "white shoe" rather than "black shoe").

You handle the agitation-propaganda, and (pointing to his half-asleep brother-in-law) we'll make Brent president." I believed him. The three of us would be an unbeatable team. Whatever Bill might dream up, I was convinced would happen. We had the future in our hands.

Bill did make conservatism "shoe." I did a lot of agitating and put out a lot of propaganda. Brent never became president, but he worked with both of us on many conservative causes over the years.

Bill's style of conservatism won me over. His orbit of friends—James Burnham (author of *Suicide of the West*), Bill Rusher (publisher of *National Review*), Whittaker Chambers (author of *Witness* and a great philosopher), John Chamberlain (syndicated columnist and critic), Frank Meyer (former Stalinist and political tactician), Brent Bozell (writer and thinker)—all embraced a conservatism that defended the primacy of the individual over the state. Out of loyalty to him, I even tolerated the excesses of many others who called themselves his followers. I did this because I firmly believe that Bill opposed any of the open or hidden anti-Semitism, anti-intellectualism, and bigotry that seemed to dog the American Right.

With rare exception, I agreed with and supported everything that Bill Buckley advocated in those early days. I never made any important professional move after 1959 without consulting him. And if I didn't have his full, although many times silent, support, I would drop the idea. I entered the 1960s with Bill and his colleagues at *National Review* at my side. Without them, I could not have accomplished one-tenth of what I did in the ensuing years.

Bill Buckley was unquestionably the most important figure in my life. We had a close and always empathetic relationship, but I can recall only a few times when we ever had a "personal" talk. Bill is shy about revealing any of his innermost thoughts. I, on the other hand, had my secret, which I could never reveal to the man I thought of as my best friend. This was only because I thought it would cause him enormous personal distress, not because of any shame on my part.

I would reveal far more to his wife, Pat, than I would ever tell Bill. Pat and I were, for many years, the closest of confidants and, by that token, the closest of friends. But neither she nor anyone else could replace that very special relationship I enjoyed with Buckley. It was almost mystical,

In 1926, at three years old, just before I started wearing glasses.

With my mother at a family picnic in 1936.

Three fellow-counselors and me, at the far right, at my first summer camp job in 1941.

Just after I joined the Army Air Corps in 1943.

OPPOSITE PAGE: Sucking a lemon for my seasickness, on deck of the *Ben Hecht*, with other refugees, in 1947 (as photographed by fellow-crew member, Wallace Litwin). The British Navy had seized the ship and was escorting it to Haifa, Palestine.

With my father, mother, and sister at the dinner in
honor of the crew of the *Ben Hecht* in 1947.

With my parents at a summer camp in 1951.

Talking with my two mentors, Harold L. Oram (left)
and Charles Edison (center) in 1956. (*Photo:* Judith Sheftel)

In a penny arcade photo booth with British comedienne Hermione Gingold, 1956.

At a rally in my honor organized by Burmese and Chinese anticommunists in Rangoon, 1957. Thakin Ba Sein, my host, is seated to my immediate left. I was traveling as a representative of the Committee of One Million and the Asian Peoples Anti-Communist League.

Sharing a laugh with Bill Buckley in 1959.

With Pat Buckley in 1960 at the Buckley family home,
Great Elm, in Sharon, Connecticut, during the
founding conference of Young Americans for Freedom.
(*Photo:* Kay Prindle)

On a receiving line in 1960 to greet President and Mme.
Syngman Rhee in Seoul, Korea.

As the emcee of the fifth anniversary dinner of the *National Review* in 1960. Priscilla Buckley is on the right, Bill Buckley is hidden behind the podium, and Admiral Lewis L. Strauss and William A. Rusher are to the left. (*Photo:* Standard Flashlight Co., Inc.)

With Chiang Kai-shek, President of the Republic of China, in Taipei in 1962. (*Photo:* Wu Chung Yee)

With Mme. Chiang Kai-shek in Taiwan in 1962. She is looking at *The Little Prince* by Antoine de Saint Exupery, which I gave her and which she "read with great pleasure and sadness." (*Photo:* Wu Chung Yee)

With Vietnamese President Ngo Dinh Diem in Saigon in 1962. (*Photo:* Phong Phim-Anh)

Accepting an award at Young Americans for Freedom
rally in 1962 at Madison Square Garden.

Donald Shafto (left) and David Franke (right), Young
Americans for Freedom activists, at my weekend house
in Southbury, Connecticut, in 1963.

Interviewing a GI in Vietnam during my 1967 tour.

Actress Helen Mirren and me on the set of my film
production of *Miss Julie* in 1973.

With starlet Julie Ege on the set of my production of the
film *Not Now Darling* in 1973.

A party I gave at a New York drag night club in 1977
for some of my London theater friends—from left: Diana
Rigg, me, Siobhan McKenna, and Robin Phillips.

With Carol Buckley and Christopher Buckley at
Patricia Buckley Bozell's 60th birthday party in
Washington, 1987. (Photo: Jan Lukas)

Greeting Nancy Reagan at White House State Dinner
for Egyptian President Mubarak, January 28, 1988.

Greeting Ronald Reagan at White House State Dinner
for Egyptian President Mubarak, January 28, 1988.

sort of ESP, between us. We didn't have to articulate it in words, but we both knew that it was there.

I remember a time when I was deeply troubled. I can't remember what about, but it was serious enough at the time for me to breach the unspoken taboo and pour my heart out to Bill. We were sitting on the terrace of his home in Stamford, looking out at the lawn and the pool and the ocean. He listened, as always, attentively, with a sad expression on his face as I told my tale of woe. When I finished, I looked up at him expectantly, convinced that he would be able to solve whatever problem I had. He looked at me with great sympathy.

"Well, *Vieux*, life is a vale of tears, you know," he said.

"What?" I replied.

"Life is a vale of tears," he repeated. And, that was that. Not very comforting, but exactly what he believed.

Bill, and Pat, opened a whole new world to me, one that I never would have experienced without them. This was the world of the rich and famous, sailing trips throughout the Caribbean and the Greek islands, ocean liners to every part of the world, trips to Morocco, Spain, the Soviet Union, Italy, Switzerland, South America, everywhere, wonderful fun people. For a boy from Brooklyn, this was heady stuff, and I relished every moment.

As we worked together, we watched ourselves move from being the younger generation of conservatives to the middle generation, with a new generation of Young Turks too ready to see us as their elders. They saw Bill and me, whether we liked it or not, as "up there" with Charles Edison and Walter Judd, although *we* knew these wise old men as the elders who had taken *us* under *their* wings.

I had first made contact with members of this younger generation of conservatives through two young men—Douglas Caddy, a student at Georgetown University, and David Franke, a student at George Washington University. Working from their campuses, they started an activist conservative-oriented youth group weighing in against the liberal establishment—the National Youth for Goldwater for Vice President. The chairman of the new organization was Robert Croll, a graduate student at Northwestern University in Evanston, Illinois. The other officers were Caddy and Franke and Richard Noble, treasurer of the

California Young Republicans. At a press conference in May 1960, Croll announced that forty-five chapters had been founded at various colleges and universities. He also stated two main objectives of the new organization: "The first was to assist in securing the GOP Vice Presidential nomination for Senator Goldwater; the second was to build within the Young Republican National Federation a permanent, nationwide union of youthful supporters of the same Conservative political and economic philosophy embraced by Senator Goldwater as set forth in his recently published book, *The Conscience of a Conservative*" (which was ghost-written by Brent Bozell).

The organization of the Goldwater youth movement was further evidence of young conservatives' dissatisfaction with the Republican party. Barry Goldwater had become the hero of the nascent American conservative movement. The young activists, unlike many of their pro-Goldwater elders, believed that Goldwater could not win the Republican presidential nomination against Nixon. But they believed that Goldwater had a chance of getting the vice presidential nod. Most important, their effort would focus even more national attention on their man and his conservative politics. Caddy and his young colleagues were ambitious, sophisticated, smart, and, I was soon to learn, ruthless in pursuing their political agenda.

Shortly after the press release was issued, Caddy and Franke graduated from their respective universities. Bill Buckley and I decided to bring both of them to New York, one to serve as an intern at *National Review* and the other to work with me on the McGraw-Edison account. Charles Edison was Chairman of the Board of the company, and I was hired to write and send conservative newsletters and other material to America's business leaders. Both young men had potential, so Bill and I tossed a coin to see who would get whom. I won Douglas Caddy. Bill won David Franke.

Caddy came into my shop like a dynamo, and I let him have his head. In addition to putting time in on the McGraw-Edison account, he was active in a dozen other groups, particularly the Goldwater vice-presidential organization. It was fascinating watching him operate.

I saw the full power of these new young conservatives at work during the Chicago GOP convention in July 1960. There I found myself sandwiched between two generations of activists—the upcoming kids and the older men who were my mentors. I wanted to work with the kids by keeping a hand in Youth for Goldwater through Caddy. And I wanted to support Walter Judd, who was scheduled to deliver the keynote address, a significant honor. I asked Charles Edison to go with me, but he demurred. "I don't have any function in active politics any more," he told me. "Nobody knows who I am or who I was or gives a damn." I was sorry for him. I vowed to myself that I would find a way to make him want to go. I wanted to see him get some of his self-confidence back, to feel important.

So, of course, I started an organization, Americans for Walter Judd for Vice President, with Edison as Chairman. I took the usual organizational steps and had Edison write to a number of VIPs to serve on the committee. His letter went out on June 25, 1960, only four weeks before the convention. The recipients were asked to sign an open letter to delegates to the Convention that vigorously supported Judd as Nixon's running mate. The response was overwhelming (as I expected), and the letter and signers were published as a full-page advertisement in the *Chicago Daily News* on the morning after Judd's keynote speech.

But more importantly, Edison was excited by the whole operation. It served exactly the purpose I wanted. Caddy, Edison, and I—three generations of conservatives—were all going to Chicago with important roles to play. I took Caddy and the Goldwater kids under my wing, and I was paying back the men who had been my own mentors.

I put up the money for the Goldwater office, and we rented two adjoining meeting rooms at the Pick-Congress Hotel in Chicago, one for Goldwater and one for Judd. Hats, buttons, bumper stickers, balloons—the usual campaign paraphernalia—were ordered on my American Express card for both Goldwater and Judd. This was probably the only time two national vice presidential campaigns were charged to the same American Express account. In years to come, I would charge the initial costs of campaigns for Goldwater, Reagan, and two Buckleys all to American Express.

The Judd campaign had no volunteers or staff except me. The young Goldwaterites were my troops; they would move from one office to the other to make Judd's headquarters look active.

Judd delivered the keynote address on Monday night, July 25. It electrified the convention and was received with a thunderous ovation. Young people from the Goldwater camp were immediately out with our signs and banners. Suddenly, Judd for Vice President became a real possibility.

The activity at Judd headquarters became frenetic. Edison was in his glory. It was like old times. By the time the Tuesday night session was over, the entire convention was talking about the possibility of Walter Judd as Nixon's running mate. All the delegate hotels had Judd signs in their lobbies, and many of the delegates were wearing Judd buttons. Our campaign had snowballed in just a few hours.

Telegrams urging Judd's nomination were pouring in to the Nixon headquarters from all over the country. None of this would have been possible, of course, if Judd had not captured the imagination of the entire convention with his keynote address.

At 7:30 that evening, Nixon summoned Judd from the convention floor and sent a special car for him. Edison, Mrs. Judd, and I piled in with him and went to Nixon headquarters at the Blackstone Hotel. We waited nervously in the lobby as Judd went up to confer with Nixon. This was really exciting! Judd came down about twenty-five minutes later and said, "Dick asked whether I would be willing to do it."

"What did you say?"

"I told him that I wasn't really sure." This drove all of us mad. In fact, he had told Nixon that he was willing to run but thought that Henry Cabot Lodge would pull in more votes from the northeast. With pressure from President Eisenhower, Nixon chose Lodge for his running mate. What had started as a lark, and to help my old friend Edison have a good time, almost changed history.

The Youth for Goldwater forces, who had all pitched into the Judd effort, were now concentrating on Goldwater. Nixon was a shoo-in; Rockefeller was in there pitching; Goldwater was the outsider who was rapidly gaining enormous ground among the delegates. When Goldwater spoke on the opening night of the convention, he was greeted with a tremendous ovation, which greatly heartened the young people.

The Goldwaterites were doing a tremendous job. Signs, banners, balloons—every possible Goldwater promotional item—were now in hand. There was a crowd estimated at close to three thousand gathered outside the convention center, ready to join in the demonstration. On Wednesday night Nixon was nominated. His orchestrated demonstration lasted approximately twenty minutes. Then Governor Paul Fannon of Arizona went up to the podium to nominate Goldwater as his state's favorite son. When his too-long speech ended, the young Goldwater operatives on the floor—and the true feelings of the convention—erupted into a massive ovation, even though many of the demonstrators outside were not permitted into the Chicago Amphitheater. The Nixon forces tried but couldn't diminish the power of this demonstration. It was a great triumph for the leadership of Youth for Goldwater.

Right after the demonstration, a bombshell dropped. I was watching the convention on TV with Brent Bozell, Bill Buckley, and some other Goldwater tacticians in our Pick Congress hotel room. Goldwater came up to the podium, thanked everyone, then asked that his name be withdrawn and told his supporters to "grow up." He said, "We are conservatives . . . This great Republican party is our historic house . . . I am going to devote all my time from now until November to electing Republicans from the top of the ticket to the bottom of the ticket, and I call upon my fellow conservatives to do the same."

Bozell turned to me and all he could say was, "That son of a bitch."

And so ended the Goldwater balloon, deflating like the thousands of Judd and Goldwater balloons as the convention came to an end.

It did not, however, deflate Caddy and the leaders of the Youth for Goldwater movement. Watching them work during that frenetic convention week made me nostalgic for my Young Communist League days. They were exactly like the kids in high school, with the same anger and the same passion and the same enemies: fighting the press, the ruling establishment, and their venal and hypocritical elders. The only real difference was in their dress—fewer jeans, more blazers and neckties— and that they saw me as one of their elders.

Toward the end of the convention, Edison told me how impressed he was by the leaders of Youth for Goldwater. "It is in their hands now," he said almost wistfully, hating to be old. "If anything is going to be done, they are going to do it. I am an old crock now who's had his day." "And," he said to me, "you've been around the track too many times even at your age. You can put things together, but it is the kids who will have to carry the torch." He told me to get as many of them together as possible, and he would host a luncheon—not only to express his appreciation for their efforts, but, he hoped, to keep them going in some sort of organized way.

Following the convention, I was privileged to play an integral role in the organization of two groups that served to give shape to the entire American conservative enterprise: Young Americans for Freedom (YAF) and the American Conservative Union (ACU). YAF, a national conservative youth organization, was the first to break away from the liberal-leaning Republican party as an independent conservative political force. This laid the groundwork for the Goldwater nomination some four years later and the subsequent "conservatizing" of the Republican party.

The ACU was organized soon after the Goldwater defeat in 1964 and served to cement a conservative GOP for the next two decades. The historical importance of these two groups in American politics and American society should not be underestimated. It was not so much the actual organizations that had such a tremendous effect; it was the *perception* of strength, influence, and power that we were able to evoke.

The precursor organization to the YAF began to take shape the day after the 1960 convention, when the executive committee of Youth for Goldwater and about six or seven other young conservative activists met in the Columbia Room of the Pick-Congress with Edison and me. The old man spoke. He wasn't Goldwater, he wasn't Buckley, but he was a hero to them. Edison urged them to keep in touch with each other through some sort of committee of correspondence, similar to that of our own Revolutionary War. He told them that, like the colonists in the 1770s, they also had a chance to make a revolution. Edison gave the rallying cry!

In just a little over a month, working out of my New York office and using all the facilities I could provide—mimeograph machine, clerical help, postage meter, mailing house and, most important, money—Caddy, with the help of a few others, set about starting a new organization. They contacted students all over the country—even over the summer recess—and invited them to attend a conference over the weekend of September 9 to 11.

I suggested to Bill Buckley that we have the meeting at Great Elm, the Buckley family home in Sharon, Connecticut. After discussing the logistics with his mother and sisters (it is no small thing to have fifty or more college kids over for a weekend, even for a family with ten children and countless grandchildren), it was agreed, when I assured them that nothing would be damaged.

The Buckley name was a substantial lure. Coordinating the logistics with Bill and his sisters Priscilla, Aloise, and Jane, I organized the meeting. An Interim Committee for a National Conservative Youth Organization was set up in my office under the direction of Caddy.

About ninety activists representing forty-four colleges and universities from twenty-four states made their way to Sharon on chartered buses and on their own. The very first gathering was in the large central hall, the Patio, in Great Elm, with the entire Buckley family, the *National Review* editors, and all ninety students in attendance. Those of us present from the older generation—Frank Meyer, Charles Edison, Brent Bozell, Bill Rusher, Buckley, and I—resolved to give no advice unless it was asked for and to keep our mouths shut, which was extremely difficult for such an articulate group.

The young activists had already started wheeling, dealing, and politicking. M. Stanton Evans, one of the older "youths" (at twenty-six!) was busy drafting a statement of their aims and aspirations. This came to be known as the Sharon Statement. Bill Buckley made some editorial changes, and the statement was adopted by the conference as was the name Young Americans for Freedom. Bill Rusher recalled "I remember not liking the acronym (YAF) much—and liking it even less when Liebman . . . became the first to point out this made the rest of us 'Old Americans for Freedom' or 'OAFs.'"

Charles Edison was in his glory. This was everything he had ever hoped for. I took great personal satisfaction in this because I loved him and felt this was all a fitting gift and tribute to the work he had done.

While Bill Buckley was speaking at the first event, Edison and I were sitting on the balcony that surrounds the patio. Next to us was Bill's sister Aloise Heath. Her beloved and elderly dog, Boykie, was given to fits of panting—as was Governor Edison. Edison was sitting on a low stool, panting away, and Aloise softly patted him on the head and said absentmindedly, "Now be quiet." Edison, chastised, did as he was bid and ceased panting.

Edison was quite deaf and used a hearing aid, a box he held and aimed at the person who was speaking. When one of the kids was speaking a mile-a-minute to Edison, the governor held out his hearing aid trying to get the words. "No thanks, governor," said the young conferee, "I don't smoke!" Edison turned off his machine, and just smiled blandly through the rest of the conversation.

In the ten months following the weekend conference at Sharon, Young Americans for Freedom, working out of my office at 79 Madison Avenue and with an advisory board I made up of every conservative VIP I could think of, became an overwhelming success. Over 180 young conservative clubs sprang up on the nation's campuses. Widespread publicity in major newspapers and magazines focused on the formation of YAF chapters.

In March 1961, YAF began publishing its monthly magazine, *The New Guard*. The same month we staged the first YAF National Awards Rally in Manhattan Center, which seated 3,200 people inside; more than 5,000 were turned away from the doors. The main speaker of the evening was Barry Goldwater. Awards went to Bill Buckley, Ambassador George K. C. Yeh of the Republic of China (I was still looking after my old friends), and the columnist George Sokolsky. YAF even set up its own front organizations: the Committee for an Effective Peace Corps, and the Student Committee for a Free Cuba.

Bill Buckley and I were impressed by YAF's rapid growth, early achievements, and dedication. "What is so striking in the students who met at Sharon," Buckley wrote, "is their appetite for power. Ten years ago, the struggle seemed so long, so endless, even, that we did not dream of victory. . . . It is quixotic to say that they or their elders have seized the reins of history. But the difference in psychological attitude is tremendous."

YAF was doing so well that even I began to lose interest. I loved to start organizations, but got bored when it came to running them. This one was already running under its own steam. And although I tried staying out of the limelight, my role in the organization was beginning to receive criticism. In his *Rise of the Right*, Bill Rusher gently chastised me by saying, "Liebman . . . had innocently fallen into the role of a sort of rich and adoring uncle who could deny these youngsters nothing, unwittingly spoiling a number of them badly." That was the story of my life then: the rich and adoring uncle to all the bright young men.

As the organization grew, it developed cliques and became the battleground for power struggles. In the early summer of 1961, these divided into three camps: the John Birch crowd, the Rockefeller crowd, and the *National Review* crowd. It was during this struggle that I began to see again the latent bigotry in the American Right and once again became its target.

Scott Stanley, Jr., a YAF director, was close to Robert Welch of the John Birch Society and was later to edit the society's *American Opinion* for a number of years. Stanley wanted to bring YAF into the Birch orbit. On the other side was Doug Caddy, the executive secretary, who had indirect ties to Nelson Rockefeller (through New York's lieutenant governor, Malcolm Wilson), and wanted to move YAF into the more liberal Rockefeller camp. In the center were me and the forces closest to *National Review*. Stanley and Caddy joined forces and tried to take control of the national board of YAF from the *National Review* supporters. It was a strange cabal—the right-wing Welch and the liberal Rockefeller—rather like the right-wing America First Committee twenty years earlier, which, ironically, enjoyed clandestine communist support.

My strategy was to strengthen the power of *National Review* in the organization. I put a classified ad for a full-time executive director in *National Review* sometime in June 1961. Richard Viguerie, down in Texas, replied to the ad, and his response caught the eye of Bill Rusher who—after checking out Viguerie's credentials and reputation with his Texas political friends—recommended that I see him. Viguerie would be a new force, loyal to *National Review*, and he, I hoped, would keep the organization together.

When Viguerie arrived in my office, I liked him immediately and realized he was perfect for the job. I got sufficient votes together on the board for him to replace Caddy, who was "kicked upstairs" as national director of Young Americans for Freedom.

At the national board's meeting in my office that September, Viguerie was our stalwart ally against the unsuccessful attempts of the Birch and

Rockefeller camps to take control of YAF. The losers went off to nurse their wounds, and the winners didn't gloat.

But the Birchers didn't give up. Underneath the John Birch Society's façade of anticommunism squirmed the worms of bigotry. As the Communist party had enlisted a number of decent Americans to its cause, so the John Birch Society was enlisting decent conservatives. But the Birchers were dangerous people. And they started to attack me.

The occasion for their attacks was the YAF's second Annual Awards Rally on March 7, 1962, which, thinking big and taking a gamble, I organized at Madison Square Garden. The two featured speakers were Senators Barry Goldwater and John Tower of Texas. The problem was that among those to be presented awards—Senator Thomas J. Dodd, John Dos Passos, Charles Edison, M. Stanton Evans, Herbert Hoover, John Wayne, and I (lobbying for me were the *NR* winners of the last YAF power struggle)—was General Edwin A. Walker. A Korean war hero, Walker was heavily involved with the John Birch Society, which was causing consternation in responsible conservative circles. Its extreme political stance (including the belief that Eisenhower was a lifelong agent of the Soviet Union) put it outside the kind of movement we were all working toward.

The board decided to withdraw the invitation to General Walker. I had led the troops opposed to Walker, and this ensured the enmity of the pro-Birch forces, who insisted that I also be denied an award. Nothing would have made me happier than to forgo the honor. But this time it was a matter of principle.

Although they denied it, the Bircher, Scott Stanley, and the Rockefeller agent, Douglas Caddy, combined forces to mobilize a virulent anti-Semitic campaign against me. The first story appeared in *Spotlight*, the publication of the anti-Semitic and racist *Liberty Lobby*. The story was headlined "Kosher Konservatives" and had a cartoon of Barry Goldwater, George Sokolsky and me kicking a young boy captioned "YAF" over a cliff to join other patriotic organizations destroyed by the Jew-Zionist cabal.

Next the "National Patriotic Research Association" issued a widely circulated report on Young Americans for Freedom that attacked me personally. "The most influential single individual in YAF holds no office. He is one Marvin Liebman who, like so many others associated with *National Review* magazine, had an extremely enigmatic record. His 'conversion' dates from 1952, when he is said to have repudiated communism. He currently describes himself as a 'radical liberal.'"

"Liebman, a fanatical Zionist, hates Arabs. His background includes a mysterious trip to Israel, which he steadfastly refuses to explain. He has bragged to friends, however, 'I am a killer.' Perhaps his strong pro-Zionist sentiments explain the fact that most of his office staff (except for front men like Viguerie) is Jewish or Negro."

I was shocked and angered to discover that many of our contributors—and distinguished letterhead names—received, read, and were influenced by such garbage. Even my good friend Edison's response was disappointing. Although he really loved me, it was hard for him to disengage himself from his own beliefs about Jews. When I asked him for support, he said he would deal with it on his own, refusing to show me his correspondence, as if he were going to defend me to his friends as one anti-Semite to another. This was a cultured, genteel style of anti-Semitism. None of my friends called me "Jew" as none called me "queer." But I had learned to accept the fact that many heterosexuals disliked homosexuals, and that many Gentiles had a streak of anti-Semitism, even those who were my friends.

I sent a memorandum to Bill Rusher, with a copy to Bill Buckley, asking for assistance. "I think that this is the time," I wrote, "for *National Review* to take up a cudgel or two in my behalf. These rumors and gossip are getting out of hand. Not only do they affect me personally; they also considerably damage my potential usefulness to the Conservative movement." Bill Buckley, who was in Switzerland at the time, sent me a letter in response. "I am terribly saddened by your memorandum," he wrote. "People are such—perhaps one of your lady secretaries is reading this . . . To look at Caddy and Stanley—and see their base ingratitude. So they lost the power quarrel: and you are the *corpus vile* (will translate on my return) . . . If it makes you feel any better, I have received some really vile mail too since I got here . . ."

"But I started out to console you," he continued, "not to weep over my own dilemma: in a curious way they are related. The more you accomplish for the cause, the more the least member of that cause thinks you belong to him, heart, mind, and soul: and the least deviation is treated as a personal betrayal."

The affair blew over, but from then on I have been alert to and aware of the anti-Semitism that continues to lurk in the American right wing and that can be used as a cudgel at any time and against anyone if gay-bashing and other bigotries don't work.

The Birchers did not get their way at the rally. Walker stayed home in Texas, and I gave a two-minute address that brought the throngs to their feet, though, in honesty, they would stand for anyone in that atmosphere, and did. Goldwater made a great speech, part written by Brent Bozell, and was well on his way to the Republican presidential nomination. Eighteen thousand people attended. The rally was a major triumph for YAF, for Goldwater—and for me.

With the success of the rally, I decided to rest on my laurels and slowly withdraw from participation in YAF. The organization moved its headquarters to Washington and set up a burgeoning bureaucracy whose alumni soon spread into all aspects of the American conservative movement. For the next six years or so, I could always call on them for any help I needed. The organization continued, but it was torn by dissension and purges and lawsuits and acrimony and God knows what else.

Meanwhile, my brushes with anti-Semitism on the Right continued. Early in 1961, George Sokolsky wrote a column that quoted a letter he received from the National Renaissance party, one of the overtly anti-Semitic organizations still around. The letter was about a "mass meeting to oppose Jewish leadership of the conservative movement." It described "Jewish intellectuals, some with former Communist records," as having been ordered "to infiltrate and capture key positions of leadership within the conservative hierarchy."

The letter then went on to name the "phony Jewish conservatives" who wanted to "divert public attention from internal subversion" and focus it "on the activities of foreign Communist governments" instead. "Are you aware," it asked, "that every effort is being made by Jewish 'Conservatives' like Barry Goldwater, Roy Cohn, Dr. Fred Schwarz, an Australian Jew who grosses over one million dollars per year through his 'Christian Anti-Communist Crusade,' George Sokolsky, and Liebman to discredit and undermine such Gentile patriots as Major General

Edwin Walker and Robert Welch of the John Birch Society?"

Calling the accusations absurd, Sokolsky ended his column by defending his own anticommunist record along with that of the others who had been attacked, including mine. "Marvin Liebman is a young man who has devoted himself brilliantly to anticommunist causes in recent years," he wrote. "To my knowledge, he has done this at considerable personal and discouraging sacrifice."

Sokolsky was an influential columnist for the Hearst newspapers and a strong anticommunist. He was also an opinionated and arrogant man. But I liked him—not only for defending me, but because he was a tough old bird.

So I was interested when Roy Cohn later telephoned and said he wanted to organize a dinner to honor Sokolsky. He wanted to revive the dormant American Jewish League Against Communism as the vehicle for sponsoring the dinner. Cohn considered Sokolsky to be his great friend, advocate, and mentor. He wanted desperately to please George as some sort of father figure. Certainly a public dinner would help accomplish this.

I first met Roy Cohn when we got together to plan Sokolsky's dinner. I had heard much about him, little of it favorable. He had a reputation as a paranoid red-baiter and a brilliant but unscrupulous lawyer with ties to the underworld. Gossip in the gay grapevine had it that he was "one of us." I agreed to work on the dinner only as a favor to Sokolsky. I didn't much like Roy Cohn then, and my dislike grew over the years.

Some time later, in 1976, Pat Buckley and I were in Bermuda awaiting Bill's boat from across the Atlantic. Bermuda was the refitting stop. Pat and I had arrived carrying all sorts of heavy and clumsy nautical equipment, and I hate to carry anything. We got through customs, changed, and went to the hotel pool.

Pat grabbed my hand and whispered, "My God, I can't believe it!" There was Roy Cohn with a pretty young man, both in T-shirts and bikinis. Roy's T-shirt read "SuperJew." This, in the bastion of Bermuda WASP gentility. We managed to say a few words and then did everything possible to avoid Roy and his current young man. He was an obnoxious show-off.

I met with Roy and George Sokolsky and organized a "temporary committee" to revive the League. The rest of the year was devoted to some minor activities, all leading up to the dinner, which was scheduled for February 13, 1962. It was hard to get Roy to do much of the work—he was too busy doing other things.

About a month after the dinner, I was approached by Dr. Fred Schwarz, an Australian who was running an organization called the Christian Anti-Communism Crusade. He was establishing various one- or two-day "schools" around the country in which he would teach the facts about communism—political revival meetings. I agreed to help him set up a school in New York that would meet in Madison Square Garden and be followed by a big rally. Cost seemed to be no object, so I wasn't put in the position of having to raise money, which was great by me.

The name of Schwarz's organization became controversial in Jewish circles, yet he refused to change it, despite accusations that he was an anti-Semite. I tried to arrange a meeting between him and the Anti-Defamation League so that they could come to some understanding. I firmly believed that Schwarz was not an anti-Semite. But Sokolsky loathed Schwarz. When he found out I was working with him, he telephoned to berate me for daring to contact the Anti-Defamation League without his okay. In telephone calls and in letters, I tried to defend Schwarz, but that only made things worse.

Sokolsky replied by letter two days later, continuing his attack and accusing me of dealing with Schwarz "for money." It was a ghastly letter. He shocked me when he referred to "your utter lack of personal discipline and your desperate pursuit of an impossible sybaritic life which ceases to be your private affair when it damages others."

Did Sokolsky know something about my sexuality? That's the thing that worried me. Not his intemperate attack. His psychotic hatred of Fred Schwarz was shown in column after column. Sokolsky never spoke to me again.

Almost immediately after YAF began to operate, I started thinking about a senior organization of the same type. I made a few attempts, with the help of Frank Meyer and Brent Bozell, but to no avail. Then, in October 1964, Robert Bauman, who was chairman of Young Americans for Freedom and one of its founders along with his wife, Carol, tele-

phoned me from Washington with an idea. Agreeing with me that
Goldwater couldn't win the presidential election, Bauman—one of the
most astute and brilliant young political operatives I have ever known—
said that we should be ready to turn the upcoming defeat into grounds for
positive action. He proposed a group that YAF "graduates" could join, a
conservative umbrella group. This coincided nicely with my earlier
idea, and I was enthusiastic.

Bauman had heard Buckley speak at the YAF national convention in
New York City a few weeks previously, and was particularly impressed
when Buckley said, "Our morale is high, and we are marching. But the
morale of an army on the march is that of an army that has been promised
victory. . . But it is wrong to assume that we shall overcome; and
therefore it is right to reason to the necessity of guarding against the utter
disarray that sometimes follows a stunning defeat: It is right to take
thought, even on the eve of the engagement, about the potential need for
regrouping, for gathering together our scattered forces."

I arranged for Bauman to come to New York later that month, and we
had breakfast with Bill. Bauman was charged with coming up with a
plan. On November 9, I sent Bauman the background material on the
plans that Frank Meyer, Brent Bozell, and I had drawn up two years
earlier for such an organization. These included a Conservative Acade-
my, which would mobilize conservative intellectuals into a think tank
along the lines of today's Heritage Foundation, and a Council for an
American Foreign Policy, which was to provide a conservative alternative to the liberal Council on Foreign Relations. Building on these
proposals, we developed a plan to start a new organization—the American Conservative Union.

I told Bauman that Meyer and Bozell would be interested in signing
on with us. Frank Meyer was a former communist, an Oxford-educated
philosopher, and an eccentric. He didn't trust the American educational
system and so kept his two boys out of school, educating them himself.
He slept most of the day and kept in touch with his many friends by
telephone late at night. He was a revolutionary with a libertarian bent, as
were most ex-communists. Like me, he loved to shake up situations and
people and to stir the pot—just to see what would happen. Brent Bozell,
too, also detested communism and loved reflection, discussing transcen-

dent values and acting on whatever he considered the great moral and political questions of the day. We were an interesting team.

Bauman and I enlisted Buckley, Meyer, and Bozell, relied on Edison to raise the initial funds, and put together a board of directors that included all of us.

At the board's first meeting, the issue most affecting the conservative movement was brought up—the John Birch Society. Buckley (with me supporting him from the sidelines) was almost alone in fighting for the exclusion of Birchers from ACU membership. The board instead voted to exclude them only as board members and advisers. Buckley wanted to publicize at least this limited exclusionary policy, but Bauman moved that the policy be kept confidential. Bauman, the consummate political strategist, didn't want to alienate any potential support from individuals also in the John Birch Society. The next day, after intense lobbying through the night, board members rescinded the exclusionary policy altogether, and instead approved a public statement that merely declared that the John Birch Society and the ACU were "wholly distinct" organizations.

All this indicated the pervasive fear of the John Birch Society among conservatives in those days. The Birch Society represented to Buckley —and certainly to me and a few others—the absolute worst in American right-wing thinking. It was a resurrection of the know-nothing bigotry that largely made up the American Right before Buckley came on the scene.

The actual conference took place around all this back room wheeling and dealing. Forty-seven leading conservatives were present. They included the absolute cream of the American Right as epitomized by the *National Review* crowd. A Statement of Principles was adopted to serve as the philosophical base of the organization. After the conference, we set up an office in Washington and started to raise funds. The efforts to create a conservative organization to counter the powerful influence of the Americans for Democratic Action were finally bearing fruit. We aimed to be the ADA of the Right. The American Conservative Union was well on its way.

In September 1965, I met with Richard Viguerie, who was now in business for himself, and turned over to him all the direct mail responsibilities of the ACU. As in YAF, the bickering was beginning. Factions were being formed. Colleagues became enemies. I quit the ACU in October 1965, sick of the intrigue and the attacks on me. It was the YAF scenario replayed.

The ACU went on to create the Conservative Victory Fund, the American Legislative Exchange Council, and the National Journalism Center under the direction of M. Stanton Evans. This latter group is still functioning and is one of the best things to come out of the ACU.

These early days of the new conservatism, when YAF and the ACU were first being organized, were exciting moments in my political career. A new generation of activists inspired me as they invigorated and transformed the organized conservative movement, at a time when it was still a cause to which good people could repair and not the fund-raising business it seems to have become. These were also days, however, of disillusionment, a time when I first began to fight from within— sometimes defending myself—against the bigotry that is relatively pervasive on the American Right.

Disheartened by what I considered to be the total collapse of YAF in later years, I tried several times—always unsuccessfully—to get another youth organization going. One of my last tries was in the mid-1980s with a group called United Students for America (USA). I was working with a bright and attractive youngster, Ralph Reed, who was assistant to Jack Abramoff, chairman of the College Young Republicans. In starting the organization, I cautioned Reed to state in his bylaws that his organization must never be headquartered in Washington. Washington is a seductive place that devours young men, either destroying their integrity or turning them into politicians or political hucksters or lobbyists.

Reed took my advice, and set up his new organization in North Carolina, where it was quickly gobbled up by the Jesse Helms organization and became a fundamentalist Christian youth group called Students for America (SFA). My final connection with both YAF and SFA was a report I received to the effect that the executive director of SFA telephoned the executive director of YAF several days after my "coming out" was publicized. "So, I hear that your founder is a faggot," he said, quite unaware that I had a hand in setting up his group as well.

Chapter 12

Political Campaigns

*I*N THE 1960s, CONSERVATIVE activists increasingly
focused their attention on local, state, and national political campaigns.
From the axis of conservative activism at my office and at the nearby
National Review, we played an important role in organizing and promoting this.

During these years my social life—when I had one—was still split
between two worlds. One centered around the Buckley family and the
National Review crowd; the other, around my gay friends and their
"fellow-travelers" I met in Manhattan and during my summers on Fire
Island. I developed a number of crushes (one of them on a woman who
moved in with me for about three months), and my sexual life was active
but always anonymous with strangers I would pick up.

Starting in 1953, I spent my summers on Fire Island. The first time I
went there was for a weekend with Betty Berzon when she came from Los
Angeles to visit me in New York in 1952. I was still thinking about the
possibility of "curing" myself by getting married again, although I
didn't tell Betty of my vague plan. We decided to get a weekend place,
and a friend told us that Cherry Grove on Fire Island was absolutely
charming. Betty went out and rented a house before the season started.

We had no idea that Cherry Grove was *the* homosexual resort town on
the East Coast, surpassing even Provincetown (which didn't have its
current reputation yet). Our weekend there quite unnerved me—I could
not deal with such open homosexuality. I got Betty to break the lease, and

we ended up in Southhold, Long Island, which was straighter and more to my taste then.

At a party early in 1953, I met Bertha Case, a literary agent for the Music Corporation of American (MCA). We became friends, and decided to rent a summer house together at Ocean Bay Park on Fire Island. We took on two housemates, both of them great-looking actresses. One worked on a TV soap opera; the other took whatever parts came along. Ocean Bay Park had been established for about seven years. On one side was Ocean Beach, more developed and a favorite summer spot during Prohibition days. Polly Adler, the famous Madam, had had a summer house there. On the other side was Point O' Woods—a WASP "restricted" community (no Jews allowed). Charles Edison would spend some weekends there in the next few years, and I would visit him. He loved meeting some of my more outrageous friends.

The rent for our three-bedroom house was three hundred dollars for the season. Ocean Bay Park had no running water or electricity. Water pumps were placed strategically along the wooden walkways, and one had to carry water by pail for drinking and flushing the toilets. At night we lighted our house with oil lamps. For fun we'd go to Cherry Grove on Saturday nights and dance at Duffy's, the favorite haunt of the Thai prince I met on my first world tour.

Thanks to my housemates, I made a great number of show biz friends —actors, directors, writers, agents. Every Saturday night before we went to Duffy's, we put on shows using our back porch as a stage, performing for audiences of about fifty neighbors and friends. I was producer—getting the talent together and handling the oil lamps for lighting. Among my artists that season were Hermione Gingold, the British comedienne; Jimmy Kirkwood, who later received a Pulitzer for writing *A Chorus Line,* among other plays and novels; Jimmy's mother, the silent screen star Lila Lee. Christopher Hewett, who was to make a success as TV's Mr. Belvedere, did his first American skit on my porch during his first week in the United States.

Two years later, we emigrated to Fire Island Pines, which was just being developed on the other side of Cherry Grove. It was even more primitive than Ocean Bay Park, which was getting too crowded for us. I spent three summers there in various houses with various housemates.

Again, we'd go to Cherry Grove Saturday nights. When Flynn's closed, the gentlemen—including me—would wander down to the Meat Rack just below the wooden walks on the sand. This was where one could go for faceless sex with unknown strangers, in the pitch black of the warm nights with only the lights of cigarettes burning, like fireflies. When the rare police patrol jeep came along, the "fireflies" would disappear until the jeep passed and the cigarettes would be lighted again.

One time, Bertha Case said she would like to come and see what it was like. I said it was for men only, but she begged me to take her. So one night, she dressed up in slacks and a warm sweater, and we went out to the Meat Rack. As we strolled along the wooden walkway, she said, "I think I'll go down to the beach and take a look." She walked down the stairs and disappeared into the blackness while I waited for her. Suddenly I heard a shriek. It was Bertha yelling "Stop! Stop! I'm a woman!" She rushed back to me and demanded to be taken home.

The year 1961 ended with Young Americans for Freedom temporarily safe from the Rockefeller and John Birch forces. The Conservative party —which was creating an alternative to the four parties in New York state (Democrat, Republican, American Labor, and Liberal)—was ready to go public. I was happy to have had a hand in helping it get off the ground. It showed conservatives all over the country that we didn't have to jump on someone else's bandwagon but could run a party of our own. The movement to draft Goldwater was beginning to coalesce. A conservative candidate running on the GOP ticket! With Goldwater conservatives could advance their philosophy within the Republican party and ultimately take it over.

A Draft Goldwater campaign gathered momentum among conservatives as the 1964 election year came closer. The Draft Goldwater Committee was first organized in Chicago on October 8, 1961, by members of the "syndicate," a national network of young conservatives who had been activists in the Young Republicans (YR) during the 1950s. They had been invigorated by the organization of Young Americans for Freedom and the formation of the New York state Conservative party. Their logical leader was Barry Goldwater.

These "syndicate" members included Bill Rusher (publisher of *National Review*); Ohio Congressman John Ashbrook, a former Young

Republican chairman; and F. Clifton White, former president of the New York Young Republicans and a brilliant political operative. Rusher, like me, preferred to stay in the background and let others take the stage. White formulated the plan of action.

I first met Barry Goldwater at the March 7, 1962, Young Americans for Freedom rally that I organized in Madison Square Garden, where he was featured as a speaker. There I witnessed his short fuse and hot temper. He was in the holding room behind the stage while Brent Bozell delivered a brilliant and endless speech to an increasingly restive audience. Goldwater was scheduled to speak last, and he was furious. He strode up and down the room, cussing out Bozell, YAF, and just about anyone else he could think of. But when he went on stage, he was terrific. The rally focused national attention on Goldwater as a politician with a growing constituency and a man to be reckoned with.

The Draft Goldwater Committee picked up steam. The only problem was that Goldwater did not want to be drafted, or to be president, or to fool around with the "political amateurs" and New York intellectuals who were trying to get him involved. Even though his book *The Conscience of a Conservative* (written by L. Brent Bozell and published in 1960) put him on the political map, Goldwater was happy being a senator. He was a mercurial man with no real sense of loyalty, as most of his friends were to find out. The moment the campaign started to look good, Goldwater called in four of his close friends—Denison Kitchel and Dean Burch, both from Arizona, and William Baroody and Edward McCabe, Washington wheelers and dealers—and slowly the four took over. The Arizona mafia pushed Clif White and his "syndicate" colleagues to the rear.

On April 8, 1963, the Draft Goldwater Committee was officially launched by Clif White at a press conference, and offices were set up in New York. They held their first rally at the National Guard armory in Washington on July 4, 1963, where nine thousand Goldwater backers cheered and yelled. But Goldwater's public reaction was, "It's their time and their money, but they're going to have to get along without any help from me." White moved his offices to Washington, and Draft Goldwater became a political reality.

The assassination of John F. Kennedy was a tremendous blow to the Goldwater campaign. The great outpouring of sympathy for Lyndon

Johnson, the Democratic candidate, made it difficult for Goldwater to campaign against the Democrats. It was as if he were campaigning against the martyred John F. Kennedy himself.

But the conservative activists could still try to win the Republican party. If Clif White and his "syndicate" could control the apparatus of the party after the convention, the cause of American Conservatism would be put way ahead. From that time on, the quiet agenda of the Draft Goldwater and the Goldwater for President operations was to take over the GOP. Goldwater formally declared his candidacy on January 3, 1964, and started entering the all-important primaries. His politicos ran the campaign, while we tried to promote conservatism behind the scenes.

And that is where I became involved professionally with the Goldwater campaign. The Clif White forces were frozen out of the national Goldwater operation by the Arizona mafia. Early in March 1964, moved back to New York and set up the New York Goldwater for President organization at the Hotel Shelburne on Lexington Avenue and Thirty-seventh Street. Once again, I used my American Express card to open the headquarters and arrange for telephones, and so on. I launched a statewide fund-raising campaign, sparked by Eddie Rickenbacker, former chairman of the board of Eastern Airlines, Congressional Medal of Honor winner, World War I flying ace, and American hero.

Then, for the big event, I booked Madison Square Garden for a national Goldwater rally on May 12. This would be my second Goldwater rally. These rallies gave me a chance to combine a flair for the theatrical with my conservative politics. Putting a rally together was like putting on a show—and showmanship was my forte.

First you get the star. This time it was Barry Goldwater, who assured good attendance. Then you build everything around your main attraction to show him or her off. The stage was important. Money was no object when we decorated Madison Square Garden as patriotically and as vulgarly as possible. Everywhere you looked you saw more flags and bunting. At the most dramatic moment, the nets hanging from the ceiling would open, and red, white, and blue balloons would engulf the arena.

As the rally drew closer, activity in my office reached a frenetic peak. A journalist and author, John Gregory Dunne, visited me to cover the rally. His article captured the excitement of those hours: "Our conversation was interrupted fitfully by telephone calls and the arrival of youthful volunteers in chinos and pimples who had come by to stamp the envelopes and generally do their bit . . . 'Get an elephant and walk it around New York with a lot of signs on it,' Liebman said into the receiver. 'Maybe he can pull a Goldwater bandwagon or something. Hey, how long can an elephant walk much without getting tired?'"

Being the impresario of a massive event like the Goldwater rally was exhilarating. As the throngs come in and the noise gets louder and louder, the band starts playing, the resounding applause is heightened by the cheers—I felt in total control of a powerful mass experience. I stood on the floor of the Garden where I personally supervised the entire production.

When Goldwater finally entered—escorted by the "Goldwater Girls," the band playing the "Battle Hymn of the Republic," and the balloons descending from the ceiling—the crowd went wild. I was so overcome that I started cheering like a lunatic myself! I lost control for a moment, but I got it back to direct the rest of the show.

The rally and its sell-out crowd gave final credibility to the campaign to nominate Goldwater: The front page of the *New York Daily News* carried the banner headline 18,000 CHEER BARRY IN GARDEN. If he could win New Yorkers in the bastion of liberalism, he could win anybody. The excitement and success of the rally carried him through to the GOP convention in San Francisco two months later.

Having been dumped by Goldwater as his campaign took off, Clif White and company asked me to run a Bill Miller for vice president operation at the San Francisco convention. This would help them play a role in the campaign. Miller was an upstate New York politician who had been chairman of the Republican National Committee and was being supported by the New York Conservative party. If Miller was nominated and won, he would then owe Clif White and company something in return. This would further their agenda of promoting conservative politics in the GOP.

For me, as for Clif White, it was a sharp drop in status from Goldwater to Miller, but once again, I was to promote a vice presidential candidate.

On my way to the West Coast in early July, I hooked up with Bill and Pat Buckley and his sister Priscilla, to take a holiday trip to Mexico. This was one of my many, many trips with Bill and Pat over the years.

As always, Bill was our tour guide. He took us to every obscure town in Mexico. We ended the trip in the Hilton Hotel in Mexico City. Bliss! Air-conditioning! All of us were sick to one degree or another—Bill, of course, felt fine.

In my room, I had finally fallen asleep, looking forward to my trip to San Francisco the next afternoon. Suddenly, I felt myself being shaken by someone. I opened my eyes, but there was no one there. Weird! Then, the large mirror in front of my bed slid off the wall with a great crash. Poltergeist? Then, the window blew in. I felt as if the floor was dropping below my feet, like a plane was falling through a large air pocket. I always sleep with my clothes by the side of my bed (I don't know why, but I do). I dressed hurriedly—for some reason I remained calm—and went to rescue my friends.

Priscilla's door was wide open, but no Priscilla. Pat and Bill's room was empty too, except for Pat's jewelry box on the bed with their two passports laid neatly on top. They had deserted me! The building was shaking even more. I collected the jewelry and passports and ran out to the stairwell. It was jammed with shrieking people in various stages of undress.

I rang for the elevator—which actually came—and took it to the ground floor, where I stepped out, calm, cool, and fittingly dressed, to find absolute chaos. I spotted Bill in his undershorts, with his wife's negligee thrown over him and his sleeping mask on top of his head. (On his way down he forgot to take if off and told Pat, who was leading him, that he had obviously been blinded). No one was hurt, but the hotel was literally split in half. I have never seen Bill so discombobulated before or since.

When I arrived in San Francisco, I set up the Miller headquarters and arranged for flags, balloons, hats—all one needed to create an instant vice presidential candidate. (See my detailed scenario for a rally later in this chapter when Bill Buckley runs for mayor.) Many of the YAF kids there —and there were plenty—also helped out on our Bill Miller operation, which proved successful.

Goldwater won the nomination, and Miller was nominated for Vice President. The Eastern establishment, under Rockefeller, was routed, and Goldwater supporters took over—at least for a time. They were not able to keep control for long, but several significant players and trends emerged. The GOP was opened to the West for the first time, and that's where the new votes and the new money were. Ronald Reagan went on national TV on October 27 with a Goldwater campaign speech and enhanced his own national image. Richard Nixon served as chairman of New Yorkers for Goldwater/Miller. But the party lost the election, and the conservatives would not regain control for another fifteen years.

In early 1965, conservatives were licking their wounds from the Goldwater defeat. There was no national political leader in view who could capture their imagination. But in New York, Dan Mahoney and Kieran O'Doherty, who had organized the Conservative party, were casting around for candidates, this time to run in the upcoming New York City mayoralty and other off-year election races in New York.

The incumbent mayor, Robert F. Wagner, was on his way out. He was beset by fiscal problems, corruption, and the Tammany Hall machine run by Carmine DeSapio. The probable Democrat candidate would be Abe Beame, the city's comptroller. The Republicans and Liberals would certainly field the personable, good-looking, and ambitious Congressman from New York's silk-stocking district, John V. Lindsay.

Lindsay was the darling of both the Republican and Liberal parties. The Liberal party bosses, David Dubinsky and Alex Rose, had the same hopes for Lindsay that they had had for Rudolph Halley some fifteen years before: the presidency of the United States. Lindsay had a real chance—mayor, then senator, and certainly a candidate for the 1968 Republican nomination for president. Big dreams!

The Conservative party felt the mayoralty election could give them political clout. The idea that Bill Buckley might be persuaded to run followed a speech he made to the Annual Communion Breakfast of Catholic policemen at the New York Hilton Hotel on May 4, 1965. Buckley defended the police against charges of brutality.

The cops greeted Buckley's remarks with thunderous and enthusiastic applause. He became an instant hero and received considerable publicity. Buckley considered John Lindsay a political poseur. When on

May 13, Lindsay announced that he would run, Buckley was ready to go.

But first, and most important, he had to convince his wife—who was vigorously opposed to his running for anything, anytime—and to resolve the problem of his residence. Although he spent a good deal of time in New York at *National Review*, and had an apartment on East Sixty-eighth Street—his main residence was in Stamford, Connecticut. Jim Leff, the able elections lawyer who got the Conservative party on the ballot, was asked to investigate.

I spent the weekend of June 4 with Bill in Stamford. Pat was in Vancouver with her sick father and nursing a broken leg from a bad skiing accident earlier that year. She was not in good temper.

Dan Mahoney, head of the Conservative party, telephoned Buckley on Friday evening, June 4, and reported that Jim Leff had looked into the matter; Buckley was eligible to run.

Bill spent that weekend on the telephone, speaking to his friends, confidants, and family. He telephoned his brother Jim, in Hawaii, where Jim was on vacation with his wife, Ann. Bill wanted his advice and, more important, to find out if Jim would be willing to help run his campaign.

Between the telephone calls, I urged Bill on. "Why not?" I said. The only real obstacle was Pat. After a long telephone conversation with her, he said, "Well, I convinced her!"

As with the many other times that he convinced Pat, he didn't.

She came back from Vancouver in tears, not speaking to either of us. She accused me of being the mastermind behind her Bill's incredibly stupid move (as if I—or anyone else—could ever convince Bill Buckley to do anything he didn't want to do!).

With Pat still unconvinced, Bill telephoned Dan Mahoney on Monday June 7 and said that he would be the candidate of the Conservative party.

I had already organized a rally for Public Action at the Manhattan Center for the next evening as a tribute to Mrs. Seth Milliken and her small public interest organization. She was the matriarch of the conservative and generous Milliken family who had supported *National Review* and so many other causes. Senator John Tower spoke, but Buckley was the main attraction and the draw.

Although he hadn't publicly announced, rumors were rife. His speech that night was basically the beginning of his campaign. He used the platform to talk about New York City. He ended by saying, "The people of New York [are] owed, by good government, the security of their liberties: to work without harassment, to live without a crushing fiscal overhead, to educate their children with minimum interference from extrinsic distractions, to walk confidently in the streets, and sleep quietly at night. Public action is needed to secure these private ends."

The overflow crowd responded with cheers. Although he hadn't officially announced, they knew they had their candidate. The next morning, the *New York Times* headlined BUCKLEY IS EXPECTED TO RUN FOR MAYOR AS CONSERVATIVE.

A few days later, Jim Buckley returned from Hawaii. He had formally committed to serve as his brother's campaign manager, but only after he wrote to his friend and classmate, David Lindsay, John Lindsay's twin brother, who was serving on John's campaign team. Jim Buckley, the most amiable man in the world, never had any problems with David, although their two brothers fought each other with increasing bitterness as the campaign went on.

We had our first informal meeting of the still very informal campaign committee in my offices at 79 Madison Avenue: Bill and Jim Buckley, Dan Mahoney and Kieran O'Doherty, and Neal Freeman, a bright young staff member of *National Review* who became Buckley's personal aide during the campaign.

At this meeting, Buckley said, "Listen, gentlemen, I want this to be a campaign of ideas. We are here to articulate ideas. I don't want or need any of these bumper stickers, balloons, or straw hats. We don't need that kind of stuff. We will just do it on ideas, and we'll save a lot of money." Several weeks later, at another meeting, Bill complained bitterly at the absence of posters and bumper stickers, "I see Lindsay's stuff all over town and nothing for Buckley." Bill had turned into a candidate before our very eyes.

Our first task was to plan the public announcement. We picked June 24 as the day, and I booked a room at the Overseas Press Club on Fortieth Street. The press conference was covered by more than fifty reporters. It was a stifling hot day, and the room was not air-conditioned. Pat was still not speaking to me. She had reached some mild rapprochement with Bill and grumpily sat in her wheelchair, fanning herself vigorously and casting her eyes to heaven with her special "What am I doing here?" look. Bill read his announcement, which was published in its entirety the next day in the *New York Times*.

At the question-and-answer period following Buckley's statement, a reporter asked, "How many votes do you expect to get, conservatively speaking?" Bill replied, "Conservative speaking? One."

From another press conference a week later to introduce his Conservative party running mates came another famous line. He was asked by a reporter, "What would be the first thing you would do if you were elected?" Bill answered, "Demand a recount!"

These two press conferences unnerved the Conservative party and delighted just about anyone else. Bill was amusing and flip. He would not bow to boring political mores and the classic way of doing things.

I was assigned to handle the fund-raising and the logistics of the headquarters—the telephones and all the other details that go into a campaign. My first coup was to get enormous space on East Forty-second Street near the UN. It was air-conditioned, carpeted, and in a brand-new building and would cost—nothing! It was unused office space and would be made discreetly available by the Chinese delegation to the UN at no charge to the Buckley campaign.

Jim Buckley quickly, firmly, and politely declined the offer. Starting political campaigns with my American Express card was sufficiently outrageous; accepting headquarters space from a foreign government was simply not done! I finally located space at 25 West Forty-fifth Street, and we moved in on August 15.

The political pros found Buckley a difficult candidate. He didn't follow any rules. But to everyone else, he was marvelous. Pat's sister, Kathleen "Bill" Finucane, came to New York to make peace between us, and Pat even began to enjoy the race. As she accompanied Bill from time to time in the limousine, she'd wave to "my people," who were thronging around. She was the reigning queen of New York, a position she would really achieve some twenty years later as doyenne of "society." The crowds loved her imperial look and manner.

I worked closely with Dan Mahoney, Kieran O'Doherty, and Jim

Buckley in setting up the campaign organization. I tried to make our tenth-floor offices on Forty-fifth Street like the film versions I had seen of campaign headquarters. I had tired old bunting hanging around, balloons, and signs, and I arranged for the great mass of telephones to ring constantly, especially during our official opening when the press was there. To the great annoyance of the candidate during his brief remarks, they continued ringing for the rest of the press conference. We hired a staff and borrowed others from the *National Review*. Another "cause" was under way.

Among the events that remain in memory were the television debates arranged because of the newspaper strike. The participants were Democrat Beame, Republican/Liberal Lindsay, and Conservative Buckley. Buckley walked away with all three debates. He was great on TV—wonderfully witty and totally self-assured—and the debates helped in large part to launch his television career.

Buckley went up even more in my estimation by keeping up his battle against the John Birch Society during the campaign—against the advice of those who thought he would lose right-wing votes thereby. We thought that *National Review*'s 1962 denunciation of the Birch Society was sufficient. It wasn't. The August 1965 issue of *American Opinion*, the Birch Society's publication (which was soon to be edited by one of my early YAF nemeses, Scott Stanley), repeated its conviction that most of the United States government was communist dominated, and that we should withdraw from Vietnam because the communist enemy was at home rather than abroad.

Buckley wrote an August column labeling the Birch Society's views "drivel," and *National Review* published a special issue condemning the Society, devoting the cover and fourteen pages to it. *National Review* called the Birch Society "a grave liability to the conservative anticommunist cause." The issue caused dissension among NR editors and great concern in the Conservative party. Instead of hurting Buckley's campaign, however, it added to his luster as a "responsible" conservative.

By late September, the campaign was really catching on. Bill became more involved in the race. We all started thinking, My God, maybe—what if—he wins? He started taking it more seriously. I became more interested in working with the endless parade of young volunteers. One of them was Daniel Oliver, who later became my boss in Washington when he served as chairman of the Federal Trade Commission. Bill was huddled in boring meetings with politicians, economists, social scientists, and experts of every sort working on "position papers." He really did want to add something to the discourse on New York City's problems.

The opposition accused him of racism, insensitivity, and just about everything else. And, like any politician, Bill was often wounded by these attacks. Lindsay and Beame hurled the final javelin; they both accused Buckley of racism and, an even more heinous charge in New York, anti-Semitism. On August 26, Lindsay publicly accused Bill of advocating "deportation camps for welfare recipients."

This attack had to be answered, and we called on Clare Boothe Luce. This was the first time that I met that fabulous woman, who went from being a stimulating acquaintance, to a friend and finally a great pal during her last days in Washington in the late 1980s. Clare was one of the giants of our century: editor, playwright, writer, congresswoman (from Connecticut), ambassador (to Italy), and wife of the powerful publisher Henry R. Luce. She was beautiful, accomplished, and amusing.

On October 29, 1965, we put out a press release in which Clare denounced Lindsay's charges that "any New Yorker who, like myself, favors a vote for Mr. William Buckley is a bigot, or a racist, or is trying to destroy the democratic process. Mr. Lindsay's flat refusal," she went on, "to grant the sincerity and good faith of those who oppose him is more in the tradition of a Huey Long or a Senator Bilbo, than of a man who seeks election in a City that prides itself on its liberalism."

On October 2, I organized the ubiquitous rally, this time at Manhattan Center. It was an enormous success. I was by now the best producer of conservative rallies in the country.

I filled the stage with Conservative party celebrities. Then Pat and their thirteen-year-old son, Christopher, made a grand entrance, followed by Bill, who acknowledged his mother, Aloise. She was sitting on the stage feeling rather uncomfortable but inordinately proud of her son. Bill then delivered his usual rousing speech, which brought the overflow crowd to their feet and caused my favorite rally band to break spontaneously into my favorite rally number, "The Battle Hymn of the Republic."

I tried to organize my rallies like clockwork. At this one, I gave the following instructions to the MC, Jeffrey St. John, and to the other principals:

7:00 P.M. Doors open.

7:30 Band starts playing patriotic, march and "sing-along" quick tempo songs.

8:00 Band leader conducts a flourish. Lights are lowered. MC (Jeff St. John) comes on stage alone and asks all to rise for the "Star-Spangled Banner" and to stay standing for a prayer.

8:03 Band conducts "Star-Spangled Banner" and everyone sings (we're trying to get a Negro singer). St. John introduces him, and he takes mike to lead song.

8:08 St. John asks everyone to bow their heads in prayer for the nation and the candidates, etc. etc. But, not too long!

8:10 St. John makes a few introductory remarks and calls on platform guests (there were 40!) to come on stage. He calls out their names and titles; the band plays "When the Saints Come Marching In"; the platform guests file on when their names are called and take their seats. The ones that should get the most applause will come on last—the Buckley family, especially his mother. All speakers stay off the stage until they are called for.

8:20 St. John introduces Kieran O'Doherty, Chairman of the Conservative Party City Campaign Committee. Band plays "It's a Grand Old Shillelagh" during some applause.

8:23 O'Doherty speaks for 5 minutes and ends up by introducing Hugh Markey (candidate for Comptroller). Band plays "What I Couldn't Do with Plenty of Money and You."

8:30 Markey comes on and speaks for 10 minutes. There probably won't be much applause for him, poor thing.

8:43 St. John calls on all Conservative party candidates, wherever they are sitting, to stand up for a big hand.

	House lights go on for this. Band plays: "There'll be a Hot Time in the Old Town Tonight" during applause. Do this quickly, because they're all hogs for the limelight.
8:50	House lights go down, and St. John introduces Rosemary Gunning (candidate for President of the City Council). Band plays a medley of "School Days" and "Oh, you Beautiful Doll" during applause, and there should be plenty for her.
8:52	Rosemary Gunning comes on and speaks for 15 minutes.
9:10	St. John introduces J. Daniel Mahoney. Band plays "East Side–West Side."
9:12	Mahoney comes on and speaks for 5 minutes ending up by introducing BILL BUCKLEY. Band starts playing a medley of "Billy Boy," "Boola-Boola," and "Happy Days are Here Again."
9:20	Buckley comes on with Pat and Christopher for a thunderous at least 5-minute ovation.
9:25	Buckley speaks for 25 minutes. He's good at keeping on schedule.
9:50	Meeting is adjourned.

Beame lost the election, and Lindsay won. But the real winner was Bill Buckley. He received massive national exposure on television, in magazines, and the press. He had become *the* American conservative alongside Goldwater (although Bill had the benefit of not suffering a humiliating defeat in a national election).

Bill was catapulted—along with Pat—into the rarified precinct of American celebritydom. This was to change both their lives radically, along with the lives of their friends, especially this one.

I continued working for the Conservative party and maintained my personal friendship with its leaders over the years. In 1966, the Conservative party surpassed the Liberal and became the third largest party in New York state, winning line C on the election ballot. The Conservative party was well on its way.

But I was busy with other things and really not that interested in politics, except in organizing campaigns. In 1968, I became involved in two more: Jim Buckley made his first race for New York senator on the

Conservative party line, and Ronald Reagan, his first race for the Republican nomination for president.

It was just before election day that year when Priscilla Buckley, her mother Aloise, and I were returning from a short holiday in the Caribbean. There was an enormous line waiting to get through customs, and Aloise said she would try to get us out quickly. She approached one of the custom officers and said, in her usual sweet, Southern way, "Excuse me, sir, we're in rather a hurry to meet my son, the candidate for senator from New York." He smiled at her and said, "Right this way, Mrs. Javits," and ushered the three of us through.

Jim Buckley was prevailed on to run against the veteran liberal Republican Jacob Javits and the ultraliberal Paul O'Dwyer in the 1968 New York senatorial race. There was no possibility of Jim winning, but the Conservative party had to field a credible candidate so as to keep line C on the ballot and keep the party in the public eye. We all did the best we could, and ran an effective campaign with most of our old Buckley for Mayor troops on hand.

Jim was and is a private man, quite different from his brother Bill. He never really liked the spotlight, but he deeply cared about the issues, and the only way he felt he could really contribute something to his country was to run for public office. So he did!

Jim Buckley received 1,139,402 votes or 17.4 percent of the votes cast in the three-man race that Javits, naturally, won. This was more than twice as many votes received by the Conservative party two years earlier, which had earned them line C. The Conservative party was now very much a force in New York state politics, and Jim Buckley had become a political figure of some importance. Two years later, in 1970, he was to win a seat in the United States Senate as the candidate of the Conservative party of New York.

In August 1968, the Republican National Convention was scheduled to be held in Miami. Ronald Reagan and Richard Nixon were running for the nomination. I never liked Richard Nixon personally, nor did I ever have much respect for his political career. He had shifty eyes. Nixon would try to look directly at you, but his eyes would wander. I also didn't much like Barry Goldwater, because of his poor treatment of the people who got him the nomination in 1964. There was only Reagan. I felt almost as if I knew him because of my brief acquaintance with his wife, Nancy, some eighteen years earlier. There were a lot of pro-Reagan YAF kids going to the convention, and it would be fun.

This time, I didn't have to urge Edison to go. He was enthusiastic about Ronald Reagan and had generously supported his gubernatorial campaign.

I arrived three days before the convention opened to set up liaison for Governor Edison. I wanted him to feel important, to be noticed and have a good time, even though he didn't have any real function. Edison was coming down by train. We had booked a large three-bedroom suite for himself, me, and his nurse, Alice Stevenson, who had had to start accompanying him everywhere since the death of his wife, Carolyn, five years earlier.

I arrived at night and went down to the hotel coffee shop the next morning for breakfast. When the tourists were in residence, there was a fashion show each morning in which models would go by the tables and show clothes available for sale in the hotel's boutique. Three elderly women were sitting at a table. They were wearing plastic shower caps, which were de rigueur for ladies who still had their curlers on. They were waiting for the fashion show to begin, but instead the delegates started to arrive. A tall, distinguished lady wearing a tailored gray suit was standing with her back to the trio of old girls. On her copious bosom were the badges of a California delegate.

One of the old women looked at her skirt and ran the material through her fingers. "How much?" she asked.

The startled delegate turned around and said, "I beg your pardon?"

"How much, darling, how much is the dress?"

"I am a delegate," said the California lady haughtily. "Oh, excuse me," said the old girl and went back to drinking her tea with the other two. They would see no fashion show for another five days.

I knew that Reagan would be a favorite son candidate of California. What I didn't know was that Clif White and the old "syndicate"—now known as the "hard core"—had been politicking for many months. Roger Milliken had also been politicking among the Southern delegations and had made some real inroads. I arrived to an absolute frenzy of disorganization.

I was approached by David Jones, the executive director of YAF, to help a Youth for Reagan for President operation. Milliken, White, and others were so busy wheeling and dealing that they had done nothing about organizing the crowds, the banners, and all the other stuff that brings a candidate to the attention of the convention and the public. David Jones asked me to help. He had the troops. All he needed was money. Out came my trusted American Express card, and we started the Reagan Youth operation.

I housed a number of the kids with me in the Edison suite, cautioning them that they had to be out the moment the Governor arrived. Edison's train derailed, however. He was badly shaken, and Alice Stevenson suffered a broken hip. They never got to Miami. Room service was kept busy day and night, and the young Reaganites all had a wonderful time— and Edison picked up the tab.

Watching Dave Jones work was a revelation. I have never witnessed such rapid organization in such a short time. Wherever Reagan went, there was a crowd of cheering young people waving Reagan signs. The overwhelming majority of the YAF board were pro-Reagan, with only two pro-Nixon. But of course Nixon handily won the nomination.

My spirits were down, suffering from more than a convention loss. I resolved not to get involved with any more candidates' campaigns. It all seemed pointless to me. Even when you won, you lost, sooner or later. I was disillusioned with politics. I was also becoming increasingly disheartened by the Vietnam war.

Chapter 13

Vietnam

AS THE SIXTIES progressed, the war in Vietnam dragged on, and I struggled to come to terms with its realities. I remained firmly anticommunist, but became more dismayed about the war itself and the politicians in Washington and abroad involved on all sides of the debate. Hypocrisy and political expediency were the rule.

On previous tours to Asia, I had traveled a number of times to South Vietnam. I was especially impressed by President Ngo Dinh Diem, whom I first met in 1957. As I listened to him that first time, he seemed more the poet than the politician. He talked of the sufferings of his people—North and South—and all the young soldiers who were willing to die for freedom and all the innocents in the country who were dying for no reason at all. He was a dedicated patriot who made the needs and future of his country his absolute priority. I saw Diem several times again, and I was deeply saddened to hear of his assassination in 1963. Because of my personal dealings with him, I was convinced that his country's fight against communism was worthy of support and that he was the man to lead the fight.

In 1964, I decided that something should be done to focus attention on just what we were doing in Vietnam and on the thousands of American "technical assistants and instructors" who were in that beleaguered country. So I launched another campaign—this time on my own and pro bono.

In mid-March, I wrote to the Department of Defense and asked for the names of Americans killed in Vietnam and the names and addresses of their next of kin. They sent me the names of 132 Americans who had been "killed as the result of hostile action" in Vietnam from January 1961 through March 1964.

Studying the list, I saw that the next of kin closest to New York City was that of a Corp. Charles P. Tuthill from Uniondale, New Jersey. On April 2 I wrote to Corporal Tuthill's father, Charles. "This is a most difficult letter to begin," I wrote, "but begin I must. I hope, after reading what follows, you will see fit to cooperate in an undertaking which I believe to have great national importance." I told him about my idea of making a public statement expressing concern over the situation in Vietnam and how I had obtained his name. Then I outlined the plan.

The statement we wanted to publish as a full-page ad, I explained, "poses a single question: Why? It raises a specific point: If American lives are to be sacrificed in Vietnam, there must be a definite plan. To date, there is no plan and it is difficult to justify the supreme sacrifice made by so many of our young men. We are certain that sufficient attention will be paid to the publication of the statement—particularly as it will be signed by the parents, wives and children of the Americans who gave their lives —to bring the question to the fore and prompt decisive action on the part of those in Washington." Then I asked him if he would be willing to sign a statement addressed to President Johnson to be published in Washington, D.C., and sign a letter to the other families asking them to join with him.

Mr. Tuthill telephoned immediately after receiving my letter. He said that his son, a Marine photographer, died in a helicopter that was shot down October 8, 1963, by the Vietcong guerrillas. "We felt Charles' death was not any use to the world," he said. "We felt we were being let down." He agreed to my plan.

By May, thirty-one next of kin had signed the statement, and it was ready to go to press. It read:

> The undersigned—parents and wives and children of Americans killed in Vietnam—have a question for the President of the United States and the Nation:
>
> # WHY?
>
> *WHY* are the young Americans who are fighting Communist aggression in Vietnam—shoulder to shoulder with free Vietnamese soldiers—forced to withstand the onslaught of the Communist enemy without having the opportunity to attack the enemy's own territory in the North?

WHY must young Americans give their lives in the jungles and the rice fields in Vietnam in the fight against a Communist enemy when the Government of the United States authorizes trade with Communist countries—trade which is utilized to strengthen Communist power in Vietnam and throughout the world?

WHY must our young men die in far-off Vietnam, fighting the Communist enemy, when their government authorizes "cultural" exchanges with the Communist world—the exchange of ballet dancers to entertain Communist leaders in Moscow while a young American does the dance of death in Vietnam?

WHY must we repeat the tragic error of Korea—where 54,246 Americans gave up their lives in a war that we had no intention of winning? Must the same number be sacrificed for the same empty reasons in Vietnam?

WHY do we fight Communism with one hand—at a terrible cost of our loved one—and help Communism with the other hand? If international Communism is the enemy of our Nation, then we must fight. If it is not, then let's bring our young men home—from throughout the world—and submit to international Communism's ambition to control the world. We can't have it both ways—it must be one way or the other!

These are only some of the questions that we have—and these questions demand an answer in the name of our national conscience and honor. The men whom we lost were precious to us—our sons, our husbands and the fathers of our children. They died in the service of their Nation. That they died in vain would be a national crime.

We call on you, Mr. President—and on the Nation—to see to it that the sacrifice of those whom we loved shall not have been for naught. And the only way to make their sacrifice meaningful is to rededicate ourselves to the eternal struggle for freedom against all who would threaten it. If we do not, then these empty sacrifices will continue until our final defeat at the hands of an enemy who has a plan and is willing to implement it in every way.

When freedom is under armed attack—as it is in Vietnam—we must fight back with everything we have. We must destroy the enemies of freedom wherever they are—and not stop at some artificial border created by diplomats in a far-off country who possibly have never known the pain of battle or the loss of a son or a husband.

To make the supreme sacrifice in a war that cannot be won is too great a sacrifice to ask of anyone. If we are to battle, let's battle to win!

If we are not to do this, Mr. President, please tell us:

W H Y ?

The *Washington Post* refused to accept the advertisement; I don't recall their reasons. It was finally published in *The Washington Star* on Tuesday, May 12, at a cost of $2,521 for the full page (it was a lot cheaper in those days). Edison gave me $3,000 to pay for its publication and to help out on other mailing expenses. I put up whatever else was needed.

Working on this campaign put me personally in touch with the actual toll of this war. Each time I received another acceptance from one of the parents or one of the wives of the young Americans killed in Vietnam, I realized that this was not just another signature on an advertisement— like those in my previous campaigns—but represented another precious young life lost.

The ad created a national furor. The Pentagon was annoyed at this public criticism of its policy. Liberals didn't like my call for a more aggressive war and played up their "discovery" that I was really a conservative. Surprise! *The New York Herald Tribune* headlined a front-page syndicated story GI KIN PROTEST EXPOSED. Their "exposé" was the fact that I was the "central figure in the attack on Washington's Vietnam policy," and that I was "active in ultra-conservative circles." On the same day, Richard Dudman, the Washington correspondent of the *St. Louis Post Dispatch*, headlined a story RIGHT-WINGER BEHIND AD ON VIETNAM WAR: Got Relatives of Dead Americans to Urge Attack on North. But the ad received substantial editorial support as well. Bill Buckley, in his column "ON THE RIGHT," called it "the most poignant full-page advertisement I have ever seen."

The ad was a one-shot deal. We sent each signer the names and addresses of the other signers so that they could correspond with each other if they so chose. It had little effect on the Pentagon's war policy.

As my concern for our country's soldiers and my opposition to the Pentagon's policies grew, I became more upset by the rising tide of militant, leftist, anti-U.S. activism on the campuses. Their opposition to the war, unlike mine, seemed too often to be pro-communist and anti-American. They were the new know-nothings of the Left. So I became involved in launching a worldwide effort to demonstrate that many more American students supported the war's anticommunist cause than opposed it.

In late 1965 Walter Judd and I met at my office with David Keene and Tom Charles Huston, a director and the national chairman, respectively, of Young Americans for Freedom. The boys were deeply concerned about the growing anti-Vietnam war "protest" movement on U.S. campuses. We discussed what might be done to counteract the increasingly successful attempts of the communists to infiltrate, establish, and use youth organizations for their own ends in the United States and abroad. We set up the World Youth Crusade for Freedom in Vietnam.

I contacted responsible anticommunist groups abroad. Tom Huston took time off from his law studies in Indiana and left for the Far East in December for a three-week tour. My Chinese friends paid the round-trip ticket to Taiwan, and I supplemented the cost in order to fit in other Asian countries.

Huston was welcomed enthusiastically by youth and senior anticommunist leaders wherever he went. As a result of our efforts, pro-U.S. demonstrations and projects were organized early in 1966 in Australia, Taiwan, Malaya, Korea, Vietnam, Hong Kong, India, Belgium, Denmark, Norway, Sweden, France, Italy, and the Philippines. It was the beginning of what seemed to be a strong organizational base. In the United States, rallies were held in connection with the World Youth Crusade for Freedom on campuses in Boston, New York, Philadelphia, Washington, D.C., St. Louis, Cleveland, Houston, and Los Angeles. These demonstrations marked the first time that youth groups from many nations participated in a *coordinated* joint anticommunist venture.

Our next step was to begin recruiting volunteers for an International Freedom Corps that I set up, an activist, anticommunist response to the Peace Corps, as the first major project of the WYCF. As a pilot project, we sent young Americans to eight countries of the Far East to work directly with anticommunist youth groups there at the grass-roots level. Ten volunteers who were particularly articulate exponents of the anticommunist cause were chosen to represent the WYCF in Asia during July and August of 1966.

The volunteers traveled to Asia to let young people know that the majority of American youth were anticommunist; to report back to young Americans about the true situation in the country to which they went; and to lay the local groundwork for organizing coordinated anticommunist youth action throughout the world.

Despite our great hopes and rhetoric, by May of 1967 I considered it fruitless to continue the WYCF. There was no organized anticommunist movement anywhere in the world except in the committed anticommunist nations: Korea, Taiwan, and Vietnam. The youth groups in those countries were sanctioned and supported by their governments. The WYCF had no one of any real substance to work with in other countries, neither senior nor youth. I did not want to be involved in building another facade, especially one that could be exposed as such. I was all for "perception" but not when I had something real to accomplish. In May 1967 I resigned as secretary. The WYCF continued for several more years, mostly sending young Americans as summer interns to Taiwan.

The failure of our attempt to organize a movement of anticommunists on campuses highlighted my own ambivalence about the young generation of peace activists. Although I disagreed with their opposition to the war on moral, political, and military grounds, I had a sneaking admiration for them. Filled with frustration and rage, they took to the streets and campuses of the nation to fight for something they believed with all their hearts and with no reservations or sophistry. I could never find that passion in the activities of the conservative youth, even though I supported their aims. I missed and envied the passion and excitement of the opposition.

The war in Vietnam had become a national crisis in the United States by October 1967, when I had the opportunity through the APACL to visit the country again. I wanted to go to where the fighting was and see what was going on for myself. I had an accreditation from *National Review* that would allow me to travel outside Saigon.

My first night in Vietnam was spent in the Majestic Hotel in downtown Saigon, where I had drinks with some journalist friends in the top floor bar with the big windows. As we sipped our iced drinks and nibbled at hors d'oeuvres, we could watch the flashing lights of the war in the distance. And, I knew, people were being killed and maimed under those lights in the distance.

I hired a Vietnamese photographer, and we both went looking for the war. Most of the next four days were spent around Da Nang. One night I stayed in Con Thien when it was under heavy bombardment. We couldn't get out by truck, helicopter, or anything else.

As I lay there on the muddy ground in the rain under a makeshift shelter, surrounded by sleeping GIs, I recalled vividly both my plane trip home from Cairo and my trip on the boat to Cyprus. The memories were as sharp as they could be, and it rather frightened me to be in exactly the same position at this time—surrounded by sleeping men. I tape-recorded interviews with about forty young GIs and took photographs of all of them. Their stories and predicament touched me deeply.

"After spending time with these boys," I wrote in a report to friends and colleagues when I returned, "and that's what they are, I experienced a deep sense of guilt which I ask you to share so that some constructive action may result." My guilt was over these men being called on "to face enemy bullets in defense of their country" while they heard about growing dissent and opposition at home. "They read of demonstrations and statements, in direct and indirect support of the Vietcong, by students, professors, politicians, and clergymen . . . They see reruns of TV news specials which seem to crow over the supposed growing strength of the enemy and to demean their own efforts." Once again I called for a "public dedication to pursue the war in Vietnam to victory."

But in my report, my anticommunist politics seemed to pale against my descriptions of the young American casualties of this war. "There are now some 500,000 American troops in Vietnam," I wrote. "The great majority are under twenty-one years of age. According to official figures released by the Pentagon, they—and the young Americans who preceded them—have already suffered more than 100,000 casualties. And what do 'casualties' really mean? Young men shot to death in Da Nang, Pleiku and Con Thien; boys with their legs blown off in Chu Lai and Bien-hoa; youngsters coughing themselves to death in the rains of Vung Tan and An Khe; teenagers racked by dysentery in Nha Trang and Binh Thuy." They represented to me all the young men I had loved over the years.

It broke my heart when I thought of our troops in Vietnam. The war seemed more confusing and rotten to me. I got fed up with the rhetoric and political manipulation of these young men's lives on all sides of the political spectrum.

I didn't realize the war would go on for so long, and be so devastating to our soldiers and to the Vietnamese people. When I went there and saw the anger, the courage and suffering, I became increasingly but privately opposed to the war. I didn't have the courage to speak out publicly because I was afraid of alienating my conservative family—and losing them as I had lost my communist family years before. Nor did I want such a protest to give comfort to the communist enemy. Either way, I knew that the war would go on and take more lives. I felt helpless.

When I visit the Vietnam Memorial in Washington today, I have a gnawing sense of grief and failure, of having made a mistake along the way, and I wonder if there was something more I might have done. I once took Clare Boothe Luce to the memorial. It was a gray drizzly day. Under her umbrella, she began to weep softly. "So useless, so useless," she said.

On November 30, 1967, a dinner in my honor was given by Bill Buckley, Charles Edison, Lee Edwards, and Walter Judd at the Union League Club in New York in recognition of the tenth anniversary of my firm, Marvin Liebman Associates, Inc. That afternoon, a major blizzard swept through New York. In spite of the snow, all my friends in the city pushed their way to the club. There were no planes from Washington, so we lost Walter Judd as one of the speakers.

It was a wonderful occasion, and Bill Buckley and Charles Edison outdid themselves in their testimonials to me. I was pleased to hear their tributes, and especially to see my mother sitting next to me on the dais. She was thrilled beyond belief.

My mother died two months later. During her last years, I was able to make sufficient peace with myself to give her whatever pleasures she expected. My therapist intimates that I should be angry with my mother for "what she did to me when I was young." But I have never been able to be really angry at her. She was beset by her own demons, as was my father, as am I. She did the best she could. So I was happy to watch her basking in my glory. Like my father watching me speak at the dinner for the crew of the *Ben Hecht*, she saw her vague dream for me fulfilled at that moment.

Each guest was given an oversized printed program that had a picture of my head fixed to Charles Atlas's body holding up the globe. Surrounding this image were the names of endless committees and causes and events that I had organized.

The dinner was meant to herald the future of Marvin Liebman Associates. But to me, it seemed a more fitting conclusion. I was tired of the war, of causes and political passions. I was ready to retire, to leave the field to younger people. Just a year later, I left the United States for London.

Chapter 14

London and the Theater

*F*OR THE NEXT five years, I created a new life for myself in the London theater world that was a dramatic change from my political activism.

The door to the theater first opened in Athens during the summer of 1968—after rioters had stormed the Democratic Convention in Chicago and Nixon had been nominated at the Republican Convention in Miami.

I had flown to Athens with Pat and Bill to rendezvous with some friends for a yacht tour of the Greek Islands. The night before we were to sail, we were having dinner in a restaurant in the Athens seaport of Piraeus. It was a balmy night, and we were eating outside and having a good time. I heard my name called. I looked up to see Marjorie Steele, a friend and poker-playing buddy from Hollywood and New York. With her was her current husband, Constantine Fitzgibbon, the English-Irish writer. It was a grand reunion made even better by happening in a foreign place by accident.

As we were talking, Fitzgibbon told us that he had written his first play, *The Devil He Did*. It was going to be produced in Dublin at the Gate Theatre if he could put up the money needed for the production, five thousand pounds (about $12,500 in those days). I had invested in several Broadway shows over the years, so I was amazed to find out how little it cost to produce in Dublin. Hilton Edwards, the noted Irish director and head of the Gate Theatre, would direct the play. His good friend and partner, the spectacular Irish actor Michael MacLiammoir, would star and play the Devil. I asked if Fitzgibbon had a copy of the script, and he did.

I took it on the boat and read it the next day. But the story didn't matter to me. If it was good enough for Hilton Edwards, Michael

MacLiammoir, and the Gate Theatre, it was good enough for me. I fled the boat and (as was my wont in just about all the many sailing trips I took with the Buckleys) flew by helicopter to Athens several days later to telephone Fitzgibbon that I would put up the money for his play—provided I would be billed as producer. He agreed. I returned to New York and could think of nothing but the show, Dublin, the theater, glamour—my new life had begun!

I arranged to meet with everyone in Dublin in late September. I arrived at Kennedy Airport to discover that the plane was packed with Catholic priests and nuns. I thought they would not be the liveliest company, so I upgraded to first class with my trusty American Express card.

I found myself sitting next to a distinguished gentleman whom I was sure I had met, but couldn't place. We were talking about Vietnam. He was drinking rather heavily, which, I discovered later, he was prone to do. He had lost a son in Korea and was revealing all sorts of personal matters the drunker he got.

I asked him what he was going to do in Dublin.

"I'm going to buy a bank," he replied. The man was George Champion, then chairman of the board at the Chase Manhattan Bank.

He asked me why I was going to Dublin. I said, "I'm going to produce a play."

"Well," said Champion, "we have just about the same chance of turning a profit." These words were to prove prophetic. Champion was an investor in my first London production.

Marjorie and Constantine met me at the airport and took me to their lovely house just outside Dublin overlooking the bay. The next day, I met Fitzgibbon's literary agent, Robert Fenn (who was also the agent for Ian Fleming, creator of James Bond). Fenn advised me that I should establish a formal relationship with an active London producer—in case the play was successful and could move to London. He recommended his friend John Gale, who had produced the very successful currently running London play *The Secretary Bird*.

I telephoned Gale. He and his wife Lisel came to Dublin the next day. It was their tenth wedding anniversary, so I booked a room in my hotel to host a party in their honor. Michael MacLiammoir, Hilton Edwards, and the great Irish actress Siobhan McKenna (who would soon star in one of my productions) were guests at the party.

Michael MacLiammoir was considered by critics throughout the world to be one of the great actors of our century. He made an international success playing Oscar Wilde in a one-man show. I first met him one morning when I called at the house where he and Hilton Edwards lived. Hilton opened the door, ushered me in, and offered me a drink—a neat Irish whiskey before noon. I had heard that Edwards and MacLiammoir were longtime lovers. Edwards and I were chatting and then, as if on cue, we stopped. A majestic presence entered. Here was Michael MacLiammoir wearing a black satin dressing gown, a green ascot and full makeup, lipstick, mascara, a slicked-down toupee, and even a beauty mark on his cheek. It was an extraordinary entrance. I thought back to Ilona Massey and the Hungarian picket line. Why? They both had beauty marks. And they both had mastered the fine art of making grand entrances.

It was then that I realized that homosexuality didn't really matter in the theater. So long as one had talent, no one cared how outrageous one became.

The Devil He Did opened and closed rapidly. I lost my money but had a great time for a couple of weeks meeting and mixing with Irish show folk. They were all exactly like the actresses and actors and directors and writers and designers that I had met in just about every country. This was another "family" for me, and I loved it and every one of them.

During the production, I saw John Gale several times again. He told me that since I seemed to enjoy the theater so much, I ought to come to London and set up shop as a producer.

"What's required?" I asked.

"Simple. Find the play; find a star who will do it; find the director. These three steps can be done in any sequence. The fourth step, however, is the most important. Find the money to put it on."

It occurred to me that this was not dissimilar to what I had been doing: find a cause or a candidate; raise the money to promote them; then present them to the public on election day—or opening night. The result always rests in the fickle hands of the public.

John Gale was becoming my mentor and partner in my new career as theatrical producer. Just after Richard Nixon was elected president in November 1968, Gale telephoned me to say that he had optioned a play called *Highly Confidential,* an espionage drama. Gale knew that I was a good friend of the British comedienne-actress Hermione Gingold. If I could convince her to return to London, after her many years' absence in America, to star in it, success was virtually guaranteed.

Hermione's first play, *When the Rainbow Ends,* had been with Noel Coward in 1911, when they were both children. During World War II, she reached the apex of her British career in three brilliant reviews: *Sweet and Low, Sweeter and Lower,* and *Sweetest and Lowest.* She became the darling of the American troops stationed in England. At that point, she seemed only interested in gay lovers, and she had many. She became a queen among queens. Her propensity for gay men lasted until the end of her life when she was in her nineties. What they did together physically, I'll never know. When we first met in New York, she and I became fast friends.

I always thought of Hermione during the war as the epitome of British pluck. When she walked to the theater during a bombing raid, she would simply unfurl her umbrella and carry on, certain that she would be shielded from any bomb.

In January 1969 I went to London to meet with Gale and began the preliminary work on *Highly Confidential.* I found a small mews house at 12 Kinnerton Street just off Cadogan Place in Belgravia. (Pat Buckley told me that under no conditions should I live anyplace that didn't have a Belgravia telephone number.)

Kinnerton Street was delightful, lined with small carriage houses. There were a number of rather famous residents, two of whom became friends: Major Basil Neville-Willings, a diminutive and distinguished looking man who used to book acts for London's Café de Paris. He knew a number of the stars who worked there: Marlene Dietrich, Noel Coward, Liberace, and Hermione Gingold.

Also in residence was one of the most outrageous queens in London. He served as an unpaid pimp to some of England's most illustrious luminaries, allegedly including members of the royal family. His specialty were Guardsmen, who seemed to be always available for him or his friends for a few drinks and a five-pound note. They were all six feet tall or more, their height accentuated by their bearskin hats (which was sometimes all they wore to amuse their gentlemen callers). I loved the street, complete with ironmonger and greengrocer. It was my first London home.

I finally convinced Hermione to make her return to the London stage in *Highly Confidential*. She liked the script but with "some of the changes I plan to suggest." I should have seen an ominous black cloud then, but I didn't.

I had to make all sorts of accommodations to Hermione, including secret personal financial ones that I didn't disclose to my partner, John Gale, for fear he would think me too extravagant. At that point, expense was no object; I just wanted to get my first show on the London stage. Then (one of the saddest sacrifices) I had to give up my Kinnerton Street house to Hermione, who had lived on this street before and during the war and had let the Major have her own house when she left London.

Before I was able to pay her first-class QE II fare to London (return trip and all expenses guaranteed), I had to raise money. I did this in my usual way—by direct mail to a select group. I used my old list of $1000-and-over contributors. My pitch was: *here* I was in London ready to bring conservatism and anticommunism to the fountainhead of mass entertainment, the British theater. If the British theater could be changed to promote the morality espoused by the American Right, then this would filter over to American theater, films, TV, and all the mass media. We were in a crucial position to save the English-speaking world from leftist intellectual elitists who used the theater to corrupt the young. This was the only really hypocritical letter I ever sent out in my career.

It was a good letter, though, and it worked. My first investors included such conservative donors as Charles Edison, Mrs. Eli Lilly, DeWitt Wallace, J. Howard Pew, George Champion, and William F. Buckley, Jr.

Hermione took the QE II to London and moved into the Kinnerton Street house. I moved around the corner to a flat on Cadogan Place, overlooking Cadogan Square. I had a key to the private park and felt very British. *Highly Confidential* was a first play by Robert Tanitch, a very sad and earnest young man who was always dressed in black, which someone once suggested he relieve with a strand of pearls.

As Hermione got what was left of her teeth into the script, the play turned from an espionage drama to a high camp burlesque, with the seventy-year-old star playing a rather young British Mata Hari. London rehearsals were held in the Savoy Theatre on John Gale's *Secretary Bird* set. The production became more outrageous as all concerned (including me) turned matters over to the more and more demanding Gingold. She would shriek, stamp her foot, faint, and do anything else to get her way. I was enjoying it all less and less.

We had out-of-town tryouts at the Theatre Royal in Brighton. Hermione was depressed. The playwright seemed suicidal. One night I was dispatched by John Gale to rescue Tanitch, who was standing at the water's edge literally ready to end it all. His landmark drama had turned into a music-hall charade for Gingold.

On another night in our Brighton hotel, I was having a light supper with Hermione. It was the off season, and the dining room was almost empty. It was pouring outside. The three-lady band behind the palms started playing Ivor Novello's "We'll Gather Lilacs." Hermione started to reminisce about the old days. She started speaking about the war, when she had her greatest triumphs. Her eyes filled with tears, and she began to weep, her mascara running down her cheeks, the rain beating against the windows, the band playing Ivor Norvello. I, too, became depressed, knowing that the show would probably be no good. The two of us sat across from each other, alone and sad, over our very bad, overcooked supper.

We played Manchester, Leeds, Oxford, and Brighton and opened at the Cambridge Theatre in London on June 18, 1969. Hermione was enthusiastically welcomed back to London, but the show was panned. It closed some six weeks later—a total loss, except for a poster I kept as a souvenir: "John Gale and Marvin Liebman Present . . ."

On Wednesday, July 30, 1969, as I was eating lunch with Hermione Gingold in my flat, the telephone rang. It was Alice Stevenson, Charles Edison's friend and nurse, calling from New York.

"The Governor had a stroke," she said, "and has been taken to the Harkness Pavilion. It doesn't look good. I am sure he would very much like to see you."

That's all I needed to hear. Within three hours, I was on the very next plane out. I had to fly first class because there were no seats in economy. That didn't bother me a bit.

I was very distressed, but I kept thinking, as I looked out the window at the passing clouds, "If he dies, I wonder what he'll leave me?" I hated myself for the venal thought, but it kept coming back. "Ten thousand dollars would sort of be an insult. A million dollars to help the cause? Well, my only cause now is the theater. No, not a million. A hundred thousand dollars? Fifty thousand?" And, so it went.

I took a taxi directly from the airport to the Harkness Pavilion when I arrived early the next morning. Alice Stevenson and the entire entourage were there, looking weary and anxious. It was obviously a death watch. I was taken into his room. It was about 9:00 A.M. He looked very old and very frail. "Hi, Governor," I said. "How's it going." He looked up and whispered, "Hi, young feller, it's good to see you," and that is all he could say. Those were the last words I ever heard from Charles Edison.

I helped arrange his funeral and tried to do what I thought he would like me to do. The service was held at the Madison Avenue Presbyterian Church in New York. Our favorite rally song, "The Battle Hymn of the Republic," was sung by a choir, and I remembered all the past glories. Along with Bill Buckley, I was one of the pallbearers.

The previous day, I had been to the reading of his will at Glenmont in West Orange, New Jersey, the Edison family home and the place he was born. When my name came up, I listened attentively. Instead of the million, or the hundred thousand or even ten thousand, the will read that the deceased "forgives Marvin Liebman any debts he might have to the estate."

As we walked down the aisle of the church, Bill, who was in front of me, whispered, sotto voce, "*Vieux*, you sure got shafted."

I probably did materially, but I have memories of happy times with one of the giants of the American Conservative movement. Through the years, and to impress the Governor with my business acumen and trustworthiness, I repaid him every penny I ever owed him. I had no debts to forgive!

I spent the fall and winter of 1969 laying the foundation of my life in London and trying my hand at producing without my mentor, John Gale. I made new friends, and after the financial failure of our two 1969 productions (we also co-produced *The Young Churchill*, a staged reading), I had to find new backing. I kept using my direct mail letters. I took the perfect London office, right next to the Strand Theatre at 11 Aldwych. It was tiny, oak-paneled with a fireplace and room for three people. The fireplace had a gas grate that was constantly on because of the damp London chill in the winter. I thought it was the most glamorous place in the world.

I was working on two productions: *Best of Friends*, which was to star Nigel Patrick and my old friend Siobhan McKenna, *It's Underneath That Counts*, starring the comedienne Miriam Karlin and the Australian comedian Peter Jones. In the works were Robert Anderson's *I Never Sang for My Father* and Ronald Millar's *Abelard and Heloise*. This was a very busy time for me, and typical of my taking on too much too soon.

One of the people to whom I wrote was a contributor to the Goldwater campaign and to several of my old committees, David Fasken. I wrote him the usual letter but didn't hear back from him until one day in early January 1970. My secretary, Anna Welch, announced that a Mr. Fasken from America had come to visit. I warmly greeted this unassuming man of about fifty. He was impressed by the "Britishness" of my office. Anna brought us tea. I dropped every impressive name I could think of, from Lawrence Olivier to Bill Buckley. Fasken ate it up. He asked what my plans were. I told him of the four plays I had in mind, and the necessity of raising money.

"How much will they cost?" he asked.

"Oh, about fifty thousand pounds or so, I guess, for all of them—maybe a bit more, maybe a bit less," I replied.

To my horrified amazement, he took out a checkbook and wrote a check for fifty thousand pounds to "Sedgemoor Productions," the name of the company I had set up. Nearly fainting, I said, "Oh, Mr. Fasken, I couldn't let you pay for the whole thing. But I will certainly let you be one of my major investors." And I kept my word.

From that moment on, David Fasken appeared on the bills with me as co-producer. I named him chairman of Sedgemoor Productions, Ltd., and I was the managing director. I became his mentor for the next several years.

He was tremendously wealthy (I still don't know from what) and lived just outside San Francisco. When he got married that year I gave him a lavish wedding reception; major stars of the day in London came, including Ingrid Bergman, Ralph Richardson, Deborah Kerr, Wendy Hiller, John Gielgud, Coral Browne, and Diana Rigg. David was in his glory, certain that every penny he had invested in the theater had been well spent. The roster was also a tribute to me and my close friend Coral Browne. When it was necessary to impress backers, we could deliver the stars, who would always come out as a favor to either one of us.

My relationship with Fasken ended some three years later. His wife didn't want to share his money with anyone else, and turned him against me and against London. His departure was the beginning of my financial demise.

But back in 1970 I was making a great leap into London's theater, and having the time of my life. *Best of Friends* was ready to open at the Strand Theatre on February 19, 1970. John Gale's office was upstairs, directly over the huge electrical sign that advertised the play. I had a neon sign installed with a neon cupid at the bottom shooting an arrow that hit a heart at the top of the sign. (I also put my name—"Marvin Liebman Presents"—at the top of the sign, which Gale thought was typical American vulgarity.) Whenever cupid shot the arrow—every two minutes—the lights in John Gale's office went out. Until the electricians were able to fix the problem two days later. John was very angry about the sign, and later, at me for leaving him and going it alone.

On opening night, I was a nervous wreck. During the first intermission, I was in the crowded lobby trying to look calm and waving and smiling and "Hello-Darling" and "I'm-so-glad-you-like-it" and "So-nice-of-you-to-come," all the while puffing at my cigarette (which I was never without in those days). Except, it wasn't my cigarette. By mistake —and to her astonishment—I started sucking on a cigarette held by a well-dressed lady standing next to me. My cigarette was at my side. "I'm-so-very-sorry, darling," I muttered as I quickly withdrew my lips.

I became friends with the stars of *Best of Friends*. Nigel Patrick's dream was for knighthood, but he never achieved what he most desired. Siobhan McKenna was already a star and, except for her drinking, was marvelous to work with. It was at that show that I met Jill Melford and, through her, my best woman friend in London, Coral Browne, who became my English Pat Buckley and remained always dear to my heart until she died in 1991.

One night Coral and I were at my apartment at Cadogan Place and wanted some milk for our coffee. Everything was closed. So we went across the street to the swanky Carlton Tower Hotel. I asked if I could buy some milk. They sniffily said, "We're not a retail outlet" and wouldn't sell me any milk. So Coral sat down in the lounge and ordered a quart of milk. Why shouldn't a well-dressed and glamourous lady order a quart of milk if she wanted it? When the waiter asked her, "What room are you in?" she said, "Room 617," signed her name, and we left to have our coffee and milk at home, thanks to the guest in room 617.

Each year, the MCA literary agent Milton Goldman and his companion Arnold Wiesberger, a theatrical attorney, came to London with Arnold's mother Anna, and threw three parties. The "A" list party was in their large suite at the Savoy Hotel, to which only knights, dames, and the very top theater names were invited; the "B" list party was in a large reception room at the Savoy, to which all the lesser lights were invited; and the "Z" list party (always held in a private home), to which all their gay friends were invited. In 1972, the "Z" party was held in my home at 23 Chepstow Place. I couldn't believe the array of knights and superstars that attended. It was my moment of glory which was also shared by my neighbors, rather like a gala Hollywood premier.

I accompanied Hermione Gingold to the 1969 "A" party. I was looking for another apartment, and Arnold's mother, Anna, liked me a lot. She came over, "Darling, I have a woman you should meet who has a lot of apartments available." She took me to meet this tall lady and said to her, "Darling, this is Melvin Liebowitz (she could never remember my name) who is looking for an apartment, and I thought you could help him." She then left me with the Duchess of Westminster, the largest landholder in all of England.

It's Underneath That Counts went on a five-week tryout tour that started on April 27 and never came into London. *Best of Friends* closed the week after, another financial flop. During that period, I had agreed to co-produce *Abelard and Heloise* with John Gale. John handled most of the details. He obtained the services of Diana Rigg, who was a major star in the TV series "The Avengers." It opened on May 19 in Wyndham's Theatre and was an enormous success—my first and only one.

Diana Rigg had to appear nude—albeit briefly—in one scene where she dropped her cloak. Abelard drops to his knees before her, thereby beginning his "fall" from grace and as a priest. Diana demurred at first, saying she didn't mind being nude in front of the hidden theatre audience, but it was absolutely impossible for her to strip in front of her fellow actors in rehearsal or even on stage. Robin Phillips, the young director, overcame her reluctance by offering to take off all his clothes at a rehearsal and suggesting that all the other actors do the same. Thank heavens, his suggestion didn't include the producers. It was the first time that a leading actress appeared in the altogether on stage. The resulting publicity didn't hurt. Diana Rigg was and is wonderful.

I culminated my active winter and spring of 1970 with *I Never Sang For My Father*, which opened at the Duke of York's Theatre on May 26. The play was written by Robert Anderson, who also wrote the tender— and one of the very first—plays on homosexuality, *Tea and Sympathy*. Half the money required for this production was put up by Julie Dougherty, an American woman who adored the theater, and especially the people involved. I told Julie that I wanted to do this play as a "memorial to my father." When the returns came in, she said it would have been far cheaper for her to buy the most elaborate mausoleum possible for him instead of putting her money in the play.

I enticed Raymond Massey to leave his semiretirement in California to star in the play. During one of the rehearsals at the Haymarket Theatre, Massey paused. He was seated in a wheelchair on the stage, and he pointed his cane to the front of the theatre. "Do you know," he said, "that when I was a very young man, I saw Mrs. Patrick Campbell play in Bernard Shaw's *Pygmalion* across the road." He was pointing to Her Majesty's Theatre.

We had a good deal of difficulty finding a theatre; I had to bribe the manager of the Duke of York's Theatre to get in. My cash bribe was larger than that of any of the other producers looking for a theater in that busy season. Although the reviews were excellent, the show just didn't catch on.

For a brief time I had three shows going all at once in London's West End. I made it a habit before the curtain went up to visit each of my shows, saying a few words of encouragement to the casts backstage and cracking a few jokes. I had a hard time getting to all of them and still stopping for my usual salt beef (corned beef) sandwich just across from the old Windmill Theatre.

Toward the end of the run of *I Never Sang for My Father*, I was standing outside the theater attempting to pull the American tourists in through sheer willpower, trying to mesmerize the passers-by, but there were very few takers. A button-adorned busker was doing his turn outside the theater in order to earn some coins from the people passing by. He usually worked the Duke of York's, but this particular night was absolutely dismal, with no customers for either him or me. He took a break from his act, which was playing a harmonica, drum, and cymbals, and I took a break from my mesmerizing. Just for good luck, I gave him a five-pound note, which to him was enormous. He was extremely grateful. "Thanks, Guvner," he said. "Do you have anything to do with this show?" he asked.

I proudly pointed to my name on the poster and said, "Yes, I'm one of the producers." He looked wryly at me and said, "Rum business we're in, isn't it, Guvner?"

After the final curtain, the cast gathered backstage to have some champagne and say good-bye until the next show. It was a sad occasion. Massey came on wearing his shabby, good-luck wool dressing gown. Everyone applauded, and he raised his glass and toasted, "To my last company in my last show, thank you, my dear friends." Everyone said no, certainly not the last, you'll go on forever, etc., etc. Massey was very sad. I said, "Ray, what about *King Lear*?"

"No, not likely," he replied.

"You could do it in some sort of period wheelchair. That might even be more effective."

"No, no," he said, and then, musing, "*King Lear, King Lear*," he left, forever the actor, thinking about his next production. This was the last time he would appear on stage.

In 1970, I bought my house at 23 Chepstow Place. All my furniture had come in from New York. I bought Enoch, a Dandy Dinmont puppy, at Harrod's and hired Antonio and Fina as live-in servants. Pat Buckley came over from Switzerland and spent a few days to teach them how to run my house in the way that she ran hers, finger bowls and all.

In the fall, I started planning for 1971. I was working on two different productions: *Tonight at Eight*, three short musical plays by Noel Coward, and *Spoiled*, a play by Simon Gray.

I needed to raise some extra money rather quickly for the Noel Coward production. One of my constant backers was a charming woman from Texas who was in London, so we went to the Battersea Fun Fair to look about. She went into the tent of a lady numerologist. She came out happy and amazed at what the numerologist told her about her past and predicted about her future. She urged me to go in. I demurred, but she said she'd pay my way, so I obliged. As the numerologist droned on, my mind was at work. I sensed opportunity knocking.

I came out, and she asked me excitedly if I could possibly disclose what the numerologist told me. I replied, "I really couldn't understand it. She said that two letters and a number would bring me great fortune, and she repeated the word *fortune* again and again. I thought she was quite mad."

"What were the letters and the number?" she asked breathlessly.

"*C* and *N*, and the number 3," I replied.

She mused on that; then suddenly her face lit with excitement. "Heavens," she said, "*C* is for Coward and *N* must be for Noel, and 3 must be the three plays of his you want to put on—in the Fortune Theatre. Isn't that amazing?"

Needless to say, she took out her checkbook then and there and made an unusually large investment for her.

During the play's run, I met Noel Coward, who was everything I expected, even in his later years—charming, funny, witty, talented. He was at one of Milton Goldman's parties. Someone introduced him to the American actor Keir Dullea. When they said, "Mr. Coward, this is Keir Dullea, the young American actor." Coward looked up and said, "Keir Dullea, gone tomorrow!"

Tonight At Eight was a charming production and brilliantly reviewed. Everyone kept congratulating me on my second great success (after *Abelard*), but the public didn't come to the tiny Fortune Theatre, and we had to close after a run of several weeks.

Spoiled told the story of a school teacher (Jeremy Kemp), his difficulties with his wife (Anna Massey) and his attraction to one of his students

(Simon Ward). In the final scene both men fall into bed in each other's arms followed by a blackout. Very daring! The show opened at the beautiful Haymarket Theatre, which I was able to get by being especially nice to its owner, Sylvia Stuart Watson, who kept having "palpitations" and kept putting my hand to her heaving breast to help stop them. I felt very elegant having a show at the Haymarket. *Spoiled* didn't do much business and closed in April.

Despite my shows' short runs, I spent the rest of the year enjoying myself. I was now part of the London scene. I was accepted as a member of the Society of West End Managers. I also became a member of Les Ambassadeurs—an elegant restaurant and gambling club run by Robert Mills, who had previously managed El Morocco in New York. I did a lot of gambling at "Les A," as it was called, and also at the White Elephant Club, a film hangout. I would usually be accompanied by Coral Browne, Jill Melford, Anna Rudd, or any one of a host of other beautiful women.

Coral Brown and I would often go, the two of us, to Les A after dinner by taxi. I'd gamble and she'd watch. I'd have five-pound chips. She'd see the five and get nervous. I'd say they were shillings, and she'd feel better. Many a night, when I'd lose, we'd have to walk back the fourteen blocks to her Eaton Place flat with no money left for a taxi.

Once in a while, when I went gambling, my friend Geoffrey would come with me. I met Geoffrey soon after I arrived in London, and he became my guide to the gay underground in that city. He knew just about everyone. He was a charming and a wonderfully "depraved" British upper-class playboy. He was also a good gambling companion.

Many times, after several hours of gambling, Geoffrey and I would take his Rolls and go cruising for young men. We once remarked to each other that we got the same adrenaline rush (followed by despair if we were unsuccessful) cruising as we did gambling. Sex and gambling have a great affinity.

I was settling down in London. I purchased a yellow BMW. But three weeks later, I sold it at a loss. I was terrified of driving in London, especially after an incident in Westbourne Grove. I was driving along quite slowly when a large truck smacked into me and all my fancy chromium fell off.

I was furious and jumped out of the BMW to accost the driver, who was nowhere to be seen, obviously having left the scene of the crime. A small crowd gathered, and the driver finally appeared.

"Why did you swerve and hit my car?" I asked angrily.

"Swerve?" he said, "I was parked by the curb."

I have never driven since.

Geoffrey set me up with a number of working-class boys, the type he fancied. To the best of my knowledge, they were all "straight" or bisexual. He was absolutely furious with me when I gave one of the young men a five-pound note "for a taxi."

"You never pay," he said. "Never!"

Geoffrey was right. During the early seventies—if not always—there were any number of young men from all classes who would play around and experiment with other men. In spite of Geoffrey's endless private reserve, many times I would wander through the West End at night, cruising just for old time's sake. I was always successful.

When I lived on Cadogan Place, I met Jonathan, a British Navy sailor who was just about to be discharged. He lived with his mother and two brothers in Brighton and would come to visit at least once a week on his motorcycle. He liked me a lot, and I suggested that he move into the flat.

That lasted about two weeks. This venerable theatrical manager would rise at 5:00 A.M. each morning to make sandwiches and hot strong tea for his thermos jug, then wave good-bye to this young man, who went motorcycling off to work in the London docks.

It was at the end of 1971 that I met Jeremy, who was a drug addict. He had rosy cheeks, an angelic face, and long hair, the typical English schoolboy. I decided to save him. He moved into Chepstow Place and at first caused something of a scandal among my friends. As he began to recover, his sweet personality overcame everyone's doubts. He was accepted as some sort of "son." Jeremy became a major part of my life at that time. We went on a number of trips, to Morocco when I first met him and then to Venice with two very amusing girls. Jeremy may have been gay, but he was also involved with women, who found him irresistible, especially the older ones. Before we met, he had an extraordinary year in Paris, where he knew everyone in the fast set and was the pet of that crowd. I loved him very much and was able to help start him in the film industry.

By the end of 1971, I was involved in preliminary work on Frank Marcus's *Notes on a Love Affair.* I engaged Robin Phillips to direct. Frank had written the play for Coral Browne, and it was Coral who had put me in touch with him. But Robin decided that it was a project for Irene Worth, who finally got the part. Coral was furious with me for at least four weeks. To make up for everything, I had to buy Coral an expensive dress from Bill Gibbs, the hottest designer in London at the time, who designed Irene's clothes for the play.

The day the play was to open (March 23), I was checking the electric sign just outside the Globe. I felt a touch on my shoulder and turned to see Hugh "Binkie" Beaumont, London's premier producer for many years. He was a great friend of Coral's, who knew everyone.

He said, "Welcome, Marvin, to the Avenue."

That was perhaps my most thrilling moment in the London theater. I had arrived.

The show had a fair run, but we made no money.

By 1973, my finances were dismal. I had lost a good deal of money in 1972, and David Fasken was beginning to get edgy. I was concentrating more on film production and less on the theater. It was more glamorous, the stakes were higher, and when I gambled that gave me more pleasure.

Robin Phillips had directed a production of Strindberg's play *Miss Julie* for the Royal Shakespeare Company. I decided to produce it as a film to be distributed by Tigon Productions. Tigon was a "knockers and knickers" film producer and distributor. They dealt in soft-core porn, but they were trying to better their image. What better than Strindberg!

Tigon was managed by an East End Jew, Tony Tensor. He had no time for nonsense. Robin was very temperamental. I had to arrange the first meeting between Robin and Tony, and I was worried. I explained the personality of each to the other—Robin, poetic and sensitive; Tony, rough and tough. Because I wanted this picture to go on, I asked them to try to be considerate of each other's feelings.

The meeting was held in Tony's office on Wardour Street (the street with all the film companies and the only street in London—so the saying goes—that's shady on both sides). Tony was on his best behavior. Robin was a bit nervous and arrogant.

"How do you see the titles, Robbie?" said Tony, making Robin wince at his use of the diminutive. "*You* can do anything you want in the picture. But the distributor has control of the titles."

"Well, I see a bird cage and a sweet canary twittering, twittering, flinging itself against the bars of the cage twittering, twittering," said Robin dreamily. "Twittering."

"That won't do, Robbie," said Tony. "What I see are the soles of Miss Julie's feet as the titles start rolling. I see, 'Tony Tensor presents,' and as the titles continue, the soles part wider and wider until the camera zooms in on Miss Julie's cunt, and that's how it starts."

Robin, needless to say, had the vapors and had to be helped staggering out of the room. The movie was done cheaply and quickly and opened early in 1973 to no business whatsoever.

Peter Thompson, who worked for Tigon, urged me to do another picture quickly. I produced the film version of the very successful West End farce *Not Now, Darling*, and that marked the beginning of the end of my film career. David walked out on me, and I was stuck with the entire guarantee. I had to put up the money. To do so, I sold 23 Chepstow Place, which I loved, and moved to the still luxurious 82 Addison Road in Holland Park. When I later returned to New York, my lawyer gave me the definition of a guarantor: "a shmuck with a fountain pen."

Now totally on my own, I produced four more films and tried producing a few more plays, but without financial success. My favorite was *Zorba*, written by my old friend, Fred Ebb, together with John Kander. It opened at the Greenwich Theatre on November 27, 1973. While the New York production had about forty people in the cast and a full Broadway orchestra, Robin pulled it back to seventeen people with a four-piece bazuki band. It starred Alfred Marks and my friends Miriam Karlin and Angela Richards. It was absolutely superb. My date at the opening night was Lauren Bacall, who had appeared with Angela in *Applause*.

When the *Zorba* production closed just before Christmas, I had reached absolute bottom. I was deeply depressed and considered myself a total failure. During the last act of the last performance, I walked toward the river just behind the theater and wondered if I should throw myself in. I resisted only because it was so cold.

I went back to Addison Road and spent the next week going deeper and deeper into despair. What had I accomplished over the last five years? Who was I kidding? I had no money and no prospects. Everything I touched seemed to go sour. Whenever I tried something new, I failed: the army, the communists, the conservatives, show biz, everything; nothing worked.

My friends were worried. They kept calling until I turned the telephone off. All I had was my faithful dog Enoch. Each day, the mail brought more bills. It was absolutely overwhelming. Christmas was coming, and that added to the sadness and loneliness. The obvious answer, of course, was to kill myself.

Over the years, I had amassed a collection of sleeping pills. The perfect answer! The only problem was Enoch. If I died, who would look after him until they found me? I could put him out in the back garden, of course, which was just about as big as a park. But he would freeze. What to do?

I came across the American Express card. I decided to wait until after New Year's. Somehow, I got through Christmas. We all went over to the talented director Vivian Matalon's house and ate the goose he roasted. For the moment I was beginning to enjoy my public depression and everyone's attention.

On December 26 I made a decision. I would let American Express pay for my last days on earth. I called up Anna Rudd, who was the most beautiful girl in London, if not the world. "Let's go to Gstaad over New Year's." Anna had a friend there and knew a lot of people. A few days after Christmas we met with a few friends on King's Road and walked down the street looking at the sales. I was feeling very happy. It was a wonderful day. We went to a leather store, and I bought all of us full-length leather coats, all on American Express. We looked rather like Nazi storm troopers. Very expensive, but so what. Anna, Barry Quin (one of the cast of *Zorba*), his girlfriend Jane, and I flew to Geneva. I arranged a private plane from Geneva to Gstaad, and we had three rooms at the Palace Hotel: one for Barry and Jane, one for Anna, and one for me and whoever else might come along.

We had New Year's supper in a private room at the Olden, with Sir James Goldsmith as the host. There were about thirty of us in his party.

At one end of the table the guests were snorting cocaine between the courses. There were all sorts of celebs and friends of Sir Jimmy. At midnight, Jimmy Goldsmith made the most amazing toast I ever heard: "Here's to war in '74"— and he meant it!

I went back to London feeling a lot better, and it was only after I received the American Express bill that I felt like killing myself again.

1974 was the final year in London. I co-produced *Waltz of the Toreadors* with Eddie Kulikundis, which opened at my favorite Haymarket Theatre on February 14. Coral Browne starred with Trevor Howard, who, when he wasn't drunk, was terrific. Coral was wonderful in the part.

I was on a cruise around Africa with Bill and Pat Buckley when I received a telephone call on the boat from Eddie Kulikundis, who said we should close the show because it was losing too much money. I knew that one of my big American backers was coming to London in two weeks, so I said I would cover the cost of keeping the show open until he had a chance to see it. That proved to be a very expensive seat I bought him.

That year, I also took my final fling at pictures and produced a spin-off of a successful television series starring Patrick Cargill, Donald Sinden, and Beryl Reid, who played in the film, *The Killing of Sister George*, with Coral Browne. Although that, and *Not Now, Darling* were financial successes, the money was all tied up in lawsuits by Fasken and the collapse of the Laurie Marsh distributing empire.

By the summer of 1974, I was flat broke. I began to divest myself of just about everything I owned to help pay some of my debts. First the paintings, then the silver, then my collection of carved medieval religious figures, then the few bits of antique furniture—everything was sold. Geoffrey took charge, working with Sotheby's and Christie's. I was able to pay off a fair amount of debt through this. I also sold the lease to my Addison Road apartment. Just before I left London, I sat in an empty room alone with Enoch, my beloved dog. I gave him to Peter Daly, one of the dancers from *Zorba*, and over the next seven years, they had a happy life together.

So, in July of 1974, Enoch-less and penniless, I departed London for New York.

Chapter 15

Comeback

I RETURNED totally defeated. My thoughts of suicide of the previous December had dissipated, but I was still in a deep depression.

I sublet a furnished apartment for the summer of 1974 in a narrow building on Eighty-sixth Street just east of Fifth Avenue. I hated it. The furniture was ghastly. There was no air-conditioning. I was absolutely broke, except for some money my sister lent me, and I was miserable. I didn't have any idea what I would do. I was a failure, without a shred of self-esteem, and I was getting ready to mark my fifty-first birthday.

Desperate for money—and for something to do other than stare at the walls of the terrible apartment—I went to Bloomingdale's to try for a job. To my amazement, they hired me to sell socks, handkerchiefs, and underwear in the men's department. Well, I thought, at least it's a good place for cruising or, as I was quite a bit older and had no money, to observe all the handsome young men. It seemed a good way to make the days go by.

I wasn't there for more than five days when I was discovered by a friend of Pat Buckley's and a nodding acquaintance of mine. "Darling, how nice to see you. What are you doing here? I thought you were in London." "I work here," I said. "Oh my God, you can't be serious." "Oh yes I am."

Pat invited me out to Stamford that weekend. When I said that I was working Saturday and couldn't come, she said, "Quit." And I did.

That weekend was the first of just about every weekend over the next five years I spent with Pat and Bill.

The moment word got around about my situation, friends rushed to help in whatever way they could. I was overwhelmed and—at first—very humble and grateful. I quickly lost my humility but remained grateful then and forevermore.

Hermione Gingold used her influence to get me an apartment at 350 East 55th, the sister apartment building to 405 East 54th ("Faggots' Fortress" or "Four Out of Five" East 54th) where I had lived during the 1950s. Fifty-fifth Street was a little less show-biz, but it got me out of the furnished place. I had my own furniture—whatever I couldn't sell— shipped back from London.

In September, Bill Rusher got Gene Loh (my old friend and fellow propagandist who was head of the China News Service) to arrange for me to be hired by the Friends of Free China, a "soft-sell" cultural exchange operation. I started working there just after Labor Day of 1974 and started getting some of my old vitality back. I began to plunge into work as in the old days.

I was put on the payroll of the Friends of Free China at $250 a week, which gave me some walking around money. I was itching to get back into business again. In October—four months after I returned—I incorporated a new firm, Marvin Liebman, Inc., with its first headquarters at the Friends of Free China offices. My old boss, friend, and mentor Harold Oram agreed to help. He provided me with office equipment, furniture, and money for the installation of telephones and two months' rent at offices at 95 Madison Avenue, the building just next to my previous operation. Harold got 25 percent of the stock of the new company (which eventually proved quite worthless). We worked together on a number of accounts. He had come through for me when I really needed help.

The Friends of Free China faded away, and I went on to other things. The most catastrophic to me was my work for Chile. In October 1974, when my funds were at their very lowest, Bill Buckley received a call from the Chilean ambassador to Washington. This was soon after the Marxist Allende regime in Chile was overthrown by the anticommunist and free-market advocate, General Augusto Pinochet. The right-wing coup caused enormous consternation in United States liberal circles. Allende was the darling of the liberals, a gentrified Castro. They abhorred the new Pinochet regime and were joined by much of the media. Nena Ossa, a Chilean friend of Bill's—who became an intimate and beloved friend of mine—suggested that the embassy get in touch with Buckley, who knew everyone and everything, for the name of a public relations firm that might help them out. Bill saw this as an excellent chance to help out his old friend.

He recommended me even though I didn't yet have a "firm," a staff, or anything else. On October 28, I had lunch with some Chileans, including Nena Ossa and Mario Arnello (a lawyer who later became Chilean ambassador to the United Nations) to discuss in general how Americans perceived Chile and its new government. Bill arranged the luncheon for only one reason: it was his way of helping me out. He would put me in touch with the Chileans, and then he would withdraw.

The very next day, I submitted a proposal to Arnello. I suggested organizing the American Chilean Council (ACC), which would be funded by American firms doing business in Chile so that the council would be completely independent of the Chilean government.

In March I wrote to a group of personal friends, asking them to help me out by joining the ACC. I did my best to explain to them that the ACC would be receiving money from the Chilean Council of North America (CCNA), which Nena Ossa had set up in Santiago to support our effort. The CCNA would be funded by Chilean and American firms, rather than the Chilean government, and the money would be routed to us. We would also raise money from American anticommunists. This was all perfectly legal and aboveboard—or so I thought.

I registered with the Foreign Agent Registry Unit of the Justice Department as an agent of the CCNA, which I felt legally obligated to do. (If you represent any foreign company, government, or group, you have to register.) To the best of my *public* knowledge, the CCNA was privately supported and had nothing whatsoever to do with the government of Chile. Of course, I was pretty sure that the Chilean government gave the effort its full moral support.

My first major task was to counter the myth of Allende with the facts. The American media made him out to be a democratic socialist who would lead Chile back to prosperity following the pattern of the workers' paradise in Cuba. In truth, Allende was a close collaborator of Fidel

Castro and, if not an agent, certainly a willing pawn in the international communist apparatus aimed at taking over all of Latin America. Left-wingers of every stripe from every nation flocked to Chile. It was the Nicaragua of the 1970s.

The ACC embarked on a major program of propaganda: publications, speeches, full-page advertisements, a monthly newsletter, the usual. I hired a number of my old friends and colleagues in Washington to help. Although we raised some money through direct mail from private Americans, this didn't begin to cover our expenses. It was difficult getting money from the CCNA, but we got it sooner or later, thanks to our liaison Mario Arnello.

The assassination of Chile's former ambassador to the United States, Orlando Letelier, caused a great furor. The word was that he was assassinated at the direct order of Manuel Contreras, who was head of the Chilean secret police.

I hired Robert Shortley, the brother-in-law of Terry Dolan (who was then making a big name for himself as head of the National Conservative Political Action Committee—NCPAC), to investigate the matter. He could find nothing to suggest that Letelier had been assassinated by other leftists or by Castro or by anyone other than on orders from Chile. I hoped that this story would die. It didn't.

I received a telephone call early in 1977 asking me to meet "an important Chilean." I went and met Contreras himself, who was illegally visiting the United States. He was wanted by the Justice Department for complicity in the murder of Letelier. Contreras was charming and spoke in a low voice as if the place were bugged. He asked how the ACC was going and, although terrified to be talking to a man who shouldn't be there at all, I was my usual polite self and answered his questions as best I could, desperate to get out of the room. I mentioned the Letelier affair and the difficulties it was giving us. He said, almost contemptuously, "Letelier doesn't matter and never mattered. It will all blow over." At that moment, I realized that Contreras probably did have a lot to do with the assassination.

I made several visits to Chile during this period. Mario Arnello was head of Lan Chile, the Chilean national airline, and he was able to facilitate a number of trips, not only for me but for various American and

British journalists. My mother's brother and his family lived in Santiago, and I enjoyed visiting with them. One of the trips I made was with Bill and Pat Buckley, an extension of a South American cruise (which we paid for ourselves). Nena Ossa had arranged an interview for Bill with President Pinochet.

The president was at his summer home in Viña del Mar, the beach resort just outside Valparaíso. Pat and I whiled away the afternoon at the casino and then returned to a friend's apartment to wait for Bill. When he returned, he looked absolutely exhausted. It was a lengthy interview of two hours. He demanded an aspirin, sank into his chair, and muttered, "After two hours with Pinochet, I know that there is no danger of a cult of personality in Chile."

Things went along reasonably well, the only problem being getting funds from the CCNA on time to pay the bills. Then the U.S. government started turning up the heat on us. This was during the Carter years, and if the Democrats could embarrass conservatives, they did. Here was a perfect opportunity. In 1979, the Justice Department demanded to see all the books and records of the ACC. Throughout my career, I have never been known for discretion, and never really threw away anything. The Justice Department's premise was that I—and the ACC—should be registered as an agent of the Chilean government and not the CCNA.

Of course, I objected to this. I knew that if we were registered as an agent of the Chilean government, whatever effect we had would be lost. It was imperative that we have no official connections with any government. Also, I was personally reluctant to register as an agent of a foreign government. I had never done so before, even though many of my activities were exactly that.

I was distressed and anxious. I had involved many of my closest friends, especially Bill Buckley, and I didn't want to cause them any grief. Bill's involvement at the very beginning was just to do me a favor. I didn't want him to suffer because of it. I didn't know what to do.

Once again, the old feeling of defeat swept over me—rather like London in 1974. I couldn't use my charm or humor or jokes or kidding around. This was real.

I was called to make a deposition in Washington, and Steve Umin, a partner in the law firm of Williams and Connolly, represented me there.

There was great consternation among all those who had worked with me and for me, and among those who had accepted trips to Chile. I went to the Justice Department with Steve to make a deposition. My interrogator was a bright young black female attorney.

Steve told me not to answer any questions. I still have the little slip of paper he gave me, which has printed on it, "All That Jazz!" with music lines over it. He had torn it out of some publication. On it is written, "Upon the advice of counsel, I respectfully decline to answer upon the grounds of Fifth Amendment privilege."

The Justice Department attorney asked me a number of questions, and I really got tired of repeating the disclaimer. Steve asked, and she agreed that all I had to say after that was, "Decline," and the entire response would be put into the record.

Steve was a sharp attorney who embarrassed me by yelling at my persecutor to throw her off balance. I really felt bad for her. "How dare you waste the taxpayer's money on such frivolous stuff," he shouted. "Mr. Liebman is a busy man, and I don't know what he is doing here or what you people are trying to do."

The Justice Department ordered me to sign a public "consent agreement" saying that I neither affirmed nor denied that I was an agent of the Chilean government. I had to pay for its publication in the *New York Times* and *The Washington Post*. This implied that I was guilty without stating it. I was once again publicly humiliated, embarrassed and apologetic to all the friends whom I had involved. That experience was yet another rung down the ladder and helped make up my mind to get out of New York and try something else—even though I was getting pretty old to start another life.

Early in 1975, I was asked to organize the Friends of Jim Buckley. Jim was up for election the next year, and I wanted to set up a base of operations for him. I approached Leon J. Weil, who had been treasurer of Jim Buckley's successful 1970 campaign and suggested he start building a campaign operation as early as possible. I knew that Jim would face a tough battle in 1976 no matter who the Democratic nominee was. The Friends of Jim Buckley would build a base to raise money for next year's election. Lee, as a matter of charity (of which he is a master practitioner) and in order to give me an "account," agreed. So I started working on Jim Buckley's campaign for re-election twelve months before it began.

Bill Buckley caused a lot of consternation during the campaign when he endorsed the liberal Democrat Allard Lowenstein, who was running against incumbent Representative John Wydler in Long Island, but Bill and Al Lowenstein were great friends despite their ideological differences.

Lowenstein had a reputation in some quarters as gay, and he was later murdered in his office by a man who claimed to be his lover. I liked Al, who was funny and bright, but we never discussed sex. The only indication I had—besides the gossip and rumors—were the very attractive young men who constantly surrounded him as adoring supplicants. But then, it was no different with me, except Al had more. Jim's campaign staff considered Bill's endorsement of Lowenstein a major setback to Jim's faltering campaign. I disagreed. Nothing could save the campaign by then.

The part of the campaign that I remember best was election night. We were in a private suite in the Waldorf that was reserved for Jim, his family, and top campaign workers. It was a sad occasion. The election was lost. What does one say after so much effort ending up with nothing? Some of the women were teary. Jim's sister Carol, who was in charge that night, was smiling bravely, her dimples showing, trying to act as if nothing awful had really happened. She was chatting with someone, trying to be her usual vivacious self. Standing next to a table on which rested some gelatinous dip and rather limp vegetables, she leaned over for balance and put her hand, up to the wrist, into the bowl of dip. That almost did it for Carol. She almost lost her composure, but recovered— the dimples still valiantly flashing.

I saw Jim Buckley, the defeated candidate, sitting on the couch, alone for a moment. I went over and said, "Well, Jim, that's politics," or something stupid like that. He looked up at me and said, "Marvin, you know it has always been difficult for me to communicate with my children." I nodded. "I love our country, and I just wanted to let my children know that and how it works and what it's all about. I thought that being in politics might show them what I could never really say to them. I hope it has."

I was deeply touched. I remembered Governor Edison, who would have liked what Jim said. I said, "I am sure it has, Jimmy; I am sure it has."

In 1980, Jim Buckley was prevailed on to run for senator again, this time from Connecticut against Congressman Christopher Dodd, the son of my old friend Senator Thomas Dodd. I was retained to organize a national committee for Jim. He lost, and this was his final campaign for elected office.

Things started picking up for me by the end of 1975. Word of my availability was getting around, and there were many calls for my services. I was still operating in the same way as I had promised Governor Edison—providing a resource for anticommunist and conservative public interest groups.

Although I had lost interest in politics for the most part, I still required money to live and to pay the bills. So I took just about everything that came along. One of the more interesting jobs was something called the Committee of Single Taxpayers—CO$T. Robert Keith Gray, a charming Washington insider and one of the top executives at Hill and Knowlton public relations company, called on me for help. He told me of a small group he had organized in 1971 to end tax inequities for single people. There were two bills in the congressional hopper that year, and Gray wanted to organize some public support for them.

I was intrigued by the possibilities, and agreed to organize a National Committee of Sponsors. CO$T's purpose was "to end the tax inequity" and "to explore and fight other discrimination against single people, such as home buying and credit rating (especially leveled against single women). Such action is part of our national heritage, started some 200 years ago, when individuals banded together to fight for fair and equal treatment for all regardless of race, color, creed or marital status." I wanted to add "sexual orientation," but that might have required my coming out publicly, and I wasn't nearly ready for that yet.

This account provided me with an interesting challenge. It was directed at affluent single persons, but it was also aimed at mobilizing individuals outside the establishment of "couples"—gays, lesbians, and bachelor men and women included. This would be fun. I enlisted several of my friends, and I organized a committee second to none with emphasis on show biz. The honorary chairmen were Eugene J. McCarthy, former senator and presidential candidate, and George Murphy, Hollywood star and former senator.

I was membership Director. Among our sponsors (many of whom were my personal friends) were Larry Kramer, Edward Albee, Lauren Bacall, Lotte Lenya, Kaye Ballard, Joan Bennett, Sylvia Miles, Candice Bergen, Dyan Cannon, Craig Claiborne, Dotson Rader, Fred Ebb, Rex Reed, Chita Rivera, Jerome Robbins, Ned Rorem, William A. Rusher, Katharine Graham, Cybill Shepherd, Bobby Short, Priscilla Buckley, Frank Sinatra, Liz Smith, June Havoc, Stephen Sondheim, Goldie Hawn, Gloria Steinem, Loretta Swit, Christopher Isherwood, Diana Vreeland, Gene Kelly, and James Kirkwood. It was one of the best committees I ever organized. I thought what a terrific and glamorous party it would be if all these people got together!

By 1979, things were going rather well. I had forgotten (or at least I thought I had) my despair at my London failure. I imagined that that was behind me. There was something else that I wanted out of life, something that I didn't have. Though my everyday life, professional and personal, was going along fine, there was something lacking. Whenever I wanted to love, I could always find somebody to love. I gave my affections freely and openly. There was always a special young man in my life.

I was 55, and I wasn't thinking so much of physical love any longer. That was becoming increasingly unimportant, and it rarely took place, always as an experiment in nostalgia. But there was always emotional love. I was very good at that. I still had crushes. But I now wanted to be loved, to find out how that felt. How could I do that? I felt these questions were spiritual, and I found myself looking inward for the answers.

In my search, I started going across Fifty-fifth Street to a Catholic church, Saint John the Evangelist. I went to several other churches in New York, Episcopalian and other Protestant denominations. I went twice to a Hassidic Jewish service in Brooklyn, and even went quietly to a few services at the Bay Ridge Jewish Center where I was bar mitzvahed. But in the synagogue, I felt no real connection. It was as if I were looking at an interesting ethnic curiosity. I tried, but nothing happened.

I didn't speak to anybody about this search of mine. Someone—I forgot who—gave me a copy of Roland Knox's translation of *The New Testament*. I read it first by skimming through the pages. Then I read it a second time. I found this familiar ground, because Christianity permeates American society. Although I was brought up a Jew, and I loved every bit of my Jewishness and all the Jewish traditions, I knew as much about Christianity as any other American child. At PS 185 we sang Catholic hymns in assembly and were told the stories of Christmas and Easter. Although at home we didn't have a Christmas tree, we had Christmas stockings and the Easter bunny and eggs.

As a child I had attended Hebrew school and Sunday school, and my parents celebrated all the major holidays: Passover, Yom Kippur, Rosh Hashanah, Purim, Hanukkah. I liked going to temple on Shavuot and going to the sukkah, the rough edifice erected of twigs and straw to celebrate the harvest. As a Jewish boy in Brooklyn in those years, I had the best of both worlds. So, I was no stranger to Christianity but no particular admirer of any particular religion, including Judaism.

When I read the Roland Knox Bible translation for the third time, I wanted to feel Jesus Christ's love in the most desperate way. After several weeks of soul searching, I again went across the street to Saint John's to attend the 10:30 Sunday mass. I was on my knees and trying as hard as I could to commune with God. Then—it was almost a physical experience —I felt an overwhelming sense of being loved, an absolutely new and unique feeling for me. For the first time in my life, I felt that I was loved, and I was ready to accept it. I was exhilarated by the feeling. I was receiving the love of Jesus Christ. I was embarrassed by my own feelings and emotions.

The day after the service, I went to the office of the church and undertook to maintain the small shrine of Saint Francis in the corner. I made an arrangement with the plant store next door to keep the shrine filled with flowering and green plants for the next six months. This was my way of saying thanks. This, for the time being, would be the cathedral that I would ultimately build for the greater glory of total love.

A week later, I telephoned my friend Dan Mahoney. I don't know why, but I was awfully nervous about the whole business. I had reread the Gospels, and I was absolutely convinced. But I didn't want to tell Bill Buckley until I was sure. It was almost like preparing myself to "come out." I spoke to Dan confidentially about it, and he was thrilled.

Later that day, I received a telephone call from Monsignor Eugene Clark, an acquaintance then, a friend now, who could always be counted on to deliver the invocation or the benediction at any public dinner we had. "Hi, Marvin," he said. "Dan Mahoney told me that you might want to talk to me." I told him that I did, that I was thinking about joining the church. "Well," he said, "let's get together." I thought that he would invite me to some deep crypt at Saint Patrick's Cathedral where he worked. "What are you doing tomorrow afternoon?" said Gene. "About 5:30." "Nothing," I said. "Well," he said, "Let's meet. How about the Union League Club?"

Could it be as easy as that? I met with Gene the next day, and for the next several weeks we met a number of times. I had no problem whatsoever with any of the doctrines of the church, at least those that were outlined in the Gospels: the Virgin Birth, Mary, Joseph, the Resurrection, all of it. I accepted it without a question or doubt. But Gene gave me things to read that I hated. "Monsignor," I said, "I don't need to read these. I already believe, I really do." "I am sure you do with your heart," he said, "but unless you understand with your head and your brain, it won't be complete." Of course, he was right.

Unfortunately (or fortunately for my conversion) I never learned all the dogmas other than faith. Certainly, I was not really aware of the church's deep aversion to the practice of homosexuality. If I had realized it then, I might have had some second thoughts. Clark gave me more books to read on theology. I still clutched my dog-eared Knox. I finally told Bill about my conversion while I was on a cruise ship with him and Pat, and he was as pleased, thrilled, and happy as I have ever seen him.

I never discussed my homosexuality with him because I truly believed it wasn't relevant. His Lord—and mine—accepted me as I was, and I didn't think it necessary to "confess" or even discuss it. I had come out to God and was prepared to make a commitment to Him as I was and not as anyone wanted me to be. I was a naked child before Him, a gay child, and I knew He would embrace me.

I had a final meeting with Monsignor Clark, and he said I was ready and that he would baptize me in Saint Patrick's on Easter Saturday about a week later. "Should I tell my sister?" I asked him. I wanted to. He said,

"I know it will make her unhappy, and she will undoubtedly try to talk you out of it. I know that you can't be talked out of it, but why give her any grief? Tell her afterward."

The moment he left, and despite his advice, I telephoned my sister. "Darling," I said, "I have something to tell you. I have decided to become a Catholic." "A what?" she said. "A Catholic." She had been through enough with me, and she reacted exactly as I hoped she would, like an adult, modern sophisticated woman. "Well, dear, if that makes you happy, what can I say? Whatever is good for you is good for me."

"I'm being baptized on Saturday. Will you come?" "No, darling, I am happy for you but it would not make me feel so good." OK, I thought, that's fine. This was about 7:00 P.M. At 11:00 P.M., the telephone rang, and it was my sister. She was sobbing uncontrollably. "How can you do this? How can you betray Mom and Dad and all the millions of Jews who were killed? Don't you know what Catholics have done? How can you do this?"

Eleanor had reacted probably just as she should have. She reached back into the depths of her heart and became our mother and our grandmother and all those who came before. Jews were Jews, and any theological detour was akin to death. My sister was not ready to mourn me, but she was close to it. That telephone call was upsetting but not sufficiently so to change my course.

On the day I was to be baptized, Pat had arranged a reception for me at Seventy-third Street immediately after the ceremony. Their son, Christopher, had taken me to lunch at the Sign of the Dove. I was a nervous wreck. The baptistery at Saint Patrick's is quite small. All of Pat's servants and most of my New York Catholic friends—and just a few non-Catholics—were there. The Easter Saturday mass was just letting out, and the place was jammed. I was there, as white as a sheet, and Bill and his sister Priscilla stood up for me.

Pat, tall and resplendent in her fur, waited outside the baptistery. A woman came up to her and plucked at her sleeve. "Oh, madam," she said, "they baptize such beautiful babies here at Saint Patrick's." Pat looked down at her with her special look and said, "Madam, wait 'til you get a load of this one."

From the reception, I went up to Stamford. Bill wanted to take me to the prettiest service he could for Easter Sunday and my first communion. His favorite church had no seats available, and we went back to old Saint Mary's where they had a folk Easter service, and my first communion— to Bill's horror—was taken with a guitar strumming in the background.

I had to choose a baptismal name, and I picked Mary Magdalene, who is my absolute favorite. She was the only one of all those around Jesus who never denied Him, who accepted Him totally. "Marvin Mary Magdalene Liebman." It had a nice ring to it. But they wouldn't allow me to be called Mary. Nuns can take men's names; why couldn't a man be called Mary? That was the very first church restriction that I encountered. So I chose the name Joseph, who, like me, was a Jew who just followed whatever orders he was given, a simple and good man whom I admired greatly.

Several weeks after my baptism, Carol Buckley's oldest daughter, Anne, was about to be confirmed with her class at New York's Sacred Heart School for Girls. She called and said, "Now that you are, would you . . . could you, be my confirmation sponsor, along with Aunt Priscilla?" I was flattered and accepted immediately. In order to be confirmed, you needed a bishop, and I thought I could kill two birds with one stone—be a sponsor and receive confirmation myself. I telephoned the headmistress of the school and asked whether this was possible. She said it was, and she would see to it that the bishop was informed.

I marched down the aisle with all the pretty little girls in their white dresses and approached the bishop with Anne and Priscilla. He tenderly slapped Anne on the cheek, which was part of the ritual, said whatever words he said, and then started to turn to the next young girl.

"Bishop, sir, Your Eminence, didn't anyone tell you? I would like to be confirmed too," I said. The good man was alarmed at first, thinking that I was some sort of lunatic, but he smiled, slapped me on the face—a little harder than I thought necessary—and I was confirmed a Catholic.

The Tuesday afternoon after my baptism, Bill was being installed into the Knights of Malta at a private ceremony conducted by Cardinal Cook. Bill asked me to come, and, a Catholic for only three days, I had lunch with the cardinal in his dining room just behind Saint Patrick's Cathedral. As I remember, we had canned chicken noodle soup.

And so, I found love at last, the only kind that I was able to accept—the love of God which is unconditional and universal, even for an old gay man who was born a Jew.

Soon after I became a Catholic my faith was seriously tested. I was spending the weekend as usual at Bill and Pat's in Wallack's Point. During the night, I awoke. My right foot was cold, and I felt a "pins and needles" sensation. I recalled that when I went to the doctor for a general exam, he would always ask, "Do you feel pins and needles in your foot or your hands?" So I was a bit worried, and I tried to go back to sleep. But the cold and the tingling feeling persisted.

The next day I went to see one of the leading vascular doctors in New York. He examined me and immediately sent me by taxi to the emergency ward of New York Hospital, where I was admitted to the intensive care unit and hooked up to various machines and monitors.

They discovered that I had a clot in one of the arteries in my foot; the rest of my vascular system was a mess. I was in immediate jeopardy of a heart attack or, even worse for me to contemplate, having my foot amputated because of the beginnings of gangrene. They scheduled an angiogram for the next morning.

It was late in the afternoon by then, and I was told that there was no room for my clothes in the ICU, could I have them picked up? So I began planning the logistics, as is my wont. I didn't want to frighten anyone, but I had to take care of business. So I had the nurse call Frances Bronson, my good friend and Bill Buckley's invaluable aide. The nurse told her to please come and bring a shopping bag or suitcase and not to say anything to anyone.

Poor Frances came within the hour clutching an empty bag, looking shocked as she walked into the room and saw me hooked up in the narrow bed in a room filled with sick and terminal patients. She tried to keep her usual bright vivacious manner, but all she could say as I remember was, "Oh dear, Oh dear."

"Take my clothes to *National Review*," I told her, "and send them to my apartment by messenger in the morning. Delia (my housekeeper for many years before and after England) will be there. Then, dear, telephone my office and tell them where I am but not to worry. Don't tell my sister or even Bill. Have the office call Delia and then my sister, I'll be in touch with them directly tomorrow if they will let me use a phone" and, I thought silently, if I'm still around.

Frances, the paragon of efficiency that she is, followed instructions to the letter, but they didn't quite work as planned.

My office telephoned Delia the next morning. She was already worried that my bed had not been slept in. As they were talking, the doorbell rang. Delia opened the door to a messenger with a shopping bag full of my clothes, the sight of which caused her to become weak at her old knees. She returned to the phone and shrieked, "Mr. Liebman's in the morgue, he's in the morgue! They sent his clothes home. The poor man's in the morgue!" At which point she actually did pass out and was revived by the poor messenger boy.

My office, hearing her shrieks, went all to pieces, "My God, he's dead, he's dead." The phones started ringing. Liebman had died.

All the while, I was in the intensive care unit feeling a lot better, and bitching about the inedible food and the service, waiting for my angiogram rather anxiously.

My good doctor ordered me to stop smoking. I tried to bargain with him by saying, "Well I'll have only five today and maybe three tomorrow." He said, no, I must stop that moment and, if I found myself over the next year or so (if I lived) picking up a cigarette and smoking it, I should telephone him no matter what time or where he was. He would consider that a medical emergency. He told me a year or so afterward that it would not have been a medical emergency, but by then it had worked! I stopped smoking that moment—cold turkey—and have not had a cigarette since.

I was put in a lavish suite at the hospital that had recently been used by the Shah of Iran. I spent the next few days waiting to see if my foot could be saved. It started hurting terribly, and I was in great pain for the next four months, almost incapacitated. But I still had my foot.

I spent my fifty-seventh birthday in the hospital. The next day, I received a note from Bill Buckley. We had never talked about our "feelings" with each other, and this note was a rare and welcome exception. "Dear *Vieux*," he wrote,

> These things are hard to say, but I feel the need to record this, that the death of no member of my family would bereave me more than the loss of you, whom I have the honor to consider a member of the family.

Your kindness, your deep spiritual resources, your warmheartedness, your loving care for others' concerns have always moved me, but even if your virtues were all vices, I'd love you none the less, so bear this in mind, since you no longer have the alternative of putting it in your pipe and smoking it.

A priest came to visit me in the intensive care unit and asked whether I would like to have "the sacrament of the sick." I'd never heard of that one before, but a sacrament is a sacrament. I said, "Yes, Father, please," and he gave me what used to be called Extreme Unction.

As I lay there in the ICU, I thought of real and final death for the first time in my life—not suicide or any of that, but real, the end. To my surprise, I had no strong emotion whatsoever, neither fear nor expectation, but I had a feeling of deep peace, the feeling that whatever will come will come. It was in God's hands, and I was totally confident that it would all end up OK. Being gay, being old, or anything like that was no longer relevant. That was all of this world. Everything about it—the fears, the joys, the secrecy—was of no consequence. I felt incredibly peaceful— except for the pain. The health crisis passed, and I was back to normal in a few months.

One Sunday morning shortly afterward, I went to mass at Saint John's and heard Father Bruce Ritter deliver the sermon. I was deeply moved. He spoke of the Christian obligation to love and help all people. He spoke of the castoffs, the disenfranchised, the young people in the streets of our cities. These were children who had run away from home or had been thrown away, left at gas stations and grocery stores with their parents speeding off to God-knows-where, forced to fend for themselves in any way they could.

It was these children that Bruce Ritter was trying to help, and he was asking for contributions. He was running something called Under 21, which was on Eighth Avenue and Forty-fifth Street, a storefront where the young hustlers of the streets could come in, take a shower, have a cup of coffee, and hide if they had to from their pimps. It was a refuge with no questions asked. I went up to him afterward and asked whether I could help. He told me to visit him in the Under 21 building.

There was an armed guard stationed near the door to protect the kids inside from intruders. He directed me up a rickety flight of stairs to where Bruce Ritter had his sparsely furnished office/living quarters. Ritter, who was fast becoming my hero of the moment, was in the room. I shuffled around, and Ritter said, "Excuse me, Marvin, but would you step off my bed." I looked, and sure enough, I was standing on a blanket. He slept on the floor. Ritter was deeply religious and ascetic.

Ritter had hit a nerve when I heard what he was trying to do. For too many years, I had cruised the streets of Times Square searching, looking. Although I treated my young men well, I had a bad image of myself for doing this, for being gay at all. I thought I might atone for my guilt by serving these young boys and girls. They were like all the beautiful children I had known and loved in my life, but they had dropped to the absolute bottom. If I could help them in any way, I wanted to. What I really wanted to do was to serve food or scrub floors.

I told Ritter, and he said, "We have plenty of people to serve food, and we have plenty of people to scrub floors. What we need is money, and, if you can help us get it, that's what you should be doing. That's your contribution."

A couple of days later, I spent about three hours with Ritter. He told me how he started. He was a college teacher and lectured about the poor and the underprivileged. One of his students berated him and asked what he knew about being poor. Ritter realized that all he knew came from books and newspapers. He decided to find out and went to New York's East Village, which then was the center of the city's drug culture.

Ritter rented a small cold-water flat and somehow got several street children to seek haven there. The word got around that there was a weird Catholic priest who would take care of you if you were really down and out. So the kids started flocking to the apartment, and this expanded to Under 21. He set this up simply to provide a comfort station for the hundreds of children who came to New York and went to the streets because they had no other place to go.

Ritter wanted to give them some sort of haven and, if they wanted, whatever counseling and help he and his community could provide. His hero was Mother Teresa of Calcutta, who also sought to love and serve the very lowest of the low, the helpless and the useless. I absorbed all that he told me and became even more eager to help him.

My first job was to try to express what Ritter was doing in a fund-raising letter. I drafted one that started out:

3 A.M.

My dear friend:

I have just returned from the streets. I am weary and very sad. I wanted to write to you before I close my eyes for a few hours of sleep.

I sit here at my window, looking over 8th Avenue in New York City —they call it the Minnesota Strip—and I see children from all over the country still on the streets, trying to sell themselves in order to get some money to pay their pimps (if they are fortunate enough to get someone to protect them), for drugs to make the night go away and for a place to sleep.

I looked down at farm boys from Iowa, blond and still innocent, or beautiful young girls from Kansas, eyes half closed with weariness and despair as they push their bodies forward toward the passersby . . .

I showed the letter to Ritter, and he liked it. "This really expresses what it's all about," he said.

Who should we send this to? I didn't think it would really work with my old anticommunist conservative lists, although it might, but I didn't want to take any chances. I had offered to pay for the first mailing myself, as my contribution.

I got in touch with the Catholic List Company, which had just about every contributor to Catholic causes or subscriber to Catholic newspapers in the country. They sold me thirty-five thousand of their best names.

I now had a fund-raising letter and the names. I was ready to go ahead. I invited Father Ritter and his friend and colleague, Robert Macauley, to lunch at the Union League Club.

The Union League Club was symbolic ground for me. I had been accepted into the club in 1978, and this was a major achievement. I was one of the first Jews to be admitted, and I was pleased (and embarrassed because I was so pleased) to be a member of the club among all the WASP businessmen. It is a handsome place, and, as I sat in the grand lounge looking out one of the large windows at Park Avenue, I would think of me on a Young Communist League picket line, nearly forty years before, holding a placard and shouting slogans about one of FDR's pet hates—the Union League plutocrats. Each time I looked out those windows, I saw this skinny kid with horn-rimmed glasses shrieking, "Wages up. Hours down. Make New York a union town." It was a tender memory as I looked out from my deep leatherbound chair across the *Wall Street Journal*.

Ritter and Macauley enthusiastically approved of this first mailing. We arranged for the returns to go to the Under 21 address. They would then be sent to my office for processing.

I was extremely nervous about the response, but I needn't have been. The results were amazing. We had a response of almost 30 percent; over ten thousand contributions came in. I quickly bought more lists and sent the same letter out. The responses became too much for my office to handle, and I certainly couldn't continue to contribute the money for these additional mailings.

Under 21 quickly grew into Covenant House. Ritter took over a large building on West Forty-first Street from New York state. He was a tremendous fund-raiser. He conjoled, threatened, and did everything possible to get money, buildings, and whatever else was needed. Covenant House became a massive national and international organization, with branches in cities throughout the country and the world. Children were being helped, but this was at great cost to Bruce Ritter. As the project expanded, I stopped being a volunteer and worked professionally for Covenant House for about six months and then turned the entire operation over to Ritter and his fast-growing staff.

One day Mother Teresa came to visit Covenant House and I was privileged to meet her. What a wonderful creature she was—tiny hands like little bird's claws and a sweetness of spirit that I have never encountered before. I thought back to the Dalai Lama in the same India she loved so much. She was speaking about working with the poor. "There is nothing that I want more in this life than to nurture and love my unhappy and sick and poor people. I yearn to hold them in my arms and comfort them. I yearn to have my tears wash away some of their sorrow, for they are the people of sorrow. Bruce here," she said pointing to him, "surely feels the same. But we are on airplanes all the time and have to deal with buildings and staff and money, and there is no time left to do what we most want to. This may be God's punishment for too much love."

She was right. Saints are never left alone to be saintly. If they seek to spread their saintliness, they must cope with organizations, fund-raising, administrations, and all that goes into creating a movement. I am sure that Saint Francis had to deal with landlords and wholesalers and contributors when he set up his order. Saintliness is lost—like art—in its administration.

Only once was I able to spend several hours alone with Bruce Ritter. He had come to visit me at my apartment on Fifty-fifth Street. It was then that I told him everything that I knew about myself—my homosexuality, my not accepting it, my hating it, and all the problems and traumas that I could think of. Being a priest, he was a great listener. It was like a confession, and he drew me out. I told him about my wandering around Times Square through the years, my guilt, my feelings about his work and what he was trying to do. He was sympathetic and strangely even empathetic.

"Love is part of our lives," he told me, "and something that God has given us and Jesus has articulated for us. But love can also be a curse. To give too much of your heart is always dangerous. To let too much of yourself into others' hands can cause great grief. This is a difficult dilemma. I hope you find the answer, and I pray that you can find the limits of limitless love."

I compared this spiritual advice with the "life is a vale of tears" advice I had received from Bill Buckley some years before.

Ritter was a lot better at spiritual and personal advice, but then he was a priest.

It was this talk with Bruce Ritter, and the theology I found in Catholicism, that finally made "being loved" seem real to me. I remember back to Patsy, my wife, who said when she left me, "I know you love me, but you will not let me love you." This had always come up in my life. But I was beginning to know love and, in spite of dogma, acceptance for who I was.

I lost touch with Father Ritter. I wrote him in the late 1980s asking if he would do a favor for my friend, Terry De Crescenzo, who is the founding director of an agency called GLASS (Gay and Lesbian Adolescent Social Services) in Los Angeles that provides many of the same services that Covenant House does, but for gay and lesbian youngsters. Ritter said he couldn't do it. I was a bit annoyed with him. I had never asked him for anything before, and I thought he owed me. But Ritter had become a major national figure who even overshadowed the legendary Father Flanagan of Boys Town. That's show biz, I thought, and forgot about it.

A year or so later, Ritter was accused of sexual improprieties with some of the young men he had helped. He was ousted, creating a national scandal. I wrote to him to say that I was available to him for anything I could do to help, and I meant this with all my heart. I never heard from him.

When I discussed Father Ritter's predicament with Terry De Crescenzo, she said that she didn't know the facts of his situation. But she did know that in dealing with high-risk teenagers, one had to be aware that they would sometimes use any weapon they could if they felt wronged by an adult. One had to be circumspect in dealing with them without withholding affection, a difficult balancing act to perform well.

Chapter 16

Washington

*M*Y FATHER HAD wanted me to become a civil servant. I was like a "feather in the wind," he thought, and he wanted more than anything else for me to settle down and get a secure job. He was afraid of what would become of me. Three decades after his death, in the late 1980s, I finally achieved the security he dreamed of.

One May evening in 1981 (about three months after Reagan's inauguration), I was in Washington having dinner with John (Baron) Von Kannon. We ate outdoors at La Brasserie, a splendid restaurant on Capitol Hill. It was a lovely night. The trees had fairy lights, and we sat at a table next to the sidewalk, looking at all the beautiful young people walking by. John, who was treasurer of the Heritage Foundation, was full of gossip about the new administration.

Sitting there on that perfect spring evening, I decided to move to Washington. Conservatives had finally been elected to the White House. I would be part of the Reagan revolution with all the young Reaganauts. The move would also get me out of New York. I was sick of the city and of running my own office. I wanted something new, a different distraction, a new crowd, new work. I had been in one place too long.

Ever since the disastrous Chile experience, I couldn't seem to get things together. Whatever I touched seemed to fail. I had lost interest in causes and had been working on them mostly because that's how I could make a living. My growing lack of interest made it difficult to carry out my professional duties.

Although I was only peripherally part of the winning Reagan campaign, most of my friends and associates had been actively involved. I thought I could just about write my own ticket for a job.

Joining the migration to Washington of conservative activists who had campaigned against Big Government, I started hustling for a government job—to work for less government, of course, by getting on its payroll. I bought a copy of the "plum book," which listed all the non-civil service jobs available through presidential appointment, the definitive patronage list. Anyone who wanted to go to Washington—to escape from Des Moines or Oakland or Butte or Tampa—had a copy of the book. The jobs listed went from cabinet secretaries to the lowest clerk. I stuck pretty much to the middle level. I was certain that I would get a job; my connections were splendid.

I found a position listed under the United States Information Agency: Director of the Bureau of Educational and Cultural Affairs. Perfect! I would travel widely and use my experience in the theater and my international contacts to coordinate international cultural liaisons. I would be the czar of a new international artistic Renaissance. And I wouldn't have to do any fund-raising; Uncle Sam would provide the money.

I learned that an old acquaintance was on the transition team that handled the USIA. I telephoned and told him that I was interested in the job. He said, "It's yours!" He would see to it. I asked whether I should get my VIP friends to start writing letters. He said absolutely not, to leave it completely in his hands. I did.

Weeks passed. I was beginning to get rather nervous. Charles Wick had been named head of the USIA. Wick was a former band leader and a good friend of the Reagans. He had struck it rich in Los Angeles, and he and his wife, Mary Jane, were right up there in the crowd of Californian job seekers who flocked to Washington. I called my friend to ask whether I should get in direct touch with Charlie Wick. I had met him a few times previously, and we had a number of mutual friends and acquaintances.

"No," he said. "It's all in hand. For heaven's sake, don't rock the boat."

So I waited around, until I read in the *New York Times* that Wick had appointed *my friend* director of the Bureau of Educational and Cultural

Affairs. I was furious, but there wasn't anything I could do about it. I had learned my first Washington lesson: trust nobody.

I gave up on the USIA and decided to try the National Endowment for the Arts. Even though I was politically and aesthetically opposed to a national endowment for anything—particularly the "arts"—I thought it might be fun to work on their theater program. At the same time, I would do my best to see that the NEA was disbanded, part of my conservative belief in breaking down the bureaucracy and getting rid of extraneous agencies and programs. Big Government was stifling America. We conservatives were going to get rid of it. For about three or four months, we held on to the dream—until we were all firmly ensconced and absorbed.

I am not against public support of art. I am in favor of municipal and even state arts councils that use local taxpayer's money to support artists and artistic endeavors within their own communities. I am opposed, however, to a federal bureaucracy such as the NEA taking money from the taxpayers in, say, Portland, Oregon who already give their tax money to the Portland and Oregon state arts councils. Their money is laundered in Washington through elitist panels and screenings, and then a small portion is sent back to Portland, a waste of time and effort having nothing to do with art. And the NEA is only part of an ever-growing bureaucracy. The state and municipal councils in turn created the National Association of Local Arts Agencies and the National Association of State Art Agencies, and on and on. I always have a vision of a painter, crushed and squirming, at the bottom of a pyramid of executive directors, executive secretaries, coordinators, councils, trustees, organizations and institutions. At the pinnacle squats the National Endowment for the Arts with its eye (like the eye on the one dollar bill) darting over the landscape looking desperately for new and even more absurd things to fund. The poor painter is squashed underneath, and the only way he can escape is to return to his garret, forget any funding from anybody, and hope that somebody will buy his painting just because they like it. If an artist really wants to get funded, the amount of paper work and time required leaves no room for anything else.

Moreover, there are many talented and good people at the NEA whose time is spent as bureaucratic clerks rather than as artists. The NEA is also used as a public whipping boy by organizations who deal in bigotry. They go under the guise of "conservatism" or "family values," or whatever other hogwash they can think of to mask their real motives. The hue and cry over funding the late Robert Mapplethorpe's homoerotic photography exhibits had nothing to do with the NEA. It had everything to do with antihomosexual bigotry, just as groups objecting to various US aid programs to Israel have nothing to do with foreign policy but have everything to do with anti-Semitism. In our time, bigotry is more subtle than a cossack beating a Jew with a club for the joy of it, or castrating a homosexual just to hear him scream. Today, bigotry masquerades in many guises—conservativism, morality, religion, family—but it's the same as the barbarian's knout or Mengele's surgical blade.

If there has to be a National Endowment for the Arts in order to pacify the members of Congress and their wives who enjoy serving on boards—and to pacify the professional arts lobby—it should be limited to national institutions, for example, a National Opera Company utilizing companies already existing in New York, Chicago, and San Francisco; a National Ballet Company utilizing ballet groups already existing; or a National Theater utilizing the already subsidized Kennedy Center. These national companies would then more openly and directly be controlled by the Congress—not one of the great reservoirs of aesthetics —to suit their own constituencies. If the national institutions want federal money, then they must expect to be controlled by the art appreciators in the House and the Senate. Or let them forget federal money and get on with art.

I mobilized my troops, as one usually did in the early days of the Reagan administration, to write letters and make phone calls. The key agency to get access to was the Office of White House Personnel, headed then by Helene Van Damme, who had been personal secretary to Reagan when he was governor of California. Helene liked me and thought of me as an early Reaganaut. She had taken on the mission of seeing that Reagan supporters had jobs in all parts of the government. She was an instinctive political woman and knew the benefits of patronage, to both giver and recipient. Helene was no conservative, but she was a devoted Reagan loyalist.

I arranged a series of letters to Helene, to President Reagan, to Nancy

Reagan, to Lynn Nofziger (an important Reagan aide at the White House), and to anyone else I could think of. Among my letter writers were Bill Buckley (the most important), Bill Rusher, Roy Cohn (my old nemesis but now high up in Reagan circles), William Simon, Dan Mahoney, Clare Luce, and a host of others. Overwhelmed by the flood, Helene Van Damme assured me that I would get a job with the NEA the moment they had appointed a chairman.

With Helene's assurance, I decided to leave New York for Washington in September 1981. I closed down Marvin Liebman, Inc. (as I had Marvin Liebman Associates twelve years earlier), paid off whatever debts I had, and sublet my rent-controlled apartment in New York. I hired John Von Kannon's girlfriend to check available apartments so that I could choose one without wasting time. She lined up five, and I chose the one at DuPont Circle, where I still live. I had no idea then that DuPont Circle was the gay enclave in Washington.

I arrived just after Labor Day in 1981, with my luggage and my canary, which I had named Petey, after my mother's canary of many years, to begin my new life. I was received by the conservative community with great respect as one of the early members of the movement that elected Ronald Reagan president. It was as if a "living legend" had come to Washington, and I played that role to the hilt for the first few years.

Soon after I arrived in Washington, a young gay friend took me to three bars and two dance clubs in one night to show me what they looked like. When I was younger, I used to hate the idea of old men staring at the youngsters in gay bars. I suddenly felt that I might be seen as one of these men. I got quite drunk, which is most unlike me. Then he took me to the final place—a gay piano bar where "older" gay men sit around singing show tunes. Even that was too much for me.

My first job was at ACTION, a government agency run by an old YAF friend, Tom Pauken. I worked there a few weeks as a "consultant" while I was waiting for something else to come up. From that time on, September 1981 to the present, I have never been off the government payroll. I thought this a scandal at the beginning, a blessed sinecure now. From ACTION, I went on to the Department of Education, another agency we Reaganauts wanted to close down. I worked as a $185 per day "consultant."

In February 1982, Frank Hodsoll was finally confirmed by the Senate as chairman of the National Endowment for the Arts. My appointment to see him was on the same day in February of the blizzard that caused a large passenger airplane to crash into the Potomac.

I had to travel from the Department of Education to the NEA, twenty blocks away, to see Hodsoll at 3:00 P.M. Nothing could keep me from this appointment—not even the blizzard. I couldn't get a taxi, so I hired a vulgar white stretch limousine to drive me the distance.

Hodsoll, himself delayed by the snow, showed up an hour later. He was an enormous man with the bouncy enthusiasm of a boy. He already had somebody in mind for the theater job and he suggested that I become director of Public Affairs. Why not?

Hodsoll's idea of the job differed greatly from mine. I thought that my job was to avoid publicity for the National Endowment and get publicity for local artists and arts groups, but Hodsoll wanted publicity for himself and his job. I found this to be true of most people in top government jobs. The more publicity, the better they liked it. They rationalized this by saying it was good for the agency, but it was even better for their own careers.

There were many good people at the Endowment. Most of them were professional bureaucrats who try to keep a low profile, avoid making any waves or bringing any attention to themselves. I had always been good at staying behind the scenes, so this bureaucratic style suited me well.

Despite my personal opposition to the NEA, I tried my best to do a creditable job. As part of his reorganization plans, Hodsoll decided to merge the press, public affairs, and public information offices into one Office of Public Affairs under a single supervisor. My job was to consolidate these three different functions into a tighter and more unified operation. This gave me my chance to cut government spending.

When I started, there were fourteen employees assigned to the three offices. Through my efforts, and over a period of about twelve months, eight employees were separated without impairing efficiency or lessening responsibility. This consolidation proved an effective use of personnel and saved considerable money. Or, so I thought.

The eight people who were separated from the office were simply assigned to other jobs. Two of them were given higher grades, and consequently more money, to assuage their hurt feelings. So, nothing much was accomplished. It's just about impossible to separate anyone from the civil service. A recent survey showed that the chances of getting fired from a government job were forty thousand to one. At this late time in my life, and as one of your civil servants, I may say that I am personally delighted with these odds (though, in fact, as a "schedule C" discretionary employee, I did not have all the civil service protections). But the situation certainly compromises my conservative politics.

At the end of 1984, I was named director of special projects at the NEA. In my new role, I organized National Arts Week in September 1985, which ended with the celebration of the twentieth anniversary of the Endowment. More than eight hundred arts events were held throughout the country. I was active in the creation of the National Medal of Arts and organized a committee of distinguished musical artists for American Music Week in November 1985. This was the kind of work I knew best how to do. These were my "last hurrahs" in organizing highly visible public committees.

But I found myself in a dilemma. I was doing too good a job and bringing too much attention to the Endowment. I tried my best to focus attention on local arts agencies and events, but the Endowment got all the press. I found myself too professional to accomplish my hidden agenda of closing down the NEA. I had to control myself.

I lasted at the Endowment for four and a half years. Hodsoll and I never got along. He fired me for going over his head in arranging some sort of White House proclamation. "You are not really made for government," he told me. "You're an entrepreneur and an impresario, and you have to work on your own. This is why I have to let you go, because I need somebody to work *for* me, and certainly not against me." This was the first time I had ever been fired. For a few days, I was devastated. But I soon recovered. What difference did it make at this stage of my life?

I was saved by Nancy Reagan. She was not fond of Frank Hodsoll, who won his appointment through friends who worked closely with Vice President Bush. Through her intercession, the White House put pressure on him to keep me on the payroll until I found some other suitable job in government. I stayed for the next fifteen months; Hodsoll was not about to cross swords with the First Lady. The Endowment proved to me how very difficult it was for me to adjust to working for anyone else. As Governor Edison had pointed out more than two decades earlier, I was happier working on my own.

I went from the Endowment to the Commission on Executive, Legislative, and Judicial Salaries, which was organized basically to discuss raising the salaries of all senior government employees and how to make such raises look good. Happily, we failed that year. Four years later, everyone's salary was raised through a complicated congressional parliamentary procedure.

It was in Washington that Clare Boothe Luce and I really got to be buddies. The Watergate, where she lived, was only several blocks from DuPont Circle, so we saw a lot of each other. Clare and I talked about the theater and Catholicism. Though only recently a Catholic, I was very devout but not stuffy about it. This pleased Clare. Although she could speak endlessly about the church, she had lapsed. She was still a believer, sort of, but didn't go to church any longer. She was an inveterate name-dropper and phrase-dropper (most of the latter her own creations), and full of delicious stories.

"I remember some years ago," she told me one day. "I was sitting on the veranda of Hyde Park with Franklin. His dreadful mother and his homely wife were away, thank God. Franklin and I had a tiny 'assignation,' and we were having iced tea. Franklin said to me, 'Darling, I am thinking of this wonderful idea for the American people, a great new program. I wish I could think of what to call it.' 'Franklin, dear,' I said, 'why don't you just call it the 'new deal'?' 'That's it!' he exclaimed, 'that's it!'

"Winston and I were in my suite in the Savoy during the blitz. We had a tiny 'assignation,' and were watching the bombing through our window, which was taped against shattering glass. Everyone else was in the theater downstairs that served as an air raid shelter. We didn't bother with that, of course. We were looking at the lights of the bombing, and Winston said, 'Darling, if I could just express what the British people are doing. They are giving their all.' I looked at him and said, 'Why, Winston, why not "blood, sweat and tears"!' 'That's it!' he exclaimed happily.

"I was with Douglas in his suite at the Waldorf. His darling dull little

wife was out shopping. We had just had a tiny 'assignation.' He said
to me, 'I have to make a speech in which I am going to leave public life.
If I could only think of what to say.' 'Oh, Douglas,' I said, 'why not
"old soldiers never die, they just fade away."' 'That's it!' he exclaimed."

One evening during dinner, Clare was prattling on about something
or other, and I interrupted, "Darling, do you remember your story about
the rabbi?" "Rabbi," she said, "what rabbi?" "The one who was looking
for some idea on how to begin an address he was scheduled to make to his
congregation." "No, dear, I don't remember." "You know, the one where
you suggested, why don't you start out by saying, 'Blessed are the meek,
for they shall inherit the earth'?"

For a moment, she was thinking about where the tiny assignation fit
in, and then she got it and laughed.

Clare was one of the few people with whom I discussed being gay. She
pooh-poohed my concern and said, "Relax, darling, don't take it all so
seriously," and then went on to talk about still another tiny assignation
she had enjoyed with some VIP. She hinted once that she had "tried" it
with another woman, an actress, famous naturally, but didn't really like
it at all! "Rather messy," she said.

Pat and Bill gave Clare a wonderful seventy-fifth birthday party in
their apartment on Seventy-third Street. Just about everyone in New
York was there. I was entrusted with ordering the cake with a Statue of
Liberty, to represent Clare, of course, on top of it and sparklers instead
of candles.

The last time I saw Clare was in her Watergate apartment in October
1987, three days before she died. She was very ill. I was ushered into her
bedroom, where she was propped up on pillows in her negligee. She put
one of her old legs out of the covers and lifted her nightgown to show the
leg up to the thigh. "I do have beautiful legs, dear, don't I." Those were
the last words she said to me.

Looking back, I see women—Clare Luce, Hermione Gingold, Pat
Buckley, Mildred Allenberg, Coral Browne, Bertha Case—who were
really great ladies who gave me a lot of friendship and love when I
needed it. They demanded nothing of me except to be witty and amusing, and to give them the kind of comfort and companionship that they
couldn't get from most men. They are part of the great parade of women

of power or fame, who, bigger than life, become friends of gay men.

During this period, I became friends with the young Reagan speech writers Peter Robinson, Dana Rohrabacher, Josh Gilder, and Clark Judge. It was through them that I was able to lunch at the White House Mess several times a month. I always found this to be fun, especially when one of the boys would let me bring along some out-of-town friends.

The day before my sixty-fourth birthday, I took a permanent job at the Federal Trade Commission with the Office of Public Affairs. I was able to "career in" and thus become a permanent and full-time civil servant, the dream of my father from the very beginning.

If one works too long in government, one becomes numb—rather like being under a mild anesthesia. You start with great vigor and ideas, wanting to change the world by changing the government. You end up— certainly most of us do—being completely absorbed into the fabric and truly becoming a faceless bureaucrat.

But I had one more thing to do before I settled into the security of the civil service.

Chapter 17

Coming Out

I WAS BEGINNING to feel old, not just older. Old and restless.

Years earlier, I had befriended a young man with a serious drug problem and, as his mentor, became concerned. Carol Buckley, who is wise and experienced in dealing with people with substance abuse problems, suggested that I see a psychologist to discuss my young friend's addiction and to seek some advice. In retrospect, I realized that she probably had other motives—not so much to help him, as to help me.

I made an appointment with a psychologist. I spoke to him at length about the young man, my relationship with him, and my concern about his situation. The psychologist said he would be glad to see him, but only if he really wanted to come; otherwise, it would be a waste of my money and his time. This made good sense to me.

Just as I was leaving, he looked at me quizzically and asked, "What about you? Is this all you want from life?"

My young friend never went to see the psychologist. He lived with his addiction until it was no longer possible, and then he began the long road of acceptance and recovery on his own, without any help from me, which is as it must be.

I forgot the incident until October of 1989. "Is this all I want from life?" No, I wanted more. "This" was not enough. My life had grown increasingly meaningless. I telephoned the psychologist, reminded him of our last meeting, and began therapy.

The next months were a voyage of exploration and discovery. For the very first time in all my sixty-six years, I attempted to look at myself as I really was, not as I would like to be or as other people wanted me to be. I was trying to find *me*.

It started out slowly, with only brief sparks of light. As I went on,

more and more became illuminated. I gradually accepted what I had
made the most important part of my life: the fact that I was gay. Total
acceptance, however, didn't happen until several months later: in May
of 1990, the weekend before Memorial Day. And it didn't happen
all at once.

A decade earlier, I had a chance to see what being known as gay in my
world might mean. In September 1980, after a banquet in Washington
celebrating the twentieth anniversary of YAF, I rant into Bob and Carol
Bauman, whom I hadn't seen for some time. Bob was running for
reelection as the incumbent Congressman from the First Congressional
District of Maryland. He was considered the leading parliamentarian in
Congress, a great debater and speaker, and had become one of the
authentic leaders of the conservative movement. No one knew just how
high he would go, but he was going up.

I was delighted to see them both again. I was sitting on a couch with
Carol and chatting. "How's it going?" I asked. She turned to me, her
eyes swimming with tears. Had I said something wrong? "I just wish
that Bob would get out of politics. It's hurting him and hurting us both. I
just wish he'd quit."

Several weeks later, I opened my newspaper to read that Congressman
Bauman had been arrested for an alleged homosexual act with a young
male prostitute. I was stunned and upset. I telephoned Bob's congressional office in Washington to offer him any help he needed. He was, of
course, unavailable at the time. I called anyone I could think of who was a
mutual friend or acquaintance. Nobody I spoke to had had an inkling
that Bob was gay. It was unbelievable.

There wasn't anyone I could speak to about it, not even Bill Buckley.
Just as Bob had hidden the major part of himself and fought the demons
that come with living a lie, I had to battle the demons of my own hidden
life. I couldn't even discuss this with my gay friends, because they would
have no sympathy with Bauman, as they had no sympathy with my
conservative politics.

Bob made a public statement in which he blamed everything on
alcohol. He still refused to admit his homosexuality. On October 9, Bill
Buckley wrote a column entitled "The Ordeal of Robert Bauman." In it
he said, "Robert Bauman should resign from Congress and resign, also,

his various positions in conservative organizations, conspicuously his chairmanship of the American Conservative Union."

This column was devastating to both Bob's ongoing campaign and to him personally. It was also totally devastating to me. Should I resign from everything with which I was connected? Was my moral mentor, William F. Buckley, Jr., saying that you could stay on and serve the conservative movement so long as you didn't get caught? I was deeply wounded by that column, but I didn't have the guts to tell Bill why.

I was also ashamed. Should I now stand up and say to Bill, "Look, old friend, I am gay too and have been gay a lot longer than Bob Bauman. What do you want me to do?"

I telephoned Bill, and for the first and last time I criticized something he had written. I said that I thought it was unnecessary and judgmental and something he should not have done.

When I moved to Washington some months later, I "came out" to Bob. Of course, he wasn't surprised. I still felt guilty—as if I should do something more—but I didn't yet know quite what to do.

In the months that followed, I did my best to get the gay community to utilize Bob's services and talent through Betty Berzon and her partner Terry De Crescenzo, in Los Angeles—but to no avail. Many in the gay and lesbian community wanted no part of Bob, because he had voted against two specific measures that would have provided homosexuals and lesbians the same rights as any other American. Bob is now living an openly gay and sober life.

To this day, I feel that I should have shared some of his pain, but I didn't have the courage and didn't really know how.

In 1990, several things happened that began to pry open my own closet door and I realized, much to my surprise, that I was finally ready. In February, my friend Betty Berzon telephoned and asked if she could include some stories about me in the autobiography she was then writing. I was alarmed for a moment. What could she say? What stories might she tell? I asked her to send me the part of her manuscript about me. She sent me a chapter entitled "Marvin, Europe and the Aftermath." In it, she told some amusing stories about our adventures, all of which presented me openly as a gay man. Well, I thought. And then, why not! I loved and respected Betty and knew she would never do anything to hurt me. I telephoned her and said it was perfectly fine, and I complimented her on what I was sure would be a wonderful book. I was beginning not to care any longer who knew about me, especially if I didn't have to articulate it myself. And I wouldn't have to cope with any reaction to the news about me until after the book was published, which would be far in the future.

That was the beginning. A couple of months later, Betty sent me a clipping from the *Los Angeles Times* that reported on some outrageous and openly homophobic actions taken by Young Americans for Freedom in California. She said, "Can you do something about this? After all, you founded that group." She was angry and rightfully so. I telephoned her and said that I would do something soon. I wasn't quite yet ready, but I thought that I had to "come out" publicly. This news pleased my old friend enormously. "About time," she said.

Events were moving along.

I had arranged to spend the weekend in Boston and Cape Cod with a twenty-two-year-old non-gay friend from Alabama. I had met him the year before when he served as a summer intern in a Congressman's office in Washington. Craig was the typical all-American boy—fraternity brother, soccer player, beer drinker—bright, good-looking, and a lover of women. He had those rare sexual vibes that drew females of all ages to him, and he was always ready to oblige them. I greatly enjoyed his company and was flattered that he reciprocated.

When he was in Washington the previous year, his parents had visited him, and the four of us had had dinner and a brunch during their stay. His mother wrote me a thank you note. "I am at a loss for words in thanking you for all that you have done for Craig. You not only entertained him spectacularly but more importantly, you encouraged him to grow, to explore, and to *think*. Because Destiny saw to it that you were to become a very important part of my son's life, he will be a different, and I think, better person. Craig is a very lucky young man to have you as a friend." How could any mentor resist a note like that? It's what we all dream of.

We were driving up the Cape toward Provincetown and planned to spend Saturday night there before taking the alternate route back to Boston on Sunday. As it was pre-season, everything was pleasantly uncrowded. Craig was driving our rented car, and each time I saw a sign saying "Antiques" I'd tell him to pull over. Though he was getting increasingly bored by antiques, he'd always oblige.

At one stop, a charming Cape Cod house with the shop where the sitting room would have been, the two proprietors greeted us. They were rather elderly queens—their hair dyed blacker than black, effusive, flamboyant, and delighted to see customers on this quiet weekend. They were particularly happy to see Craig, and they made an instant assumption about us, undoubtedly envious of either my good luck or my money, most likely the latter. The young man was beginning to get extremely nervous.

"Where are you boys headed for?" one asked.

"Provincetown."

"That's the gay capital of the world. Oh, you lucky things," said the other.

Craig's eyes nearly popped out of his head. He was seriously offended and obviously wanted to get away. I was embarrassed for him, for the two old men, and most of all for me.

They saw Craig's discomfort and said to him, "Oh dear, aren't you gay?"

"No," he barked, and he fled outside.

A great sadness suddenly engulfed me. I felt bereft, as if my heart were breaking. I didn't know why I had this overwhelming reaction. I apologized for my young friend and went out to join him as we drove away.

"Ugh, I hate faggots. God, how I hate them," he said through clenched teeth. I could tell that he was really frightened and repelled. "God, if one of them touched me, I'd break his nose. I'd just bash his face in." He shuddered.

I was shocked by the vehemence of his loathing and the depth and extent of his fear. I began a fifteen-minute lecture about "them." "They" were like anybody else; you shouldn't use words like *faggot*, it's like saying *nigger*; "they" couldn't help the way "they" are. On and on I went about they, them, they, them.

For the next hour or so when we'd pass through a town, and Craig saw a man or two men together, he'd say, "Look at the faggots, look at them. This place is crawling with them. My God, how disgusting. Ugh!"

"How do you know they're homosexuals?"

"Mustaches! They all have mustaches. Didn't you know?"

In response to what he knew was my disapproval, he stopped after a while. I could sense though that he was still upset about the experience in the antique shop.

What was that all about? Was it possible that he knew about me, about my secret? No! I could tell as he spoke about "them" that he separated me from those people. Why was he so frightened? Why are most heterosexual boys almost physically, and certainly emotionally, frightened by gays?

It was later on that day, as I stood at the edge of the Provincetown dunes watching young Craig skip barefoot along the incoming tide, that I finally broke through my own barrier and stopped thinking of "them."

It was "us." It was "me."

I had the same feeling of liberation in that moment as I had some forty years before listening to Eleanor Lipper in the lobby of the Algonquin Hotel. The dust and cobwebs and the shadows were swept away. What was the sense of keeping the secret any longer? And was it really a secret? Who did it serve? Who did it benefit? And who did it hurt? Only one person—me. Me!

And on the dunes, as evening approached, I felt that I had stepped over a threshold, through a door that suddenly opened from the shadowy darkness to a brighter technicolor world filled with possibilities.

What do I do about it? Do I start then and there with Craig? Do I say, "Listen, I am one of them. Look at me. I don't have a mustache, and I am still one of them—a faggot, a newly born and lucky faggot."

Although I didn't say any of that, I experienced a very real sense of joy and liberation in the knowledge that I could if and when I wanted to.

I was itching to take some action, and I was desperate for someone to talk to. My thoughts and plans weren't yet sufficiently formulated to talk to Bill. There seemed no one else. I missed my old friend and mentor, Charles Edison. In a strange way, I realized that I might have been able to discuss all this with him.

But, I didn't have the Governor, and so I had to do it on my own. I drafted an op-ed piece that I was going to send to the *Washington Times*, the right-wing alternative to the *Washington Post*. It was overly sentimental, full of polemic, and not very good. But I didn't think so then. I thought that this would be the best place for me to "come out" publicly and would create something of a sensation in the Washington "conservative" establishment.

The night before I planned to send it in, I went to the movies with my young friend John Buckley. John is a nephew of Bill's who has made a great career for himself as a novelist and public affairs specialist. He and his wife, Anna, and I had become good pals. We were to go from the movies back to his apartment where Anna had dinner waiting for us.

I told John that I was planning to "come out." Aside from Betty, I guess he was really the first person to whom I confided my decision. "That's terrific," he said. I told him that I was going to do it by writing an op-ed piece for the *Washington Times*. Would he like to see it, I asked?

We stopped off at my apartment and picked up the manuscript, and he read it immediately after dinner. He made two important suggestions: "If you want to reach the conservative community, send it to Uncle Bill for *National Review*"; then he suggested my statement be in the form of a letter. That was the letter published in *National Review* and the *Advocate*.

I had thought hard and long before I made my final move. What would Bill think? My thought then was not so much for me but for him. Would it hurt him? Could he finally admit to himself that I was gay? Amazing that in a crisis in my own life, I thought of the feelings of another person. This was not a saintly act on my part; it was just helping to get my thoughts away from me onto somebody else. I felt sorry for Bill, and guilty about adding to the weight of his always heavy burden as he takes on the problems of his family and friends and makes them his own.

After much thought, I decided to telephone Bill in Stamford early Saturday morning. I had arranged an appointment later that day with David Walter, a reporter from the *Advocate*. Two days earlier I had told Betty that I was planning to send Bill Buckley a letter and wanted some particularly scurrilous homophobic statements from presumably "conservative" sources. She telephoned her friend Mark Thompson at the *Advocate* for help. He told her he'd call her back within the hour. After a hurried meeting with his colleagues, Thompson called Betty back to say that they would like me to be the "cover boy" for their July 17 issue. By that time, I was willing to do anything I could to make a splash in both the conservative community and the gay community, and I concurred.

I told Bill that I would be faxing something to him that morning and he should make every effort to read it as soon as possible. "It is very, very important to me," I told him.

I then went over to the Dupont Plaza Hotel across the Circle and used their fax machine to send the letter that I wanted him to publish. I remember it was a hot day, and I was perspiring not only with the heat but with nerves. I returned to the apartment to find Dave Walter of the *Advocate* waiting and we started our interview. The telephone rang.

"Are you certain that you want to do this, *Vieux?*" Bill asked. "Yes," I said. "I'll have to write a reply, you know." "That's fine," I said. "Would you like me to edit what you wrote? Without changing one iota of its meaning, of course." "OK," I said. "You can do the same with my reply." "Fine," I said. I was really feeling weak.

The fat was in the fire! I was out!

When Bill agreed to publish the exchange, I sent copies of the letter, with a handwritten covering note, to about forty-five friends, family members (including my sister), and conservative colleagues and to my boss, Janet Steiger, the chairman, and the four commissioners at the Federal Trade Commission where I am employed:

> I wanted you to see this (uncorrected) exchange between Bill Buckley and me before it is published in *National Review* the end of this month. I have also given an interview to the *Advocate*, the national gay publication, which is scheduled to appear very soon after.
>
> I hope all of this does some good for both the conservative movement and the gay community. I know that I felt very good about it—an exhilarating feeling of openness and fresh air after 67 years of being inside.

This is the way I came out to the people who mattered to me the most.

A few days after he received my letter, Craig telephoned. "I got your letter. I wanted to say that I'm sorry about the things I said on Cape Cod. I just wanted you to know that I'm still your friend. I hope you are still mine."

Jim Buckley telephoned and asked me to have dinner with him as Ann was out of town. I accepted, and we had my usual table at the window of I Ricchi, a chic and splendid Italian restaurant a few blocks from where I live in Washington. It took us about two hours to eat, and we had a spirited conversation about this and that, one of the most interesting and amusing I had ever had with Jim. Not a word about the letter, which I knew he had received. The check came, and I reached for it, knowing Jim's financial prudence. "No," said Jim. "I talked to Ann, and this is on us."

"Well, thanks a lot, Jim," I said, and he looked me straight in the eyes, raised his glass, and said, "This is just to salute an act of courage." And that was the only reference to my letter or to my coming out. But it was enough from this usually taciturn friend.

It was what I had expected, but it still made me happy. The same was true, in one way or the other, of all the people who received the letter. Either they said that they were proud of me, or, "We always knew, why did you have to do it so publicly?" I was feeling free and unfettered, as if a massive weight had been removed from my soul.

After the publication of the letter in *National Review* and the interview in the *Advocate*, my life became a circus. My "fifteen minutes" of fame lasted for over two months. I was in a whirl of publicity and appearances. I hoped that I was doing some good for the gay community (especially those still hiding in the closet) and also for the conservative community. I had no time for reflection.

In October 1990, *National Review*'s thirty-fifth anniversary dinner was held to celebrate the success of Bill Buckley, the young man who had wanted to make conservatism "shoe." It was at this dinner that Bill resigned as editor-in-chief of *National Review*. He was sixty-five, and he turned the dream over to younger people. Bill Rusher had also resigned.

I had already come out by the time I went to the dinner. As part of the program, a video was shown about the past thirty-five years of the *Review*. Each time my name was mentioned, the guests applauded. Without exception, I was greeted warmly by all the old friends I saw. Perhaps some in that throng might not have wanted to see me. But if they were there, I didn't notice them.

And so, in my sixty-seventh year, I had embarked on yet another new beginning. This one, I know, will be the final one. Because now I feel safe, finally free, and home, at last.

Epilogue

I DEDICATED this book to Wing Biddlebaum. He is the main character in a story entitled "Hands" from Sherwood Anderson's *Winesburg, Ohio,* published in 1919. When my high school English teacher Bernard Malamud showed me this story over fifty years ago, I didn't see the meaning in it that I see so clearly now.

The story, which takes place in the fictitious town of Winesburg, Ohio, describes Wing Biddlebaum as an "old man walking nervously up and down . . . frightened and beset by a ghostly band of doubts." His name had been Adolph Myers before he had come to Winesburg twenty years before. He was nicknamed "Wing Biddlebaum" because of his hands and "their restless activity, like unto the beating of the wings of an imprisoned bird."

In his youth, he had been a schoolteacher in a small Pennsylvania town. In the evenings, he sat on the schoolhouse steps talking with the boys, "lost in a kind of dream." His hands would start "caressing the shoulders of the boys, playing about the tousled heads. As he talked his voice became soft and musical. There was a caress in that also. In a way," Anderson wrote, "the voice and the hands, the stroking of the shoulders and the touching of the hair were a part of the schoolmaster's effort to carry a dream into the young minds. By the caress that was in his fingers, he expressed himself . . . . Under the caress of his hands doubt and disbelief went out of the minds of the boys and they began also to dream."

One afternoon, the saloon keeper, whose son had told him about the teacher's caresses, went to the schoolhouse. "I'll teach you to put your hands on my boy, you beast," he screamed and started to beat the teacher in the face and to "kick him around the yard." That night, a crowd of men carrying lanterns came to his house with a rope to hang him. Instead, feeling sorry for someone so "small, white, and pitiful," they let him escape. "As he ran away into the darkness, they repented of their weakness and ran after him, swearing and throwing sticks and great balls of soft mud at the figure that screamed and ran faster and faster into the darkness."

This is for me the classic story of being driven into a closet full of terror and shame. As I was approaching my sixty-seventh birthday, I finally saw myself in that story. There I was, an "old man . . forever frightened." It was the grace of God—and the loving support of my friends—that enabled me to cease being afraid and finally stand up and come out.

One of the greatest dangers facing not only the gay and lesbian community, but also the country is the resurgence of bigotry as social and political forces. It is redundant but important to keep repeating the enormous change in the public attitude of the American Right after Bill Buckley came on the scene. Prior to Buckley—interrupted only by World War II and the national revulsion that came with the knowledge of the extermination of the Jews—the professional bigots had become a powerful and hidden force in American society and politics.

The Christian Front, Knights of the White Camellia, the Ku Klux Klan, the America First Committee, the Silver Shirts—these were the aboveground groups. Each had dozens of spinoffs, and there were millions more Americans who didn't join officially but secretly supported what they advocated. These groups were primarily anti-Negro and anti-Semitic. A few were anti-Catholic. Homosexuality was not an issue in those days; open homosexuals were considered freaks, and not worthy of notice by these saviors of white Christian America.

World War II brought all this to a temporary halt. The Espionage Act was passed, and all groups that were thought to be pro-Nazi were temporarily put out of business and their publications denied mailing privileges by the Postal Service.

The moment the Axis powers were defeated, the anti-Semitic and racist groups began to reorganize in an attempt to recapture the power and influence they had had before the war. Among the groups were the American Nazi Party, Identity Church, the National Association for the Advancement of White People, the John Birch Society (which was never *overtly* anti-Semitic), Lyndon LaRouche and his phalanx of organizations; the Liberty Lobby; National States' Rights Party; The New Order; Populist Party; Christian Patriots; American Free Men Association; The Covenant, the Sword, and the Arm of the Lord; The Order; White Aryan Resistance; and White Citizens Councils.

Anti-Semitic and racist groups start up, dissolve, and start again under different names. They follow the successful organizational pattern used by legitimate organizations: when a group has served its purpose, dissolve it and start another. They have fertile ground in America. Public anti-Semitism and overt racism have become unacceptable. Homosexuals are now fair game, however.

The threat to America no longer comes from the USSR. It comes again from within, from organizations that advocate racism and sexism and preach discrimination against Jews, blacks, Mexicans, Asians, and homosexuals. Their bigotry is growing along with hatred and fear of anything different.

I now have two homes and two families: gays and lesbians, both in and out of their "communities"; and "conservatives," both the true believers and even those that use the label to further anything-but-conservative aims. As in all families, you have the good and the bad, the loved and the tolerated. But the family is yours whether you like it or not. And, you belong to them.

To my gay and lesbian brothers and sisters who are "out," I say that I am proud to finally be with you. I am grateful to have been embraced as warmly as I have been. To those of you who still hide, I say come out. There is no reason whatsoever to stay in that stifling closet any longer. Leave the shadows and come out into the light. You will find that you will be welcomed, not only by your brothers and sisters but by all whom you love if they are worthy of your love.

And to my conservative friends, I say build on the efforts of the men and women of years past who have defined a new philosophy; but be vigilant against the hate-mongers who term themselves as "conservatives" but have nothing to do with its essence. Take pride in our accomplishments at home and abroad. Work to make our basic approach to life and politics more meaningful. Hold fast to the basic concept of individual liberty over the state. Accept all the different men and women who live in our unique nation with its precious constitution.

Looking back, I realize that I have achieved important things and helped to influence important events. I take great pride in this. In my failures are my successes, and are the triumphs of all of us who recognized the futility of communism and who contributed in some part to its demise.

If I have learned anything about life, it is to be yourself. Be what you are, no matter who you are or how you were born. Don't try to be what others want you to be. Accept the difference of others. Include them in your lives. By shutting others out merely because they are different, you diminish your own life and that of your children.

In 1963, I wrote a speech for Governor Edison that he gave at a testimonial dinner in his honor. The words I wrote for him at the end of his career hold true for me nearly three decades later:

> I have lived a good many years. No one knows all the answers, but I do know this: in the time that is left me, I will continue fighting for America—for what it really is and what it really means. And so must we all—no matter what the obstacles and no matter how discouraged we may become. To give up would indeed be a sin against the memory of all those heroes of the past who have given us a nation.

Fear of difference creates closets that keep us from realizing the dream. We must open the doors of the shadowy closets of bigotry and intolerance and finally come home into the bright light of freedom.

Appendix A

Letter from Marvin Liebman to William F. Buckley, Jr., and response by William F. Buckley, Jr. (Published in National Review, *July 9, 1990)*

Dear Bill:

I have given long and careful thought to what follows. It is something I feel I have to do. I urge you to give it sympathetic and immediate consideration. I send it to you 1) because you are my best friend; and 2) because *NR* is the logical publication for this statement.

It has been nearly four years since *NR* published "John Woolman's" missive, "A Conservative Speaks Out for Gay Rights." It may not surprise you to know that I have kept a clipping of that article all this time. It sits in a file which although not titled may as well be called my file on Conservatives of Courage on the Issue of Homosexuality. It is a very thin file. You were courageous to run John Woolman's letter as a prominent article, and to allow him, 18 months later, to publish his "AIDS and Right Wing Hysteria." Your doing so brought a feeling of genuine admiration in this old friend.

We've known each other for almost 35 years now, and ten years ago you served as my godfather when I entered the Catholic Church. Though the subject never arose, you and Pat, among my oldest friends, must have known that I'm gay. It never seemed to matter.

But it does matter to many "movement" conservatives—this question of who is, who is not gay; and they wonder whether homosexuals are a menace to society. Just as, too often, there has been an undercurrent of

258

anti-Semitism among even some mainstream conservatives, there has always been an element of homophobia among us. In many years of service to The Cause, I've sat in rooms where people we both know—brilliant, thoughtful, kind people—have said, without any sense of shame, vulgar and cruel things about people who through no fault of their own happen to be different in their sexuality.

Anti-Semitism is something that, happily for the history of the last three decades, *National Review* helped to banish at least from the public behavior of conservatives. *National Review* lifted conservatism to a more enlightened plane, away from a tendency to engage in the manipulation of base motives, prejudices, and desires: activity which in my view tended to be a major base of conservatism's natural constituency back then. Political gay bashing, racism, and anti-Semitism survive even in this golden period of conservatism's great triumphs: but they are for the most part hidden in the closet. I think they are waiting to be let out once again. I worry that the right wing, having won the cold war and, for all intents and purposes, the battle over economic policy, will return to the fever swamps. I see evidence of this. It disturbs me greatly. It is for this reason that I write.

I am almost 67 years old. For more than half of my lifetime I have been engaged in, and indeed helped to organize and maintain, the conservative and anti-Communist cause. The names of some of the enterprises we helped launch may bring a nostalgic tug. I name some of them to establish my bona fides as someone who has toiled on behalf of the movement.

Among the more obscure committees I was involved with were the American Committee for Aid to the Katanga Freedom-Fighters; the American Emergency Committee for Tibetan Refugees; the Emergency Committee on the Panama Canal; the Aid to Refugee Chinese Intellectuals. Among the better known, of course, are the Committee of One Million, Young Americans for Freedom, the American Conservative Union, the Conservative Party of New York, and the Goldwater and Reagan campaigns. All the time I labored in the conservative vineyard, I was gay.

This was not my choice: the term "sexual preference" is deceptive. It is how I was born; how God decreed that I should be. As with most gay men of my generation, I kept it secret. It was probably not a secret to those who knew me well—my beloved friends and family—but no one Spoke Its Name. I now regret all those years of compliant silence.

Why have I chosen this moment to go public with that part of my life that had been so private for all these years? Because I feel that our cause might sink back into the ooze in which so much of it rested in pre-*NR* days. In that dark age the American Right was heavily, perhaps dominantly, made up of bigots: anti-Semites, anti-Catholics, the KKK, rednecks, Know Nothings, a sorry lot of public hucksters and religious medicine men. I think there is general agreement that it wasn't until the founding of this publication that the modern American conservative movement was granted light and form.

I was privileged to be a part of the enterprise from its earliest days, together with such great men as Whittaker Chambers, Frank Meyer, James Burnham, Russell Kirk, Brent Bozell—all of them. This effort, combined with the groups we founded, resulted in the eight-year reign of Ronald Reagan.

Now times are changing. There is no longer the anti-Communist cement to hold the edifice together. The great enterprise, in which so much time has been invested, is in danger of sinking back to an aggregation of bigotries.

Too many of our friends have recently used homophobia to sell their newsletter, or to raise money through direct mail for their causes and themselves. This letter isn't designed to settle scores, but rather to give warning to the movement from someone who's been a part of it for three and a half decades.

I've watched as some of our conservative brethren, employing the direct-mail medium I helped pioneer, use Robert Mapplethorpe's bad taste and the NEA's poor judgment to rile small donors, provoking them with a vision of a homosexual vanguard intent on forcing sadomasochistic images into every schoolroom. . . . I have been appalled to read in newsletters by conservative leaders that George Bush, by inviting a gay leader to a White House ceremony, is caving in to "the homosexual lobby." . . . I was outraged to see a spokesman for one of the more prominent conservative foundations quoted as saying that the cost of treating AIDS patients "could be the greatest impetus for euthanasia we've ever seen."

I worry about those allegedly Christian televangelists preaching hatred and fear of gays. These are men who would deny to more than twenty million Americans even the joy of peaceful union with their own families. . . . None of this seems to me to be the purpose of the cause I joined, along with you, 35 years ago.

A personal note is in order. I am both gay and conservative and don't find a contradiction. There shouldn't be any "shame" in being gay. Moreover, the conservative view, based as it is on the inherent rights of the individual over the state, is the logical political home of gay men and women. The conservative movement must reject the bigots and the hypocrites and provide a base for gays as well as others. The politics of inclusion is the model by which what we achieved with Ronald Reagan can continue and flourish without the anti-Communist and the anti-tax movements as sustaining elements. Conservatives need to remind themselves that gay men and women, almost always residing in the closet, were among those who helped in the founding, nurturing, and maintaining of the movement. They should be welcomed based on common beliefs, and without regard to our response to different sexual stimuli. One's sexuality should not be factored into acceptance in a cause that is based on beliefs, no more than color, or ethnic origin: because sexuality isn't a belief, it's a factor of birth.

One day the conservative movement will recognize that there are gays among us who have advanced our cause. They should not be victims of small-mindedness, prejudice, fear, or cynicism. That day may be a long way off, and I sometimes think the trend is in the opposite direction. *National Review* could have an important role here, once again guiding conservatives toward the more enlightened path. I pray that it will.

As ever, your friend,
Marvin Liebman

Dear Marvin: I hope you will believe me when I say that I understand the pain you have felt. Certainly I honor your decision to raise publicly the points you raise. My affection and respect for you are indelibly recorded here and there, in many ways, in many places.

But you too must realize what are the implications of what you ask. Namely, that the Judaeo-Christian tradition, which is aligned with, no less, one way of life, become indifferent to another way of life.

There is of course argument on the question whether homosexuality is in all cases congenital. But let us assume that this is so, and then ask: Is it reasonable to expect the larger community to cease to think of the activity of homosexuals as unnatural, whatever its etiology?

The social question then becomes: How, exercising toleration and charity, ought the traditional community to treat the minority? Ought considerations of charity entirely swamp us, causing us to submerge convictions having to do with that which we deem to be normal, and healthy?

It is a vexed and vexing subject, and your poignant letter serves to remind us of the pain we often inflict, sometimes unintentionally, sometimes sadistically. It is wholesome that we should be reproached for causing that pain, and useful to be reminded that we need to redouble the effort on the one hand to understand, even as we must be true to ourselves in maintaining convictions rooted, in our opinion, in theological and moral truths. You help us to remember that a gay person overhearing relaxed chatter mean-spirited in its references to gays suffers. Suffers just as much as an unidentifiably Jewish or Catholic human being would suffer on hearing invidious locker-room talk about their ethnic or religious affiliations.

I close by saying that *National Review* will not be scarred by thoughtless gay-bashing, let alone be animated by such practices. I qualify this only by acknowledging that humor (if wholesomely motivated) is as irresistable to us, as it is to you. You are absolutely correct in saying that gays should be welcome as partners in efforts to mint sound public policies; not correct, in my judgment, in concluding that such a partnership presupposes the repeal of convictions that are more, much more, than mere accretions of bigotry. You remain, always, my dear friend, and my brother in combat.

—WFB

Appendix B

Committee of One Million Petition
and
The Sharon Statement

The Committee of One Million petition was:

We HEREBY EXPRESS our opposition to the admission of the so-called Chinese People's Republic to the United Nations for the following reasons:

1. This admission would destroy the purposes, betray the letter, and violate the spirit of the law of the United Nations whose charter dedicates the organization to insure peace by promoting freedom and respect of human rights, and subordinates the admission of new states to the Organization to their ability and willingness, in the judgment of the member nations, to carry out the obligations to the Charter as defined above. The so-called Chinese People's Republic is constitutionally unable to do so since it officially declares itself to be a "dictatorship" based on "democratic centralism". . . . This is the basic principle of Communist totalitarianism and excludes freedom of discussion or criticism of government; that is, it excludes freedom and democracy altogether.

2. Even if the so-called Chinese People's Republic were eligible for admission under the Charter the fact still remains that the duly constituted government of China exists and functions, not only as the rightful government of China but as a charter member of the United Nations. In order to give membership to the usurpers the legitimate government of China would have to be expelled. Such action would be an unthinkable outrage against human decency and international justice.

3. The so-called Chinese People's Republic has shown its un-willingness to carry out the obligations of the Charter by systematically disregarding every human right and violating every freedom.

4. By aiding in aggression upon South Korea and making war on the United Nations it has proved itself an aggressor state.

5. Its admission would destroy the prestige and the position of the United States and of the Free World in Asia. The countries of that continent, which still resist Communist aggression or infiltration, would be discouraged by the cynical surrender of the Free World to expediency and appeasement and the betrayal of the ideals of the United Nations. The Asian nations, in turn, would then make fatal compromises with the Communist bloc.

6. The so-called Chinese People's Republic violated the most elemental laws of war in mistreating, torturing, and murdering United Nations soldiers who were prisoners of war, in an unlawful war which they waged against the very organization in which their supporters now claim membership for them.

7. At a time when Communist dictatorship seems to be badly shaken inside the USSR and in its satellite Empire, the admission of the so-called Chinese People's Republic to the United Nations would restore the prestige and authority of the Soviet Government. It would help to destroy the hope of the enslaved peoples for ultimate freedom. This hope is one of the chief deterrents which has restrained the Kremlin from risking a world-wide conflict.

8. The admission of the so-called China People's Republic to the United Nations would encourage subversive totalitarian movements in the free nations of the world in the expectation that their success would be sanctioned by the Free Nations which still survive. Thus the danger of a new war would be vastly increased by the rewards offered to an aggressor.

Therefore, the undersigned Americans respectfully request the President of the United States to defend the freedom and the decency of the Free World by continuing to firmly oppose the admission of the present so-called Chinese People's Republic to the United Nations. They express the wish that their petition be communicated to the United Nations and the hope that their appeal for peace and freedom will be heard and supported by all freedom loving peoples over the world.

The Sharon Statement

The Sharon Statement represents the essence of what the conservative movement was all about then (and now):

IN THIS time of moral and political crisis, it is the responsibility of the youth of America to affirm certain eternal truths.

We, as young conservatives, believe:

That foremost among the transcendent values is the individual's use of his God-given free will, whence derives his right to be free from the restrictions of arbitrary force;

That liberty is indivisible, and that political freedom cannot long exist without economic freedom;

That the purposes of government are to protect these freedoms through the preservation of internal order, the provision of national defense, and the administration of justice;

That when government ventures beyond these rightful functions, it accumulates power which tends to diminish order and liberty;

That the Constitution of the United States is the best arrangement yet devised for empowering government to fulfill its proper role, while restraining it from concentration of power;

That genius of the Constitution—the division of powers—is summed up in the clause which reserves primacy to the several states, or to the people, in those spheres not specifically delegated to the Federal government;

That the market economy, allocating resources by the free play of supply and demand, is the single economic system compatible with the requirements of personal freedom and constitutional government, and that it is at the same time the most productive supplier of human needs;

That when government interferes with the work of the market economy, it tends to reduce the moral and physical strength of the nation; that when it takes from one man to bestow on another, it diminishes the incentive of the first, the integrity of the second, and the moral autonomy of both;

That we will be free only so long as the national sovereignty of the

United States is secure; that history shows periods of freedom are rare, and can exist only when free citizens defend their rights against all enemies;

That the forces of international Communism are, at present, the greatest single threat to these liberties;

That the United States should stress victory over, rather than co-existence with, this menace; and

That American foreign policy must be judged by this criterion: does it serve the just interests of the United States?

Index

272

United Nations, 263-64
United States Information Agency
(USIA), 234-35
United Students for America (USA), 161

Van Damme, Helene, 236-37
Verdi, Jannette, 59-60
Vietnam, 181-88
Viguerie, Richard, 153, 160-61
Von Kannon, John, 233, 237

Wagner, Robert F., 170
Walker, Edwin A., 154, 157
Wallace, DeWitt, 195
Wallace, Henry A., 68, 70-71, 87-88
Walter, David, 249-50
Washington, DC, 237-42
Watson, Sylvia Stuart, 204
Wayne, John, 154
Wedemeyer, A. C., 94
Weil, Leon J., 216
Welch, Robert, 153, 157
West, Rebecca, 96
White, F. Clifton, 166, 168, 179-80
White, Josh, 77
White, Rev. Elliot, 50
White Aryan Resistance, 255
White Citizens Councils, 255
Wick, Charles, 234
Wiesberger, Arnold, 200
Wilder, Thornton, 96
Wilmington, VT, 53
Wilson, Malcolm, 153
Woolman, John, 257
World Anticommunist Congress for
Freedom and Liberation, 136
World Jewish Congress (WJC), 56
World Youth Crusade for Freedom in
Vietnam, 185-86
Worth, Irene, 206
Wright, Richard, 30
Wydler, John, 217

Yeh, George K. C., 152
Young Americans for Freedom (YAF), 14,
129, 150-56, 158-59, 165-66, 180,
185, 246

Young Communist League, 28-29
Youth for Goldwater, 145-50
Youth for Reagan, 180